Emerging Real Estate Markets

How to Find and Profit from Up-and-Coming Areas

DAVID LINDAHL

JOHN WILEY & SONS, INC.

Published by John Wiley & Sons, Inc., Hoboken, New Jersey.
Published simultaneously in Canada.

For general information on our other products and services please contact our Customer Care Department within the United States at (800) 762-2974, outside the United States at (317) 572-3993 or fax (317) 572-4002.

Wiley also publishes its books in a variety of electronic formats. Some content that appears in print may not be available in electronic books. For more information about Wiley products, visit our Web site at www.wiley.com.

Lindahl, David.
   Emerging real estate markets: how to find and profit from up and coming neighborhoods/David Lindahl.
        p. cm.
   "Published simultaneously in Canada."
   ISBN 978-0-470-17466-1 (cloth)
   1.   Real estate investment.   I. Title.
   HD1382.5.L55 2008
   332.33'24—dc22

                                                         2007016851

Printed in the United States of America.

V006902_042418

*To my parents, Barbara and Carl Lindahl, for sharing your
endless wisdom, support, and encouragement
for all the years of my life.*

CONTENTS

Acknowledgments   **xi**

Chapter 1
Real Estate Emerging Markets: Your Ticket to Great Wealth   1
   Investing with the Four Phases of the Real Estate Market Cycle   2
   What Most Real Estate Investing Books Leave Out,
   or Don't Know   3
   Avoiding Real Estate Losses When the Market Turns Down   4
   Discover the Path of Progress, and Get Wealthy   4
   Could a Great Emerging Market Be Right under Your Feet?   5
   Why Most People Can't Recognize An Emerging Market in
   Their Own Backyard   5
   How I Discovered the Power of Emerging Markets   6
   How to Predict the Hottest Future Growth Areas   8
   How Similar Are Real Estate and Stock Market Investing?   8

Chapter 2
How to Identify Emerging Markets Using My "Market Phase"
Method   11
   How to Invest in Each Phase of the Market   11
   What You Need to Know about the Buyer's Market Phase I   12
      The Tremendous Importance of Job Growth   14
      How to Invest in a Buyer's Market Phase I   15
   What You Need to Know about the Buyer's Market Phase II   16
   How to Invest in a Buyer's Market Phase II   18
   What You Need to Know about the Seller's Market Phase I   19
   How to Invest in a Seller's Market Phase I   21
   What You Need to Know about the Seller's Market Phase II   22
   How to Invest in a Seller's Market Phase II   24
   More on Emerging Markets   25
   Characteristics of the BEST Emerging Markets   26

CONTENTS

Chapter 3

Goldmines and Landmines in Emerging Markets   29
The High Cost of Bad Advice   29
Local Investments Can Be Highly Profitable   30
Insights I Gained from the Boston Market   31
Earning Positive Cash Flow   31
Buying below Replacement Cost   32
Knowing When to Move to Another Market   32
The Importance of Courage   33
How to Manage Out-of-Area Properties   34
The Incredible Wealth-Building Power of 1031 Exchanges   35
The Compounding Factor   37
Following the Rules to Enjoy the Benefits of a 1031 Exchange   37
Emerging Markets Are NOT the Same as *Hot* Markets   39
Why Both Employers and Employees Prefer Emerging Markets   39
Why It Takes Less Money to Get Started in Emerging Markets   40
The Hardest Part of Investing in Emerging Markets   42

Chapter 4

Getting Your First Deal in an Emerging Market   44
Secrets of Great Wealth Creation   46
Where You Should Start   46
The Supreme Importance of Time Management   48
How to Save Time and Money When Investing
in Emerging Markets   48
Secrets of Successful Direct Mail Campaigns   50
Working Successfully with Agents   52
More Details on Working with Agents   53
Finding Great Investment Properties on the Internet   54
How Research Can Help You Dominate an Emerging Market   56
How to Find a High-Quality Management Company   58
The All-Important Path of Progress   58
How to Determine Where and When to Buy   59
How to Find the Money You Will Need   60

Chapter 5

How to Jump-Start Your Wealth through Single-Family Investments   63
Step-by-Step to Your First Payday   64
Get the Leads Flowing In   64
Where to Find Out-of-Town Owners   65
What the Letters Should Say   66

Screening the Deals   67
How to Answer the Calls   68
Making Offers   70
How to Approach the Seller with Your Offer   72
Tie Up the Property   73
Find Buyers   73
Assign the Contract and Collect Your Money   74

Chapter 6
Multi-Family Investing: YOU Can Make Millions,
My Hands-Off Way   76
Cash Flow Is King   77
Positive Cash Flow in Action   78
Economies of Scale   79
Start Investing Part Time   79
Who Pays for the Property Manager?   80
How to Get Lower Risk and Larger Returns   81
Two Ways to Explode Your Wealth with Multi-Family Properties   82
Finding the Best Use of Your Profits   82
How to Do Fewer Deals and Make More Money   84
How to Close More Deals with Creative Financing   84
Multi-Family Properties Have One Other Major Advantage   85

Chapter 7
How to Find Diamonds in the Rough   88
The Wealth-Building Power of Value Plays   88
How to Find—and Profit from—Burned-Out Landlords   89
A Secret Hunting Ground for Finding Burned-Out Landlords   91
Variation on a Theme: The Landlord Who Has Just Had Enough   92
A Case Study in How to Deal Successfully with a
Burned-Out Landlord   93
How to Avoid Management Nightmares   95
Red Flags in Dealing with a Property Management Company   96
How to Acquire 100 Units with Your First Deal   101
Properties that Need Repair: Polishing Those Diamonds   103
A Repositioning Success Story   104
Solving the Problem of High Vacancy . . . Once and for All!   106
More on High-Vacancy Properties   107
How the Profit Multiplier Works   108
How to Get a Steady Pay Raise   109

The Art of the Rent Increase   110
The Economic Power of Forced Appreciation   111

Chapter 8
The 10 Biggest Mistakes Investors Make in Emerging Markets,
and How to Avoid Them   113
Mistake # 1: Thinking Any Investment Is a Good Investment   114
Mistake # 2: Investing Where There's No Real
Employment Base   115
Mistake # 3: Being Too Late to the Party   116
Mistake # 4: Neglecting to Go into Every Unit   117
Mistake # 5: Getting Mired in Pollution Problems   118
Mistake # 6: Over-Paying for a Property   120
Mistake # 7: Tying up All Your Money in Only One Market   121
Mistake # 8: Ignoring Overbuilding   122
Mistake # 9: Selling Too Late   123
Mistake # 10: Paying Too Much in Taxes   124

Chapter 9
How to Find All the Money You Need to Do Your Deals   126
Four Myths that Will Keep You Poor (if You Believe Them!)   126
Five Reasons You'll Be on Easy Street When You Have All
the Money You Need for Investing   129
The Miracle of Leverage   131
The Four-Step System for Financing All Your Deals   132

Chapter 10
How to "X-Ray" Your Deals the Fast and Easy Way, So You're
Buying Right in ANY Market   146
A Properties: The Cream of the Crop   146
B Properties: Still High End   147
C Properties: Gold that Looks like Lead   147
Here's Where You Can Make a Fortune   147
D Properties: Everything Else   148
How to Grade Areas as A, B, C, or D   149
Six Easy Pieces: The Six Calculations You Can Make in
Minutes to Rate Any Property   151
How to Put it All Together, to X-Ray a Deal!   160

Chapter 11
How to Make $10,000 or More per Hour—(I'm Not Kidding)   162
The *Wrong* Way to Do Due Diligence   163

The *Right* Way to Do Due Diligence   163
The Due Diligence Process—and How to Master It   165
Looking at Property Income   166
Looking at Property Expenses   167
What to Look For, in the Pile of Stuff You'll Get   167
The Checklist: Your Best Friend   168
Finding Hidden Value   169
Finding Hidden Gold in Expenses   170
Using Others as Your Eyes and Ears   171

Chapter 12
How to Inspect Both the Property, and the Investment   173
The Property Inspection   173
The Investment Inspection   174
How Great Amenities Attract Tenants   176
Deferred Maintenance   178
What Kind of Tenants Live There?   179
Make Friends with the People Who Will Make You Rich!   180
Hazards You Must Avoid   183

Chapter 13
How to Recruit Your *Dream Team*   187
Remember: You're the CEO   187
Who's in Your Dream Team   188
  1. Brokers: Finding Ones Who Will Really Work for You!   188
  2. Your Assistant: Not an Expense, but a Profit Multiplier   190
  3. Bankers: How to Borrow as Much Money as You Want!   192
  4. Attorneys: When and How to Use Them   192
  5. Demographers: How They Can Pinpoint Emerging Markets!   193
  6. Property Inspectors: How to See the Invisible   195
  7. Contractors: How to Get Great Work at Low Prices   197
  8. Managers: Your Long-Distance Eyes and Ears   198
  9. Accountant: Finding One Who Can Save You Serious Money   200
  10. 1031 Specialist: Get One, and Defer Your Taxes as Long as You Want!   201
  11. Mentors: A Pat on the Head, a Kick in the Pants   202

Chapter 14
How to Scout, Buy, and Profit from Properties—Long Distance   205
  Don't Make These Nine Mistakes   205

Chapter 15

Know Your Exit Strategy, before You Get into a Property   210
   Flipping Properties   210
   Buy and Hold: Is this Strategy Right for You?   213
   Another Buy-and-Hold Benefit   214
   1031 Exchanges: How to Master Them   215
   Profit by the Rules   216

Chapter 16

Your Next Steps to a Fortune in Real Estate   218
   Approach # 1   218
   Approach # 2   219
      The "My Situation Is Different" Syndrome (and the Biggest
      Secret of this Book)   219
      How to Speed Up Your Progress in Becoming a
      Real Estate Millionaire   220
      A Free and Fantastic Way to Benefit from Distance Learning   221
      The Best Books and CDs   221
      The Power of LIVE Instruction from an
      Emerging Markets Expert   222
      How to Have an Emerging Markets Expert Hold a Seminar
      in Your City   223
      The Importance of Taking Action Now   223

Index   224

ACKNOWLEDGMENTS

I'd like to acknowledge Dr. Donald Moine for giving me the idea and the initial encouragement to undertake this project, and Jonathan Rozek for the dedication and tireless work ethic that it took to get all of my ideas and knowledge on paper.

I'd also like to acknowledge my brothers Jeff and Danny, my sister Tammy, and Robert Campbell, for diligently working behind the scenes in all the ventures that I have undertaken, helping to make them so successful.

Thank you to Justin Mezaros for being the perfectionist that you are; you make everyone involved and associated with The Lindahl Group live up to the Gold Standard on a daily basis.

To my aunt Edna Little for going the extra mile and being there for me at special times.

To Joan Lindahl, Jeannie Orlowski, Chris Bowser, Debbie Marino, Jennifer Crawford, Beth King, Patricia McKenna, Jill Emond, Amanda Elwood, Barry Weaver, Sandy Kwong, Doug Curley, Jackie White, and Bob Morrissey, whose dedication and day-to-day activities allow me to go off and do what I do best.

Finally, I am deeply grateful to all of the RE Mentor seminar attendees, support staff, and joint venture partners. Without you, there would be no life-changing seminars.

CHAPTER 1

REAL ESTATE EMERGING MARKETS: YOUR TICKET TO GREAT WEALTH

Two roads diverged in a wood, and I—I took the one less traveled by, And that has made all the difference.

—Robert Frost

This is the first book written about *emerging* real estate markets and how you can profit from them.

You're probably thumbing over this book in the store, or maybe online. You're wondering if it's just another thick text that's difficult to read and even harder to apply to real life. This book is different. Consider it a coaching session between you and me.

You see, I'm not out to have this book sit on dusty shelves somewhere. I built my company, The Lindahl Group, into a $140 million real estate empire very quickly because I took action on some basic principles. I developed them into an investing strategy that I want to share with you now.

This is not one of those *get rich slowly* books that's recently become trendy. Sorry. When I started investing in real estate, I was a struggling landscaper, living in a three-room apartment. At one point I was down to my last 800 bucks—I had to borrow money for my first down payment. Within 3 1/2 years my investments had made me wealthy. From my own personal experience—and now the experiences of hundreds of my students—I know that real estate can make you rich in a very short time. But the *sweet spot* is investing at the right time in an emerging market!

This book will show you how to explode your wealth in the same way. You'll discover powerful ways to invest in local up-and-coming markets, and how you can invest by *remote control* in great markets throughout the United States!

I'm not a writer by profession, so this book may not read like Shakespeare. That's okay. I only want to come across in two ways to you: I want to be clear; and I want to inspire you to do that first real estate deal.

The things I'm about to tell you are not *theory* at all. They are cold, hard, tested, and proven facts that have made money for me over and over again. Plug in the systems I've used, and they work as reliably as when you plug in your coffee pot. You don't have to be white, or black, or tall, or young, or rich, or even healthy to plug in that coffee pot, and the same holds true for my systems. As long as you have a bias for action, you're good to go.

INVESTING WITH THE FOUR PHASES OF THE REAL ESTATE MARKET CYCLE

The key to making a lot of money in emerging markets is understanding the real estate market cycle. This is absolutely vital information that most real estate investors do not yet have. Though real estate is clearly one of the best investments over time, it does not go straight up in value. But, once you know how to identify and use real estate cycles to your advantage, you can skyrocket your profits—compared to the *buy and hold* investor.

How does emerging market investing work? At any given time, any city in the United States is in one of four phases of the real estate market cycle. In fact, certain parts of a city may be in different phases at the same time! Your key to making huge profits is in knowing which phase each market is in. *The phase of the market determines exactly what actions you should take as a real estate investor.*

Of the four phases, there is one special phase that will make you wealthy faster than all the others! I have personally made several million dollars from this phase in different cities. And it's not just me: My students have made *tens of millions of dollars* from opportunities this phase presents. You can be the next millionaire! And we're not talking just profits from the eventual sale of these properties. In addition, they can mean five- and six-figure spendable cash flow coming into your house, month after month.

Sometimes there may be small pockets of emerging market opportunity that only stretch for a few blocks. Other times, you'll be surrounded by *miles of opportunity*! Different markets require different techniques and actions. Of course, there are also plenty of markets on the downturn.

That's why I always shake my head at the headlines that announce "Real estate is booming!" or "Get out now from all your real estate investments!"

That's just journalists being fed sensational *sound bytes* from amateur investors. What these headline writers fail to understand is that the real estate market is the most localized investment market of all. After reading this book, you will realize that even if the national economy and the national real estate market is soft or trending down, there are *local markets* currently in the emerging phase. In these emerging markets, you can literally make profits in 2 or 3 years, which might take a decade or longer to make in other real estate markets...never mind the stock market!

Knowing how to decode market cycles is like having secret x-ray spy glasses for real estate. Suddenly you can look at a market and where other people only see scribbles, you see opportunity! When you're finished with this book, you'll know how to identify markets in this stage, and you'll want to start buying properties with both hands. This income will give you the freedom to do whatever you want, when you want, where you want, and with whom you want! That's what I call *The Attitude*!

WHAT MOST REAL ESTATE INVESTING BOOKS LEAVE OUT, OR DON'T KNOW

Go to any bookstore and you'll find shelves full of real estate books. They cover how to buy single-family, multi-family, and commercial properties; how to flip houses and wholesale them; how to exchange properties; how to buy them at auctions and before auctions; and many other aspects. Almost all these books tend to describe *one way to buy property, near where you live*, and they ignore real estate market cycles. That just isn't logical, unless you're willing to do some very marginal, risky deals. Whenever I can, I want to shoot fish in a barrel. I want the investing odds stacked way in my favor.

As a smart real estate investor, *you want to get the highest return from your money in the shortest amount of time*. When major corporate investors such as REITs (real estate investment trusts) invest their money, they don't buy real estate in just one city. The directors and managers of the REIT look around the United States for the very best real estate investing opportunities. When they find the best markets, they spread their money across them.

Real estate investing professionals continuously look at the landscape to see if there are any new markets starting to emerge. When they spot these markets, they *take money out of their maturing markets* and put it in the emerging markets to continuously create maximum profits.

AVOIDING REAL ESTATE LOSSES WHEN THE MARKET TURNS DOWN

Many books on real estate say "There is never a bad time to invest in real estate." I take a realistic and honest stance in this book. I want to help you not only make a great deal of money, but I also want to help you to avoid losing money. When you understand real estate cycles, you understand that there is a time to avoid certain markets. Using the wrong technique in a particular market cycle could cost you a lot of money in lost profits—or lost equity. For example, the Phoenix, Arizona market was great a few years ago when many companies moved there creating a lot of new jobs (we'll explore why this happens in a later chapter). Now let's take Pittsburgh during the same period. Had you put your money in that market, which suffered a net population loss, you would have taken a bath on your investment. By absorbing the concepts in this book, you will learn how to avoid such a fate. Using the right technique in the right market will *maximize your profits.*

DISCOVER THE PATH OF PROGRESS, AND GET WEALTHY

To make the greatest amount of money from real estate in a relatively short period of time, you must understand the *Path of Progress.* This is where the greatest amount of building and development is taking place.

If you had looked at a map of Southern California 40 years ago, you would have seen that Los Angeles and San Diego were the two largest cities. Between these two giants were hundreds of smaller cities and towns, and millions of acres of farms, orange groves, and undeveloped land.

The Path of Progress indicated that soon there would be little bare land between these two great cities, 120 miles apart. Los Angeles and Long Beach moved south, and San Diego moved north. Huge fortunes were made by investors who followed this path of progress.

One man, Donald Bren, became a *billionaire* by buying up thousands of acres of bare land in a once-sleepy agricultural county called Orange County. Orange County was smack dab in the middle of this Path of Progress, equidistant between Los Angeles and San Diego.

There have been hundreds of other Paths of Progress across America, though many were smaller and created only a few millionaires! I like to call these Paths of Progress the *Paths of Profits.* That's because they will produce your highest and fastest returns.

The Path of Progress is one of the key concepts in this book. You will discover how to recognize where it is going, how to find its boundaries, and a method to determine how far it will reach. You will then be able to target your real estate investing with bulls-eye accuracy.

COULD A GREAT EMERGING MARKET BE RIGHT UNDER YOUR FEET?

Just because you'll be able to invest anywhere across America, that doesn't mean you should ignore your own backyard. I'll show you how to identify exactly what investing opportunities exist in your local market. It may even be on the verge of emerging.

If this is the case, you're sitting on a gold mine!

But watch out: That fact alone will not make you rich. You must *take advantage* of it! Investing in emerging markets can make you very wealthy, very quickly—*only if you take action.* One of the reasons my seminar students have been so successful is that I have shown them how to take action when the conditions are ripe to make maximum profits.

WHY MOST PEOPLE CAN'T RECOGNIZE AN EMERGING MARKET IN THEIR OWN BACKYARD

If your market is in the early stages of emergence, chances are that most of the local people won't even recognize it. I call these oversights *real estate blind spots.* Why do locals often have blind spots? Why can't they see what is clearly in front of them?

This blindness exists because locals have seen the downturn and stagnation of their market for several years. They've become used to thinking, "This is the way it's been, and this is the way it will always be."

As a market is ready to emerge, locals (that includes the so-called *experts*— the local real estate agents) often do not realize that *recovery and economic good times are just around the corner.* As a matter of fact, they may tell you that you're crazy for investing, because nothing good has happened in that market for years!

Here's a test for whether you'll make it as a real estate millionaire: If you seek a lot of approval, and want people to say *beforehand* "Wow, what a smart investment he made!"... emerging market investing is definitely not for you!

Instead, if you're doing it right, what you'll hear is "What an idiot! Doesn't he know that this market's been dead for years? No one else is investing now....Why does HE think he's so smart!"

You better get used to that kind of thing.

Stick with me, and I'll show you the sources of information that reveal the *true state* of your local market. The hair stylist, florist, and coffee shop owner in your town are not privy to this information. Locals will stare in disbelief as you buy properties at bargain prices and then cash in on record profits when you sell them a few years later.

Oh, and don't expect them to label you a hero then; after all, you just proved them wrong. You'll most likely hear them say "He was just lucky."

HOW I DISCOVERED THE POWER OF EMERGING MARKETS

The scenario I just described is what happened to me when I first started investing in Brockton, Massachusetts back in 1995. Brockton had been in a slump for over 15 years! Brockton was once the shoe capital of the world. Its nickname was *shoe city*.

Everywhere you looked in Brockton, there were shoe factories. Along with the factories were the tenement houses for all the workers. There were 2-, 3-, 4-, 8-, and 10-unit buildings everywhere.

Because most of the factory workers were unskilled labor, few of them could afford their own homes and most rented apartments. As the years passed, it became cheaper to manufacture shoes overseas. Material costs were lower and labor was much cheaper. One by one, companies started to move their manufacturing out of Brockton and over to those cheap overseas markets.

Factories became empty shells. Workers were laid off and couldn't afford to pay rent. People began to move out of the area to places that had jobs.

Multi-family buildings started emptying out and landlords were foreclosed upon. The banks seemed to own more properties than individuals did. The empty buildings became havens for drug dealers and crime. The once proud city of Brockton became a place where you did NOT want to be after 4pm! The downward spiral continued for almost 15 years.

When I started buying in Brockton, it wasn't because I had a crystal ball telling me that the market was about to change. I was too new at the investing game for that! I bought in Brockton because *I was buying three- to six-unit buildings for well below their replacement costs*, and these buildings had great positive cash flow!

Fortunately for me, the city was on the verge of a rebound. The first thing that happened was the city elected a new mayor, Jack Units. It takes strong will, guts, and great leadership to take a city that was a mess like Brockton and begin a *renaissance*. Jack Units possessed all three of these characteristics. He was a true turn-around artist.

The city of Brockton started tearing down the abandoned, drug-infested multi-family buildings. It sold the land at low cost to anyone willing to build a single-family home. Five new schools were built, sidewalks were paved, and the transit system was extended to connect Brockton with Boston.

Wow! This meant that people could live in Brockton and commute to work in Boston without the hassle and expense of driving and parking a car! Brockton began to emerge, and then really took off. All of those properties that I bought took off right along with the city. Property values soared. Before I knew it, I was a multi-millionaire! Just a few years earlier, I had been poor.

(If you ever visit the mayor's office in Brockton, you'll see a pair of shoes proudly displayed on the wall. The shoes have holes in the soles. They are the shoes that Jack Units wore out, campaigning for the mayor's job. Each time I see those shoes, I want to give them a big smooch!)

After several years, I started realizing that Brockton was beginning to peak. I began learning about market cycles and realized that what goes up cannot go up indefinitely. No real estate market can rise 30% per year forever. After a period of soaring prices, there is a decline in prices that brings them *back to reality*. This happens in both the stock and real estate markets.

I knew that if I continued to own my properties in Brockton, I was going to lose equity, and would have to wait for another emerging market cycle. This could take years. I didn't want to wait! And I certainly didn't want to lose any of my equity.

I started a nationwide search of other markets in the United States that had the potential to emerge and soar in value the way Brockton did. I figured I could sell my Brockton properties near the peak, and put that money in at the bottom of the cycle in other markets. Then, while the Brockton market was going through the natural ups and downs of its real estate cycle, instead of losing my equity, I was going to double, triple, or even quadruple it. Then, when Brockton showed signs of emerging once again, I would bring my money back home to Brockton!

HOW TO PREDICT THE HOTTEST FUTURE GROWTH AREAS

I was right about Brockton, and I was also right that there were other markets at just the perfect stage, waiting to give me another great ride! You see, real estate investing is not a guessing game. You *can* actually predict the hottest future growth areas.

Before you accuse me of claiming that I have a crystal ball, let me set the record straight: It's not like I'm predicting markets 10 and 20 years out. That really would take a crystal ball.

Instead, I'm merely doing what the smart guys would do in those old Western movies: Putting my ear to the locomotive rail. They could sense the freight train speeding toward them by the slight vibrations.

I'm doing the same thing. I can sense that *market freight train* coming, some months before almost anyone else can. And that's all the time I need to buy my properties!

By following my proven success formula, you'll know how to get the most out of your investment dollars. You will accomplish this by being in the right *city* at the right *time* investing in the right *property* located in the right *area* of that city. It doesn't get much better than that!

HOW SIMILAR ARE REAL ESTATE AND STOCK MARKET INVESTING?

When you hear the term *emerging markets*, you probably think of the stock market.

Many books and articles have been written on how to make money in emerging stock markets. We all remember the first Internet stocks, and also high-technology stocks, foreign stocks, and other exotics. Hundreds of billions of dollars were made—and sometimes lost—in those markets.

Emerging *real estate* markets are an even bigger and potentially more lucrative opportunity—yet they have received very little attention: Both real estate and stocks have a place in a diversified portfolio. Many of us have made money in the stock market by trying to find certain sectors of the market that are growing quickly. Unfortunately many of us have also lost money in stocks, because we got in too late. Even when we got in at the right time, the sector might have collapsed before we could get out.

Millions of Americans have reached the conclusion that selecting and monitoring stocks is an exhausting process, even when it works okay. It sometimes seems like stocks are an *insider's game*, designed to profit brokers and mutual fund companies more than the average investor. The billions of dollars worth of fines recently assessed against brokerage and mutual fund companies bears this out.

For people willing to do the work and take the risks, picking stocks can be rewarding. I've dabbled in it myself, from time to time. Today I have so much money that if I put it into the stock market, I'd be treated like a king by the brokerage firms. Yet I choose to put my money back into real estate. Why is that?

When you invest in real estate, you are making decisions based on numbers you get directly from the owner or from trustworthy public records. You do not have to trust a broker, company executive, or mutual fund company.

The numbers you evaluate when you buy a property are all *verified* during the due diligence process. You don't have to trust anyone. If the numbers hold true, you've got a deal. If the seller was shading the numbers to look better than they really are, my systems will smoke that out. In that situation, it's time to renegotiate. If you don't like the numbers, you walk away.

The stock market is fueled by so much else: speculation on management changes; tax law changes; new product launches that may or may not work...the list is endless. On top of that, the entire stock market sways under the load of rumors: What the President will do, what is OPEC's next move, and so on.

Forget that! In contrast, they don't call it *REAL* estate for nothing. You deal with reality, not gossip, hourly rumors, and wishful thinking.

The stock market is extremely unpredictable. Another company could come out with a superior technology and put your company out of business. The executives of your company could get into trouble. Or, if the executives are outstanding, they might leave and gut your company of the talent it needs to thrive. Dozens of other factors can put a once-promising company on the ropes.

Real estate is much simpler. Human beings need a place to live. Land is scarce and is getting scarcer every day. People continue to have families and the need for housing continues to rise. America—the greatest country the world has ever known—continues to attract record numbers of immigrants. People are living longer, further adding to the need for housing.

The laws of supply and demand dictate that real estate prices *must* continue to rise over the long term. There will always be bumps on the road, but real estate prices *will* rise over time. That's very reassuring to me, compared to the volatility of the stock market, and the ability to print up more stock certificates tomorrow!

IN THE NEXT CHAPTER

I am excited to share all these secrets of mine with you. Now, let's dive into the details of these amazing real estate emerging markets. We'll do that in the next chapter by talking about how to know you're looking at an emerging market when you see one.

Note

1. (Our holdings include 4,200+ apartments in multiple states and we're growing fast.)

**Special Offer for Readers of this Book:
As mentioned on the cover, you can claim
bonuses worth more than $375.00 for free.
Simply go to: www.MarketCycleMastery.com
and type in the words "Reader Bonus" for details.**

CHAPTER 2

How to Identify Emerging Markets Using My "Market Phase" Method

Like the tides of the ocean coming in and going out on a predictable schedule, real estate market cycles go up and down predictably, too. There are two differences:

1. Unlike the ocean, *in real estate, the tide always rises over time!* If you can hold real estate long enough, you'll always make money.
2. Because there are many larger and smaller markets, all with their own cycles, it sometimes looks like random movement. I can assure you it's not . . . if you know what to look for. (You soon will!)

One of the reasons I wrote this book is to show you how to make *more-money faster* in real estate. If you ignore market cycles, it might take many years to make money in a given real estate market. I'm talking *a decade or longer.*

How to Invest in Each Phase of the Market

That's way too long to wait! My students know how to make huge amounts of money in real estate by mastering the four main phases of a market cycle. They are:

- Buyer's Market Phase I
- Buyer's Market Phase II

- Seller's Market Phase I
- Seller's Market Phase II

The average time for a market to complete a full cycle will differ, but can range from 10 to 25 years. East Coast and West Coast cities tend to be more dynamic than cities in the heartland of America, and their markets rotate faster.

In fact, our coastal cities tend to have meteoric rises *and* meteoric falls. Heartland cities tend either to be slow, steady climbers, or stagnant for quite a while.

WHAT YOU NEED TO KNOW ABOUT THE BUYER'S MARKET PHASE I

Each market phase has its own characteristics. In a Buyer's Market Phase I, you will find a market that is *oversupplied with properties.* Supply is one of the key forces that can move a market from boom to bust.

Some people wonder how there could ever be an oversupply of property; after all, Will Rogers had a point when he said that real estate is worth buying, because they aren't making any more of it.

However, from my experience across America, and from what my students have also seen, that statement is not completely accurate, for the two following reasons.

Reason #1: There are very few limits to how many condominiums can be built. A small parcel of land can actually house 5,000 people or more—if they're stacked into condos. As we know by looking at any major metropolitan skyline, by building *up*, it's possible to create more real estate.

Reason #2: When you fly across our great country and look out the window, you see that *great portions of the United States are unpopulated;* and a lot of it is buildable land. To profit in real estate, you must understand that we have a tremendous ability to build more houses, apartments, condominiums, and offices. Oversupply *can* be a very real problem—especially with a declining birth rate.

I caution you to always be on the lookout for a market that is on the verge of being overbuilt. In the long run you might be dead right that the market will absorb that supply. But your investment will be dead, all the same, because your money was tied up for so many years.

It happens in virtually every city in America at one time or another: During the exhilaration at the end of an emerging market, everyone is eager to jump in and capture some of the profits that seem unlimited. Building becomes rampant to meet the seemingly insatiable demand for real estate.

Finally, the demand is met in that market—but the pipeline of deals still under construction continues to pour more supply onto the market. Very quickly, the market becomes soft.

Demand is limited, in ANY market. Most of us only need *one* house, apartment, or condo to live in. When children grow up and move out, many people find they no longer need that big house. They downsize.

Also, for the past 30 or so years, *each generation has been getting smaller in numbers.* The Baby Boomers were the biggest generation in our history. Generations X and Y, coming after the Baby Boomers, were smaller. The birth rate continues to decline.

Baby Boomers are starting to retire. Millions of people in this 78-million-person group want to downsize. Will there be enough people in the smaller post-Baby Boomer generations to buy all the homes that retiring Baby Boomers want to sell? As you can see, demand can be more limited than supply.

In *every* market, there's a time when more units come online than there are people to rent or buy them. The *time on the market* for these properties sharply increases. A home that might have taken 45 days to sell in the past might now take 70 days or longer. Prices start falling and rents start to fall as well.

These developments shock most people. However, with my investment system, it's possible to *predict this development with a high degree of accuracy.* For instance, we know it takes 2 to 3 years to plan, get permitted, and build a property. When everyone is in love with real estate, builders and speculators take out a huge number of building permits. By tracking these permits, we know which markets are at greatest risk of soon being overbuilt.

Then, as I mentioned earlier, all these new properties hit the market. Now there are many more properties on the market than people to buy or rent them. The only way to move inventory is to *slash prices.* In some cases, prices fall by 20% or more. If you put 20% down on your home or condo and have to sell in such a market, *you have a 100% loss.* That's because the bank wants its money, no matter what. So the first dollars to evaporate are your down-payment dollars.

In fact, your loss is even greater because you have to pay a real estate commission and closing costs. You could end up losing everything you put into the house; plus you may have to reach into your savings to spend more money, just to get rid of the property!

It is *essential* that you understand market cycles if you are going to prosper as a real estate investor. Other real estate *gurus* may teach some very nice techniques of buying; but without the market cycle secrets in this book, you could be applying those techniques in the wrong market, at the wrong time. That's a recipe for disaster.

The Tremendous Importance of Job Growth

Job growth is another market force with a huge effect on real estate market cycles. In a Buyer's Market Phase I, there is very little job growth. In fact, jobs may actually be leaving.

Jobs start to slow down or leave an area during the previous stage: the Seller's Market Phase II. At the beginning of a Buyer's Market Phase I, job loss is usually still taking place.

The Upper Midwest and Great Lakes region acquired the *Rust Belt* nickname, because so many jobs were lost as foreign car companies took market share from American automobile manufacturers. Tens of thousands of Americans ended up losing their jobs, and real estate prices fell for years.

No cycle continues forever, fortunately. Markets reach a certain point where unemployment peaks. Usually around this time, property values will decline to their lowest levels of all the four cycles. Sometimes, this is the lowest level in a decade or more!

For a city to move to the next phase of the market cycle—the Buyer's Market Phase II—it will have to take action to grow jobs. When jobs are finally created, people begin to migrate back into a community, population grows, and vacant properties start being filled. At last, rents start to increase.

In order to attract or create job growth, the first element needed is *strong local leadership*. If the leadership of the local government is not committed to change, or if there's a lot of infighting taking place between government officials, the area has a low probability of leaving a Buyer's Market Phase I anytime soon.

What's a sign of strong local leadership? When politicians offer tax abatements to corporations, to encourage them to build factories or hire workers in that city. They will also offer low-interest or no-interest loans to companies. Sometimes city officials offer free land.

Great leaders become creative and do *whatever they need to do*, in order to compete with other forward-looking cities and bring jobs to their area.

To find out what your city's master plan is, call the local economic development committee and speak with an official. He or she will be happy to spend time with you on the phone.

You'll hear about all the wonderful things happening in their city. If a company executive wants to visit that city, a local official will be happy to meet with that executive, provide a tour of the city, and maybe even offer a free lunch. The whole time, the executive will be pitched on the benefits the city offers to companies who can provide jobs.

These government officials also know they need investors like you to spark new growth in the city.

If the city doesn't have anyone in an economic development committee to speak with you, that should tell you something! The cities that are active in this area are the ones that will win the business, attract the jobs, and revitalize their economies and real estate.

How to Invest in a Buyer's Market Phase I

In this stage of the market, *you are buying for cash flow*. Because there is no appreciation taking place in the market, your primary concern is to *look for that strong positive cash flow*. There are two reasons for this: First, a property with good cash flow is already positioned to be a winner down the road. Second, think of cash flow as your safety margin. The higher your cash flow, the more you can adjust rents or absorb vacancies before things get worrisome.

When the market starts to rise again, you will profit handsomely from your wise investment. All the while, you will be banking money from your positive cash flow!

Unless you're buying in your own backyard, the only time you want to be investing in a Buyer's Market Phase I is when you *know that something is about to happen in that market that will create positive change*.

That positive change usually comes in the form of job growth. However, you MUST understand how long this cycle can take. When a company commits to relocate to a new city, that relocation could take 2 to 5 *years*. The company often must build a new plant or corporate headquarters, which requires major planning, a lengthy permit process, and the actual construction.

Knowing that a city will experience significant job growth a couple of years down the road is one of the best reasons to buy in an area. You can frequently pick up MAJOR bargains at this time!

One of the best places to find forecasted job growth is from the United States Census. Go online to the Bureau of Labor Statistics, and search for "forecasted job growth." Then start calling the economic development committees in the cities that have the highest forecasted job growth. You will be well rewarded for your efforts!

While you are on the Bureau of Labor Statistics website, check out which cities had the largest job growth for the previous year. Call their economic development committees to find out what they are doing to continue their growth. If they say they have eliminated incentives, avoid investing in this city. If the incentives are continuing—or if they have been strengthened—seriously consider an investment.

WHAT YOU NEED TO KNOW ABOUT THE BUYER'S MARKET PHASE II

As new jobs are created in a city, population begins to migrate back into that city. The market starts to absorb its oversupply of properties. Rental spaces fill up. The time on the market for properties and rental spaces begins to decline.

As more jobs come into the area, the pace of real estate appreciation quickens. This is an exciting time! Existing properties that were once abandoned or boarded up are now snatched up by investors, who rehab them and put them back on the market. You can make huge profits at this time.

During the earlier Buyer's Market Phase I, bank foreclosures rise to their highest levels. A characteristic of the latter stages of a Buyer's Market Phase II is that the competition for these bank foreclosures becomes fierce. Soon, there will be few, if any, bank foreclosures left.

Investors—that is, the ones who didn't bother with market cycle mastery—now realize there is serious money to be made in this market. Out-of-town investors come into the market. Even the formerly skeptical local people begin investing in real estate again. Demand increases significantly.

Rents that were at their lowest levels begin to slowly increase. Investment property values (which are tied to rents), increase as well. Later in this book, you'll discover more about the link between rents and the value of income property, and how to use this relationship to your advantage!

I have just described the very beginning stages of an emerging market. Only the savviest investors recognize these early warning signs of a market's recovery. You develop the ability to do this by conducting research and thoroughly evaluating job growth.

Local property owners frequently do not recognize the recovery at first. They are *too close to see the big picture*. They've just suffered through many painful years of a Buyer's Market I. They watched unemployment increase, and witnessed the oversupply in the market. As existing investors, they've felt the pain from reducing rents on their properties.

These long-suffering owners have watched as their apartments stayed vacant for months, as they spent money to search for tenants to fill them.

All human beings have a tendency to think that current conditions will continue into the future. When the stock market was up dramatically, Americans poured billions of dollars into it—thinking it would keep on rolling. When the stock market crashed in 2000 and 2001, more than one trillion dollars was lost, at least on paper.

Being human, real estate investors react in the same way. When prices rise, everyone wants to buy real estate. Unfortunately, many people buy at or near the top of the market. This is when, by definition, the growth has been the longest, and the most success stories are available to comfort the amateur investors. Then when prices crash, most people want to bail out.

When the market has crashed—when almost no one else wants to buy— you want to be buying with both hands! My students have made fortunes through buying at this time—and I hope you can too.

Here's a word of caution: This is by far the most profitable time to invest, but I didn't say it would be emotionally easy! You'll have naysayers and skeptics farther than the eye can see. But like a seasoned pilot who's flying on instruments and not by the seat of his pants, you must trust your instruments!

What price do you pay? At the bottom of the market, you are going to be buying properties from these investors *at or near their full asking price.* The sellers will think that you are crazy! And you will be crazy—like a fox!

It often takes local people 6 months to 1 year to realize that the market is changing for the better. However, even as prices begin to rise, many locals are just hoping to get what they paid for their property years ago. They are shell shocked from the previous cycle. They just want to get out of the property!

If you understand market cycles, you can pick up incredible bargains. It's more important to get into these properties early than it is to haggle down the sellers too much and risk losing the properties altogether.

The locals have been through all the hard times and end up selling their property, just when they could be rewarded for their perseverance. It's sad, but it's also human nature.

At this stage of the market phase, there is little or no new construction. The builders and speculators have just given up. Some builders even went bankrupt in the previous down cycle. The oversupply is just starting to be absorbed, and rental levels have not grown high enough to support the building of new properties.

If the city has an aggressive program to attract jobs, companies will be committing to the area. As these companies begin bringing jobs in, people will start migrating back into the area. This is your signal to take action!

As jobs come in, *additional* jobs are created. For every one professional job that comes into an area, another *three* to *four* service jobs are created to support that professional. These are the "butcher, baker, and candlestick maker." Remember that these people need doctors, lawyers, barbers, gardeners, housekeepers, plumbers, mechanics, computer consultants, babysitters, and innumerable other professionals and service providers. This is called the *multiplier effect*.

If a city is expecting to increase its labor force by 5,000 new nonagricultural jobs, you can expect a total employment increase of 15,000 to 20,000! Knowing this fact puts you ahead of 90% of all other investors—including local ones.

As jobs come into an area, competition for labor begins to increase. This leads to increases in salaries. More employees with more money leads to more prosperity. Then even more jobs are created. Many people have more disposable income than ever. *A genuine cycle of prosperity has begun.*

Another result of rising salaries is that the average household size will start to decrease. This is a further sign of progress into a Buyer's Market Phase II. During tough times, some people decide to live with roommates or take in renters. As incomes increase, many more people can move into their own apartments, condos, or houses. Adult children can move away from home. As more people seek a place of their own, demand is stoked for rental units.

Apartment owners (this means you!) can increase rents on those properties that were already generating cash flow, and now make even more money.

HOW TO INVEST IN A BUYER'S MARKET PHASE II

As I said earlier, this is the very start of an emerging market. When you find this market phase, buy everything that makes sense!

At this phase of the market, *buy and hold*. Do not sell too quickly! If you do, you'll be giving up incredible profits. Why settle for a $10,000 profit when you can enjoy a $100,000 one (or even more) just by being patient?

Remember: In this market phase, the strong demand for properties has not been created yet. We're only in the early stages of emergence. Therefore, *quick turning* properties is not as profitable in this phase as it will be later. If some real estate *guru* tries to sell you on the idea of flipping properties, ignore him or her at this point. Stick with me, and we'll produce much greater profits.

I do *not* recommend holding properties forever. You don't need the patience of Job to make a profit with my system. Your typical hold time in this market will be 3 to 5 years. Later in this book, I will show you how to cash out and receive huge profits from this relatively short holding period.

There's another reason why you should not have a problem paying the full asking price: It's okay, *as long as the property cash flows properly.* In a Buyer's Market Phase II, I want to see at least a *10% Cash-on-Cash Return* (that's Net Cash Flow, divided by Acquisition Costs).

Of course, I always try to negotiate the price *a little* anyway. That's because the owner will think he priced his property too low if you just open your wallet and pay the asking price! In my experience, when sellers think you would have paid a little more for the property, they try to get it from you *somewhere in the deal.* Therefore, it makes sense to negotiate a little and save a few thousand dollars or more.

Just don't try to be cheap in this market. Remember that you *are already buying at wholesale prices.* If you are competing against another investor in this deep-discount market, make a full-price offer to get the property. You will *still* make a fortune.

Don't sweat paying full price, because prices in this market have already started going up and have a long climb ahead. You should buy as many properties as you can control, sit back, enjoy the ride, and await the handsome profits!

I call this phase of the market the *Millionaire Maker,* because it tends to do that in a very short time. This has happened to me, and to many of my students. I'm hoping you'll be the next one to experience it.

WHAT YOU NEED TO KNOW ABOUT THE SELLER'S MARKET PHASE I

The next phase of the market is a Seller's Market Phase I. This is the latter half of an emerging market.

A market transitions into this phase when it makes economic sense to start building again, based on absorption and rents reaching certain points. This is called the *Point of Equilibrium.*

In this phase, local investors are now convinced the good times are here to stay. They're once again investing in the market. Outside investors have also recognized this market as a place to be buying, and they're happy to dump money into this market.

Due to this huge flow of money coming in to buy properties, demand for investment real estate is at its highest.

As demand increases, the supply of investment properties for sale on the market begins to dwindle. Properties are selling fast and the time that properties stay on the market reaches its lowest point. In some cases—at the peak of this cycle—properties are sold on the same day they are listed!

This phase of the market is very competitive for buyers of properties. *Bidding wars* start to take place as properties come onto the market. Good properties stay on the market for just a few days and—for the first time—properties start to sell *above* asking price.

The excitement is palpable. Property prices and rents continue to soar, which fuels speculation and development of raw land. Properties that were considered obsolete or "in a bad neighborhood" are snapped up, rehabbed, and sold for huge profits.

Employment continues to increase, wages keep rising, the number of people per household continues to drop, construction employment is at its height, and it becomes very difficult to get a contractor to do repairs for your property. Why? Many contractors and even handymen have become builders!

Near the end of this phase, a great deal of speculation has taken place. That's when the percentage of people who can afford to buy a home declines dramatically.

Speculators begin bidding up the price of properties based on *appreciation instead of cash flow*. In many cases, they will even buy a property with a big negative cash flow. For example, it may cost $5,000 a month to pay the mortgage, taxes, and other expenses—yet the income might only be $4,000. Why would people buy such a property? Because they *think or hope* that they can sell it for a huge profit to someone else who thinks the same!

Why do people make this assumption? It's easy to believe that current conditions will persist. When prices are low, people think low prices will continue. When prices are high, they think they'll just keep rising.

In this market, many investors have been led to believe that they can buy today, sell in a few months, and make easy money. *This leads them to buy almost anything on the market.* They will pay the asking price, no matter how high, just to own a property.

The result is that the properties they buy produce smaller and smaller returns. In the end, many are left holding properties that will cost them money and result in a loss.

How to Invest in a Seller's Market Phase I

In a Seller's Market Phase I, you should both flip properties for big profits, and hold them for appreciation and cash flow.

In this phase, demand has reached its highest point. That means there are plenty of investors ready to buy properties that you want to sell. Why would you want to sell?

If you bought a property early in the Buyer's Market Phase II—or even the late stages of a transitioning Buyer's Market Phase I—you probably have a lot of built-up equity. Now is the *perfect time* to sell this property, do a 1031 Tax Deferred Exchange (more on this later in the book), and plow *all* your profits into a bigger property, with ZERO current taxes!

Doing so will enable you to create larger monthly cash flow. Do this while the market is *still climbing*. Your property will be worth more, you'll make more money, and you'll magnify all of your profits.

An example will show just how exciting this profit potential is. Let's say you currently own a property that has a value of $1,000,000 with $200,000 in equity and the market increases 20%. Now your property is worth $1,200,000. When you sell the property, you will now have $400,000 ($200,000 + $200,000) in equity.

With a 1031 Tax Deferred Exchange, *you can take all of that equity and use it for a down payment on another even more promising property*. (Remember not to over-pay during this market cycle, though!) Let's assume we'll be putting 20% down (though, as you'll see later in the book, you can often buy with no money down). With this 20% down, you buy a property worth $2,000,000 ($400,000 is 20% of $2 million). *Now you own a $2 million property!*

Let's assume that the market increases in value by another 20%. This frequently happens at this point in the market cycle. Your old property (the one you sold) would be worth $1,440,000 ($1,200,000 × 1.2) for a total equity amount of $640,000 ($200,000 original equity + $440,000).

However, *you had the knowledge to sell that first property and you traded up to a bigger property*. During the same time span and *in the same market* your total equity is now $800,000 ($2,000,000 ×1.2 = 2,400,000). This results in $400,000 in new equity plus the $400,000 that we started with before doing the 1031 Exchange.

With $800,000, you probably feel rich. *But this is just the start!* Later in this book, I will show you how to grow this still further.

In the same market, during the same time period, because you traded up instead of staying in one property, *you are now worth $160,000 more* than you would have been if you had just held onto your old property ($800,000–$640,000). It pays to be an active investor!

You made this $160,000 *without* punching a time clock, fighting traffic jams, and having to work long hours in a boring office.

This is also a good market to buy into and hold. That's because there's still room for rents to increase and potential for your property to increase in value!

Warning: At a certain point, this market will start to cool off. When it does, I advise my students to count their profits, sell their properties, and *move onto another emerging market*. Is there sill room for the market to grow? Yes, but the longer you stay in during this transition period, the riskier your investment becomes!

Just as you entered the market when everyone around you was saying you're nuts, you'll now be leaving at a point when they think things are just fine. Get ready for more criticism—while you're walking to the bank with another fat deposit!

WHAT YOU NEED TO KNOW ABOUT THE SELLER'S MARKET PHASE II

A Seller's Market Phase II is the *riskiest* phase of the investment real estate market cycle.

At the beginning of this phase, properties will remain unsold on the market for ever-longer periods. Gone are the days when multiple offers are presented on properties as soon as they came on the market. Gone are the bidding wars. During this phase, you have to search far and wide to find a buyer! Some properties may sit on the market for a year or longer.

Because properties are not getting snapped up like they were in the previous phase, *the number of properties on the market begins to increase*. Sellers have to wait longer to get their properties sold, but in the beginning stages of this phase, *they are still getting inflated prices*. Land is still being purchased for speculation, and the amount of construction in the pipeline becomes excessive. The potential for overbuilding becomes great.

For the first time since the Buyer's Market Phase II stage, business and job growth will slow.

Investors begin to realize that the market is changing, and they put more properties on the market. They want to lock in gains, or get out of properties they just bought at the top of the market! Some sellers become desperate. The number of properties on the market continues to increase, along with the number of days required to sell each property. Now, sellers who want to move quickly out of the market must lower their prices.

This fuels the downward trend of the market even more. All investors now clearly see that *the market has topped out and is beginning to decline*. So what do many investors do? They put even more properties on the market—hoping that *something* will sell!

Smart investors have pulled their money out of this market long ago, and have gone on to other emerging markets. They did this as soon as the indicators hinted that the market was transitioning into a Seller's Market Phase II.

Two main market forces will warn you about the dangerous transition into the Seller's Market Phase II.

The first is *job growth*. When job growth becomes stagnant, that means the area will not enjoy population growth and may suffer from population loss. With fewer people, there is less demand for properties. If an area cannot create more jobs, the chances are better that it will enter the Seller's Market Phase II.

The second market force you want to track carefully is *supply*. In every emerging market, a key factor in a market losing its momentum is overbuilding. Overbuilding directly leads to oversupply. When builders create more than the demand warrants, they *must* begin to lower their prices so they can sell their inventory to pay off their loans.

At a certain point, even lower prices will not attract enough buyers. For example, if an area loses population and jobs, and if the birth rate declines (as it has nationwide), there simply may not be enough people in an area to fill all the housing units. Under these conditions we see massive foreclosures. A number of areas of the United States experienced this in the early to mid-1990s.

Foreclosures during that time were so numerous that it led to the bankruptcy of hundreds of savings and loans, and some banks. That's the extreme form of a Seller's Market Phase II. The Resolution Trust Corporation had to auction off tens of thousands of housing units nationwide.

When too many apartment units are built, rents must be lowered to attract tenants. Therefore, even if you are able to hold on to your property, you will make much less money from it. Hopefully what you make will be sufficient to cover your mortgage, taxes, and insurance.

You should always be monitoring the local building department for the number of building permits that have been issued. *This will give you the clearest indication of where supply will be in the next year or two.* In major cities that are completely *built-out*, this is less of a problem. However, in smaller towns with lots of inexpensive land nearby, overbuilding can be deadly.

Also constantly monitor the *days on the market* statistics for properties. Any real estate agent can provide you with this figure, which tells you the days between when properties get listed for sale and when they actually sell.

As soon as the days on the market start to increase, it's time to start putting your properties on the market. Don't be the last one out the door!

In a market where there is strong demand for investment properties, it will usually only take you about 60 to 90 days to sell one of your properties. However, at the end of a Seller's Market Phase II, it could take you 90 to 180 days, or longer, to find a buyer for your property—and another 60 to 90 days to close the transaction. That's 6 months to 1 year!

What happens during that 60 to 90 days *after* you've found the buyer? They are negotiating with you! They know you are desperate. They may ask for further price reductions—or maybe for new carpets in the units. They decide they'd like a new roof or sprinkler system. Gee, the outside of the buildings look like they need painting!

Not only do you have to lower your price significantly at the end of a Seller's Market Phase II, but you have to grant many of these concessions to get your property sold.

You could have had your money in another emerging market, where it would be appreciating rapidly, if you had moved OUT of this market in the Seller's Market Phase I.

By waiting too long, you end up losing equity and a lot of sleep in this down market.

HOW TO INVEST IN A SELLER'S MARKET PHASE II

In this phase, sell your properties and move on to a great new market *as soon as you realize the market is changing*. Your goal: Sell *as early as possible* in a Seller's Market Phase II.

Do you ever want to buy in a Seller's Market Phase II? *Yes*. In the final stages of a Seller's Market Phase II, there are huge bargains to be had. In some cases, properties are available for 50% of the asking price of just a couple of years earlier! Especially if this seller's market is in your own backyard, you should back up the dump truck and buy as many properties as you can afford.

Huge profits are made by those who have the courage and vision to buy at the very bottom of a Seller's Market Phase II. In the 1990s, the Resolution Trust Corporation sold off some apartment buildings for about $5,000 per apartment! Buyers of these units made millions—in some cases *more than $10 million*—in just a few years!

One of the best money-making formulas of all is to take profits early from a Seller's Market Phase II and funnel those profits into an emerging market. What do you do next? *Sit back and watch those profits multiply!*

What if you are holding a property in a Seller's Market Phase II and don't want to sell? In that case, you need my *Equity Protection Formula*:

1. Make sure you have *plenty of equity*. People with only 20% equity can easily get wiped out, or face foreclosure. Having 50% equity and a 50% loan-to-value ratio on your mortgage is a safe rule-of-thumb.
2. Make sure you can *cover your expenses* (the mortgage, taxes, insurance, and maintenance) during these tough times. You may have more vacant units than you've ever had, due to population loss. You must be prepared to pay the mortgage and other expenses out of your own pocket, if necessary.
3. *Be patient*. Some markets take a year or two to recover. Others can take a decade or even longer.

The good news is—with the exception of some Dust Bowl and Rust Bowl towns—*almost all areas do eventually recover*. Many even go on to post spectacular gains. But you *do* have to be patient. You cannot force the market to recover on your own; the market is much bigger than you are.

More on Emerging Markets

You now know more than 95% of investors do about the four key phases of the real estate market cycle. The next millionaire-maker concept you need is an understanding of emerging markets.

Emerging markets are the most exciting of all! They can happen almost anywhere, at almost any time. Even an old struggling city can have one little section that is a pocket of growth and profitability.

Emerging markets take many forms. After years of dormancy and stagnation, some big-city markets spring back to life. In rural areas, some small towns suddenly transform themselves into world-class resort destinations. Vail, Colorado is an example of the latter. Property owners made hundreds of millions of dollars there.

Emerging markets are characterized by two key things:

- people migrating in rather than leaving
- jobs being created rather than destroyed

In fact, some emerging markets grow so rapidly, they have labor shortages and must recruit workers from other cities! In an emerging market, old and empty buildings are rehabbed and put back into use.

Great wealth can be built in a very short period of time in these markets. When a market is emerging, both rents and property values rise quickly.

In the previous chapter, I explained how I went from living in a one-bedroom apartment to becoming a multi-millionaire in less than 4 years. My story is not exceptional. It is the normal result of what investors can achieve if they invest in the *right market at the right time.*

What's exceptional about my case is also a benefit to you: I developed a comprehensive, scientific system for helping other investors around the country achieve this same level of success in their markets.

To make millions of dollars in the shortest amount of time is quite straight-forward: You simply need to buy as many properties as you can in an emerging market. This is literally like picking up diamonds for a fraction of the price they will soon command. While you are investing in this emerging market, you need to develop a Sales Plan that you *will* implement, as soon as the market starts to cool down.

CHARACTERISTICS OF THE BEST EMERGING MARKETS

The best emerging markets *show—and maintain—strong leadership.* Any town can have a good few months or year. A true emerging market is strong for at least several years. It takes aggressive and thoughtful leaders to analyze a city and determine what needs to be done. They then need to have the courage and strength to implement their vision in order to help the city achieve greatness.

After careful analysis, the city's leaders develop a Master Plan. In this Master Plan you will learn what incentives the city is willing to give companies to get them to move in or expand. You'll discover how the city plans to revitalize itself and what areas will get special attention. These areas are often called Economic Zones.

The city also will put an economic package together to lure investors to certain areas, in order to rehab existing inventory or build new housing units. Incentives may include low-interest loans, tax abatements, and block grants. These incentives will be outlined in the Master Plan.

In the early years of an emerging market, two areas where you should invest are the Economic Zones and the upper socio-economic areas. It is in these two areas that you'll receive the greatest return on each dollar invested.

Aggressive incentives can motivate large companies to move into the area. Because it takes anywhere from 2 to 5 years for companies to build their facilities, move in, and hire employees, *you will have a roadmap for future growth*. The more jobs that are projected to come into an area in the years ahead, the better the market will be for investors like you and me.

As those jobs begin to move in, the city will build momentum. It will develop a positive reputation as a growth hot spot. Other smaller companies will move in to serve the needs of the larger companies. Hip new restaurants, coffee houses, and theaters will open. As quality of life improves and jobs increase, even more people will want to move in. Existing businesses in the city will expand to sell more furniture, clothing, cars, hardware, household goods, and so on, to all the new people.

You can determine exactly what jobs are coming into an area, and when, by contacting the city's Economic Development Committee. This upward-spiral of momentum feeds upon itself.

The best emerging markets have a *well-diversified group of jobs coming in*. A market that's dependent on only one job type (for example, aerospace engineering) will experience a dramatic decline if something negative happens to that one big industry in town.

Many cities that were heavily dependent on Internet jobs back in the early 2000s suffered greatly when the Internet bubble burst.

I like to see jobs well diversified in service sectors, such as health, financial, and business services. These are the jobs of the future, as our country turns ever more into a service economy.

Cities that have lots of manufacturing jobs are more vulnerable. Between outsourcing and overseas production, manufacturing jobs are continually going to shrink.

Another characteristic of the best emerging markets is some type of *barrier to entry*. And the best barrier to entry is *lack of available land on which to build*. As demand increases from people migrating into an area, and after any oversupply is absorbed, new construction begins.

If there's not much available land on which to build, then the amount of new construction will lag far behind the demand. This inevitably leads to significant increases in property values—and in rents *you* can collect.

An example of a market like this is Boston, Massachusetts. Boston is bordered by the Atlantic Ocean. Settlers have been building on the land around Boston Harbor since shortly after the Pilgrims landed in 1620. There is so little room left to build, that even back in 1890, they filled in 570 acres of bay to make room for more housing! It's now called the *Back Bay*.

Almost all construction taking place in Boston requires that someone first buy an existing property, get a permit to tear it down, and go through a long, expensive process to construct a new building. This takes a great deal of time, money, and patience. It very effectively limits the number of new properties that come on the market in any given year.

Another barrier to entry is the time it takes to get the permitting done to start new construction. Boston, New York, Philadelphia, and many cities in California have lengthy permit processes.

In some areas of California, you may have to wait several years to get a water permit! To go through the entire permitting process in Boston, when you are seeking some sort of variance (permission to do something that is not allowed in the current zoning for the property), it takes a *minimum of 3 years* to get approval. Often it's much longer than 3 years!

 You can get an estimate of permitting time by calling the local building department. Ask how long it takes to get a routine building permit for a small apartment building. Then ask how long it takes to get a variance (for example, to build extra units or an extra story).

Remember, *the longer the permitting and building processes take, the better for you!* This helps to prevent overbuilding and an oversupply of units. With fewer units, you will have less competition and will be able to charge higher rents.

Let me know about your success in mastering the four real estate investment market phases, and emerging markets. You can reach me through our website, www.MarketCycleMastery.com and type the keyword: SUCCESS. I might even feature you in a later edition to this book!

IN THE NEXT CHAPTER

We're getting into it now!

You have a solid grounding now in the nature of both market cycles and the special phenomenon of emerging markets.

In the next pages, I'm going to give you a path to follow: On the one hand, there are goldmines waiting for you. Then again, there are some landmines, too. Those mostly consist of the nonsense you'll hear other investors spout. Stick with me, and we'll hang out at the goldmines!

CHAPTER 3

GOLDMINES AND LANDMINES IN EMERGING MARKETS

"Nothing is given so profusely as advice."

—Francois de la Rochefoucauld

$\mathbf{W}$hen I first started investing in real estate, I read many books, listened to dozens of tapes, and attended numerous seminars around the country. Almost all the experts suggested that real estate investors should always invest within 30 minutes of where they lived. This is what I call the *Conventional Mindset.*

Their justification was efficiency. You would save both money and time by only investing close to home. "Think of all the gas you'll save if all your properties are within 10 to 15 miles of where you live! Think of all the time you'll save, too!"

The *experts* further explained that, because the properties will be so close, you can drive there almost every day to check on tenants, pick up rent, and do repairs.

That Conventional Mindset is wrong, and the mark of a true amateur. The little bit of money and time you'll save will be far overshadowed by the hundreds of thousands of dollars you will not earn—*unless you invest in out-of-area properties!*

THE HIGH COST OF BAD ADVICE

When almost everyone says something, you start to think to yourself, "It must be true!" During the time of Christopher Columbus, most people believed the world was flat. When Columbus announced his plans to sail west across the Atlantic Ocean, many well-intentioned people warned him that he would sail off the edge of the world.

Can you imagine the courage it took for Columbus and his crew to defy conventional wisdom and sail in a direction that many people predicted would lead to certain death?

Defying conventional wisdom can be scary—but doing so can lead to huge rewards not enjoyed by the ordinary person.

When I began my real estate investing career, the Conventional Mindset was so prevalent that I did not question it. I assumed it must be true. After all, that whole bunch of experts couldn't all be wrong!

Fortunately for me, Boston was a hot real estate market at the time. If I lived in another part of the country and invested locally, I could have lost everything! For example, in the 1993 to 1995 period, some investment properties in the Los Angeles area lost 50% of their value!

Let's say you bought a $500,000 apartment building in Los Angeles in early 1993 with a 20% down payment. Two years later, that property might have been worth only $250,000. *Your $100,000 down payment was wiped out by sticking with the* Conventional Wisdom, *and investing locally.*

In fact, your losses were even greater than $100,000. Your property would have had a $400,000 mortgage. *It was now worth $150,000 less than the mortgage!* Some property owners simply gave their properties back to the bank. Foreclosures were commonplace.

If you were lucky, the bank would just take the property back. However, in most cases, *the bank filed an IRS Form 1099 to report $150,000 in forgiven debt against you.* The IRS considers "forgiveness of debt" to be *income.*

Therefore, if you followed the Conventional Mindset and "invested locally" in Los Angeles real estate in early 1993, not only could you lose 100% of your down payment over the next 2 years, but you might also owe Uncle Sam around $50,000 in taxes on your "forgiven" mortgage debt!

LOCAL INVESTMENTS CAN BE HIGHLY PROFITABLE

Do not misunderstand my point. I am not against investing locally. In fact, I have made a fortune by investing right in my own backyard—*when the real estate cycle was right.*

Many of my students and friends have also made millions by investing locally.

One of my friends is Jeff Adams, the famous Internet real estate marketing expert. Jeff made many millions of dollars by investing locally in Los Angeles and Southern California real estate. But Jeff did so wisely. He got into his local market just as it was bottoming in 1995, and intelligently rode the entire up-cycle.

If you master the market cycles we cover in this book, you will *always* be using the right strategy, at the right time, in the *right* market, whether it's local or not. You'll *maximize your profit* in every real estate deal you do.

INSIGHTS I GAINED FROM THE BOSTON MARKET

The first year I was investing, my local market in Brockton, a Boston suburb, was stagnant. It was a good thing I did not give up! I saw the tremendous potential of the area and ended up profiting handsomely.

My area had been blighted by 15 years of both job and population loss. Many properties were boarded up and abandoned. Squatters and homeless people lived in some properties. Other properties had poor tenants who were paying below-market rents.

Why did I invest in such properties? I had two main reasons:

1. I was earning *positive cash flow* on each property; and
2. I could buy properties for *below their replacement costs*.

Let's examine each of these two major advantages.

EARNING POSITIVE CASH FLOW

If you're making money from a property, that's great. How do I define *making money?* After paying the mortgage, taxes, insurance, and for all improvements, if you're still *putting a sizable chunk of money into your own pocket each month*, you are experiencing the joy of positive cash flow!

I would personally much rather own a highly profitable, plain property in a struggling market than a gold-plated, fancy property that was losing money.

Once you've been in the real estate investment field for a while, you will meet people who prefer to own fancy properties in high-status markets. An example might be a small oceanfront apartment building in Southern California.

A five-unit oceanfront building might cost you $3 million or more. Sure, it's pretty. Yes, it is nice to smell that salt air and listen to the waves. It's great to tell all your friends at a cocktail party what you just bought.

But there is no way you can charge enough in rent to cover your expenses! You will have to reach into your savings each month to pay your mortgage. This is the kind of property you must avoid. The only people making money on such properties are investors who bought them years ago (when they cost a fraction of today's prices), and who've paid down their mortgages.

BUYING BELOW REPLACEMENT COST

This is almost as important as having positive cash flow: Buy properties for below replacement value.

Let's say land in your area is worth $500,000 an acre. If you have a chance to buy a small apartment building on an acre of land for $500,000, *give it serious consideration!* Unless there is something seriously wrong with the apartment building, *you may be getting one of the biggest bargains of your life.*

Also, if the construction costs for a building are $500,000 and if the sales price is $500,000, seriously consider adding that property to your portfolio. What do both of these examples have in common? In both cases, *you are getting the property for below replacement cost!*

In the previous examples, you are either getting the *land for free* or the *apartment building for free.* In either case, you have a fantastic deal!

KNOWING WHEN TO MOVE
TO ANOTHER MARKET

When playing cards, you need to know when to play a hand and when to fold. The mark of *true professionals* is they know how best to play a given hand. The same is true of professional real estate investors.

The hand you're dealt *in the real estate world is local conditions.* When they are not favorable, *don't* force your hand. In poker, when you start getting better cards, you bet more money—but you bet it intelligently. In real estate, when conditions start improving in a market, you put more money in.

In my local market, the conditions started to improve. Six months after I began investing, Brockton started to recover. Jobs began to come in, the state of Massachusetts built a commuter rail line that linked Boston to Brockton, and people returned in large numbers to Brockton.

My local market then appreciated *rapidly.* Boarded-up buildings were rehabbed or torn down and replaced with gleaming new properties. Vacant units were quickly rented, demand rose, supply stayed about the same, and rents soared. This is an ideal real estate market for investors!

As a few years went by, I realized that I now had a very large amount of equity in my properties. While I was building my portfolio I also continued to educate myself and learned that *what goes up must eventually level off—and then either stagnate or go down.*

That's when I came up with my *If-Then Formula for Making a Real Estate Fortune.* I realized: "*If* I could just find another market like Brockton when I first invested there, *then* I could make another real estate *fortune!*"

How would I do this? What was my plan? Here it is:

Step 1: Find an extremely promising, *high-potential* emerging market;

Step 2: *Sell my properties at or near the peak of their value* and cash out my equity;

Step 3: Move my equity to the *highly profitable* emerging market I found;

Step 4: *Double* or *triple my money* in the new emerging market; and

Step 5: Sleep like a baby at night, knowing that I *avoided* the Seller's Market Phase II and a Buyer's Market Phase I.

Unlike many other owners, I did not put my equity at risk.

I realized that if I continued to follow the Conventional Mindset of "investing locally," I wasn't going to get anything close to the appreciation I had received over the past 4 years. Even worse, if I stayed in that local market, there was a chance I would lose much of the equity I had built up!

It was these insights that led me to study *real estate market cycles* and *1031 tax-deferred exchanges* intensively. The 1031 exchanges enabled me to sell my current properties and defer all taxes. I was literally able to roll over 100% of my equity and my profits into new, super-high-potential properties.

My intensive studies led to the conclusion that at any given time— regardless of what our national economy is doing—there are cities somewhere in our great country with *real estate that is about to skyrocket in value!* Of course, there are also cities, towns, and suburbs that are declining, stagnating, or slowly recovering.

THE IMPORTANCE OF COURAGE

Earlier in this chapter, I pointed out that it takes courage to go against the conventional mindset. Though it takes courage to engage in fresh, unconventional thinking, it takes even more courage to *take action!*

Simply having a great idea is not enough. When I started to invest in Brockton, many other people were also *thinking* of investing there. Of course, those who merely thought about it and took no action never made a penny. Some of them are still renters today!

My *taking action* and investing in Brockton near the bottom of its market cycle was what enabled me to go from being a landscaper, renting a one-bedroom apartment, to owning many millions of dollars worth of property.

Brockton became my cocoon. I was very comfortable there. When I realized that property values were peaking, I knew it was time to get out and move on to another promising emerging market. However, I would be lying to you if I claimed I was confident in my actions. *It was scary!* Not only did Brockton feel like home to me, but I had no book, like the one you're holding now, to guide me in the *un*conventional, profitable way to invest.

Courage was required to take action, when everyone around me thought differently about the market. As frightening as it was to sell properties in my familiar neighborhood and invest out of the area (and out of state), I knew it was exactly what I had to do to keep growing my real estate fortune.

You've heard the old adage, "It takes money to make money." This is only partially true. If you invest in the *right* type of emerging market, *it takes relatively little money to make a great deal of money*. That is exactly what happened to me when I entered Brockton's real estate market at the bottom of its cycle. I started with relatively little money and, a few years later, I was a millionaire.

If you invest in a market when values have peaked (and everyone's saying the market will keep on going up), you may lose money. So here's my other truth: "Massive wealth comes from *the intelligent movement of money from one great market to another great market.*"

The purpose of this book and of my other real estate resources is to build a new set of wealth instincts inside you. If I can guide you through just a few cycles, you'll make so much dough that you'll need no more guidance!

HOW TO MANAGE OUT-OF-AREA PROPERTIES

If investing in emerging markets in different parts of the country is so great, why doesn't everyone do it?

It's simple: They don't know how to manage out-of-area properties.

This was also one of my biggest concerns about moving out of my local real estate market.

When I first started investing in real estate, I managed my properties myself. I soon realized that the more time I spent with *tenants, trash, and toilets*, the less money I would make. When you spend your time doing the work of a $10 an hour handyman, you will *severely limit* the amount of profit you earn and the number of deals you can do.

To maximize your real estate earnings, *you must make the highest and best use of your time*. That means *finding highly profitable deals, putting them together, and attracting the money you need to make them happen.*

You do this by creating *systems* so you can *delegate* the management of properties to others.

Some highly successful real estate investors hire outside managers. The solution for me was to hire two people who worked from my office. This worked extremely well for managing local real estate holdings. However, I pretty quickly realized this would not work for managing properties that I planned to buy 100 or 1,000 miles away.

That's when I discovered the Institute of Real Estate Management (IREM). IREM provides truly outstanding educational and training programs for the owners of real estate management companies and their property managers. The graduates of their programs are highly qualified to manage properties all over the United States.

IREM offers a complete set of courses leading to two designations: the Certified Property Manager (CPM) and the Accredited Residential Manager (ARM).

In order to earn one of these designations, five learning modules need to be completed. Each module requires 3 to 5 days of full-time intensive class work. In addition, students must pass a rigorous written test after completing each course to prove their mastery of the subject. After all modules are completed and all tests have been passed, the candidate is awarded the designation.

At the IREM website, www.irem.org, you can look up all the CPMs or ARMs in *any* city in the United States. This is where you should search for highly qualified managers to help handle your out-of-area properties.

THE INCREDIBLE WEALTH-BUILDING POWER OF 1031 EXCHANGES

At the same time I was researching emerging markets and market cycles, I learned about the IRS' 1031 tax-deferred exchange regulations. The 1031 provisions of the Tax Code enable a property owner to sell a property and defer payment of the taxes to a later date. To enjoy this benefit, you must closely follow all the rules and regulations in the Code.

One requirement is that the property be "like kind," meaning you must exchange a piece of investment real estate for another piece of investment real estate. You cannot, for example, exchange your apartment building for a luxury home in which you plan to live. Such an exchange would not be considered "like kind" and you could not defer the taxes on the sale of your apartment building.

Why are 1031 tax-deferred exchanges so profitable? Imagine that you bought a property for $500,000 and sold it for $1 million. What would your net profit be if you had to pay taxes? First, you would owe taxes on the $500,000 capital gain.

The exact amount of taxes you owe depends on your state of residence and the holding period (short-term taxes are higher than long-term capital gains). However, it's safe to say you would probably pay at least 20% ($100,000) in taxes on your $500,000 gain.

As they say in late-night infomercials, "But wait, there's more!" Whatever depreciation you wrote off on the property is taxed via a 25% depreciation recapture tax. Let's say you depreciated $200,000. This means you would have to pay approximately $50,000 in the depreciation recapture tax.

Let's add these taxes up: $100,000 in capital gains tax +$50,000 in depreciation recapture = $150,000. State taxes may also be due. However, at a minimum, most investors would be looking at *a minimum tax bill of $150,000.*

This $150,000 is more than 200% greater than what most Americans earn in a year. Why send all that money to Washington, DC if there is a way of deferring the payment of the bill? That is exactly what the 1031 tax-deferred exchange allows you to do.

In case you're thinking this is too good to be true, or some scam, it's not either. It is written right into the tax code. A long-standing theme of our economic system has been to encourage property ownership. That's what these regulations do, all right!

It is extremely important that you work with experts in structuring your 1031 exchange. Some of the rules can be quite complex. If you make one serious mistake, the entire transaction may be disallowed and the government may come knocking at your door with a demand for all those taxes—plus penalties!

Fortunately, it's not hard to find 1031 experts. These people do exchanges all day long, so they probably dream the rules at night. They can guide you with a confident hand.

THE COMPOUNDING FACTOR

1031 tax-deferred exchanges enable you to *compound* your wealth. Let's return to our earlier example to see how. We'll call the investor who uses a 1031 exchange *Investor A* and the investor who does not engage in a tax-deferred exchange *Investor B*.

As you remember, a property was bought for $500,000 and sold for $1 million. Because he engaged in a 1031 exchange, *Investor A actually now has $1 million to invest in a new property*. To keep this example simple, we will assume the mortgage has been paid off and we will ignore the effects of commissions and closing costs. In the real world, you'd have about 7% less than this, due to the commissions and closing costs.

If Investor B did not engage in a 1031 exchange, he would have about *$850,000* to invest (minus commissions and closing costs). This is because Investor B had to pay a minimum of $100,000 in capital gains tax and $50,000 in depreciation recapture.

Now both investors look for their next properties. They are each planning to use the money they have as a 20% down payment. Because he was able to defer all taxes, Investor A can buy a *$5 million property*. Investor B can only buy a $4,250,000 property.

The 1031 tax-deferred exchange enables *Investor A to buy a property worth $750,000 more than Investor B's property!*

By deferring taxes several more times on successive sales and purchases, *Investor A can literally end up twice as wealthy as Investor B!* Investor A can retire earlier, buy nicer cars, take nicer vacations, and send his or her children to the finest schools in America, due to the *wealth compounding* enabled by 1031 exchanges.

FOLLOWING THE RULES TO ENJOY THE BENEFITS OF A 1031 EXCHANGE

At one time, the IRS required that you buy and sell properties in a 1031 exchange on the *same day*. Needless to say, it was extremely difficult to coordinate all the details of selling one property and buying another in one single day.

In 1979, The IRS amended the 1031 regulations so that you now have *45 days* from the time you close on the property you are selling to *identify* the new property that you will buy. Note that you don't actually have to complete the purchase in 45 days; you only need to identify the new property.

You then have *180 days* from the time you sell the initial property to when you must close on the next property. This generous time window makes using 1031 exchanges much easier.

As soon as I learned about the many benefits of 1031 exchanges, and found an emerging market, *I took action*. I sold a property I had owned in Brockton for almost 6 years. The market was close to the top, and I sold it for $250,000. I had accumulated *$181,000 in equity* in this property because I bought it when values in the area were low.

Why did I sell the property? The *net spendable income* on this property was low—only about $600 per month. That meant I was only earning about 4% per year on my equity! I could earn that in a CD at the local bank! I had a difficult time getting the net spendable income higher because I had to pay for all the energy to heat the building. The building cash flowed great in the summer, but the bitter New England winter drained my profits. I knew I could put my equity to better use!

I traded that property for a complex in Tuscaloosa, Alabama for which I paid just under one million dollars. I accomplished this without taking *any* money out of my pocket! Now that's wealth creation! The miracle of the 1031 exchange made this all possible. If I had to pay taxes on my $250,000 sale, I could *never* have afforded to buy that property in Alabama.

By making this trade, I exchanged a $600 monthly net spendable income for a *$2,800 monthly net spendable income*. Uncle Sam let me give myself an immediate $2,200 monthly raise. *That's a $26,400 increase in my annual income from just one property, not counting growth in the value of the property.*

In addition, in just under over 2 years of ownership of the new property, I now had total equity of $370,000. That means if I had sold this property then and traded up to another, assuming that I used the entire $370,000 as a 20% down payment, my next purchase would have been for a property worth *$1,850,000.*

Imagine doing this with five or six properties at the same time! While newspaper headlines shout about over 20-cents-a-gallon gas increases, you can be quietly and legally leaping your real estate fortune by $100,000 at a time!

Let me put it in formula terms: 1031 Exchange + Emerging Market Investing + Multi-Family Properties = Astonishing Wealth

To discover more about 1031 tax-deferred exchanges, go to my website at www.MarketCycleMastery.com and type into the search box the keyword: 1031. I have a free information kit on 1031 exchanges.

EMERGING MARKETS ARE NOT THE SAME AS *HOT* MARKETS

Many investors make the mistake of investing in *hot* areas. These are the places you read about in popular magazines. Everyone is talking about them because they've performed great for several years. The amateur reads such an article and thinks "Great ... it's hot!" The professional reads the article and says "Hot = stale ... stay away!"

When you chase after hot markets, you're chasing after yesterday's winners. These markets attract a lot of *dumb money*. These are investors who are buying simply because other people are buying. They're the same people who bought Internet stocks at the peak of the stock market bubble. They're spoilers, because they bid up the values of properties (or stocks) way beyond the underlying economic realities.

In contrast, emerging markets are under the radar, not to be found in any popular magazines. They're waiting to be discovered.

Record-breaking profits happen by *anticipating the next markets that are likely to outperform*. Instead of looking at what IS hot, you must be able to determine what WILL be hot.

In parts of Florida, we saw a phenomenon of *condo flipping*. People bought condos before they were even built, in the hopes they could sell them at a profit when the building was finished.

In some new buildings in Florida, 80% of the units were bought not by residents, but by speculators!

By the time a market starts to attract national attention, it's usually a Seller's Market Stage I. When you hear people say, "You *can't* lose money if you invest in [wherever]!" it usually means property values have peaked in that area.

WHY BOTH EMPLOYERS AND EMPLOYEES PREFER EMERGING MARKETS

In many established markets, population has exceeded infrastructure— especially *transportation* infrastructure. The result is congestion and heavy traffic that many residents find oppressive.

It used to be that rush hour lasted an hour or so. Now in markets like LA, Atlanta, and New York, rush hour is pretty much all day long. As soon as they can, many residents move to less-congested, less-polluted areas. This further limits the profit potential in many established areas.

These same factors also drive away employers. Toyota had its U. S. headquarters in Gardena, California for several decades. Gardena is an LA suburb. Despite the tremendous costs in doing so, in 2005, Toyota made the decision to move its corporate headquarters and thousands of employees to Tennessee.

At a certain point, congestion, pollution, and high prices conspire to persuade both companies and individuals to move out of an area. Many of the homes near Gardena cost more than $500,000. Five miles away, in Manhattan Beach, the average home sells for more than $1.3 million. Not many Toyota workers can afford to pay $500,000 to more than $1.3 million for a home.

In Tennessee—where Toyota single-handedly created an emerging market—you can buy a great home on a large lot with clean air for less than $250,000. In some cases, a mere $20,000 down payment will move you into one of these beautiful homes!

The ability to expand operations in the future is another reason that emerging markets outperform their more mature counterparts. As I already said, mature cities are already built up. The land has been taken long ago. There IS no acreage to be found for a company to build a 5,000-person manufacturing plant in Boston or New York.

Larger companies look years down the road and move to cities and towns with room for expansion. That is one reason Toyota moved to Tennessee, and why Honda opened a huge facility in Marysville, Ohio.

Remember that one of the keys to investing in emerging markets is to *first sell off your properties in maturing markets*. Equity that is tied up in a stagnating market is *dead money*. Sell your properties at or near the peak of the market cycle, do a 1031 tax-deferred exchange, and *compound your wealth* in the next emerging market.

Remember, *wealth is built by getting out early, then getting in early*.

WHY IT TAKES LESS MONEY TO GET STARTED IN EMERGING MARKETS

You're the owner of a property that's been stagnant in a Buyer's Market Phase I for the last 7 years. You've struggled to create cash flow. Your city has lost jobs and you've lost tenants. You had to *decrease* your rents just to keep the tenants you have. Because of it, the value of your property has declined.

At one time or another, every major real estate market in America has experienced *significant* declines. Most markets have had numerous declines.

Seattle had one such downturn in the early 1970s, when Boeing and other major manufacturers had massive layoffs. Someone even put up a billboard outside Seattle saying, "*Will the last person who leaves Seattle please turn off the lights?*"

When markets are in a severe downturn, it's common for investors to have to *pay someone to buy their properties*. Let's say your mortgage is $500,000. The most anyone will offer you is $450,000. To get this property sold, you may have to hand the buyer $50,000 in cash (to pay the bank)—plus pay the real estate agent a commission of 6% ($27,000). To sell this property, you just burned up $77,000 of your life savings.

People do these desperate things to *protect their credit*. If the bank records a foreclosure against you, *your credit may be ruined for up to 10 years*.

In the midst of this bleak investment environment, some investors suddenly get a letter in the mail from a person interested in buying their properties. They think, "Who in the world would be interested in buying *my* property, in this lousy city? They must be crazy!"

That letter might very well be from me, or one of my students! If we've detected that the city has bottomed and is about to begin its up cycle, we may be very interested in buying many properties in the area.

These sellers in the beginning of an emerging market simply don't realize the market is changing. They have no clue that the city has a new master plan, with jobs coming in soon.

Instead, in these kinds of markets, many sellers will allow a buyer simply to take over the mortgage. This means the new buyer assumes the mortgage *that is still under your name*. If the new buyer does not pay the mortgage, you're still liable for the full unpaid balance! Thousands of such deals are done by desperate sellers.

Or, buyers may offer to make you an *equity partner* in whatever profit they make. Why would buyers make such deals? So they can buy your property for *no money down*.

In emerging markets, early investors get *sweetheart deals, left and right*. It's easier to get started in emerging markets with *much* less money for the following reasons:

1. You will be among the *earliest* serious investors in that market;
2. Sellers are going to regard you as a *savior*, and will cut great deals with you;
3. Because sellers don't realize what's about to happen in their market, they will sell properties for much less than they'll soon be worth; and

4. Because sellers are so motivated to sell, they will give you special terms, like bringing cash to the table, allowing you to assume a mortgage under their name, and may even give you a second mortgage that they will carry at *below-market interest rates*.

Whatever money you have for a down payment is going to buy *a lot more property for you*.

A very popular way to purchase properties with *no money down* is to use *private money*. We'll discuss how you can do private money deals in depth in a later chapter 9. It's a great technique.

The knowledge you will gain from this book will enable you to speak with private money investors intelligently. You will be able to show these private money lenders *exactly* where this emerging market will be in a few short years. They will understand that your in-depth research has taken most of the risk out of the investment. Many will be eager to lend you money.

The ability to use private money in emerging markets allows you to get started quickly and to *rapidly expand the size of your portfolio* with little or none of your own money!

THE HARDEST PART OF INVESTING IN EMERGING MARKETS

If you're a pilot, you know the term *vertigo*. It means disorientation while flying. In this state, pilots are SURE they are going to hit the ground, and they make adjustments—only to fly into the ground. That's why pilots are taught to trust their instruments. Looking out the window in a cloud bank, at night, at 500 miles per hour is no way to fly.

As I said earlier, to make the most money in emerging markets, you also need to trust your data *instruments*. There will be investors and back-seat drivers all around you with advice on how you should invest.

If they're filthy rich from real estate investing and giving you advice, then perhaps listen to what they have to say. If not, then nod and look interested, but ignore their advice!

To invest in emerging markets initially means to be uncomfortable! It all seems so counterintuitive. That is, until you've made a pile of money from hopping out of one market cycle, and into another. Pretty soon, you'll get your instrument rating for flying your real estate empire, and you'll be fine.

Here's one way to make the transition easier: Associate with like-minded people. You may find some investors at your local real estate investment association who know a bit about emerging markets. But be careful: For every such investor, there will be a dozen that either know nothing, or will give you bad advice!

Another way to find the right people is to attend one of my live events. Because I'm so utterly sure of the value of my events, I always guarantee them unconditionally. While other *gurus* have these wimpy partial guarantees, mine are 100% guaranteed from the first minute to the last.

I know that you are reading this book because you want to achieve something great in your life. I commend you for that. You're taking the time to discover new strategies and ways of thinking. The knowledge you gain will enormously benefit you and your family.

You're a knowledge seeker and *knowledge seekers who take action with their knowledge* usually become highly successful.

I look forward to hearing about the successes you achieve by using this knowledge!

In the Next Chapter

We're now going to change gears. Until now, it's been necessary to explain how things work and where to look for emerging markets.

In the following chapter, I'll show you how to put that good information into action—we're going to go out and find us an emerging market!

CHAPTER 4

GETTING YOUR FIRST DEAL IN AN EMERGING MARKET

"The way to develop self-confidence is to do the thing you fear."

—William Jennings Bryan

Before you invest in emerging markets, you need a plan. This will be your roadmap to success. Investors who simply jump into an emerging market—or any market—without a well-thought-out plan are usually not very successful.

In developing your success plan, first decide what type of property you most want to invest in. You have a wide range to choose from: small single-family homes, luxury rental homes, apartment buildings (three units up to hundreds of units), office buildings, industrial buildings, shopping centers, and so on.

Even though money can be made in all of these property types, the main focus of this book is on apartments. For reasons I explain in Chapter 6, apartments make you the most money the fastest, with little or no money down.

I want to make the point, though, that you CAN start with other property types. I'm not one of those guys who says "MY property type is the ONLY kind that works." That's just baloney.

So let's say you settle on apartments as your main focus (with an eye out for great deals in other types, should they come along). The next *essential* factor that many newer investors overlook is *the ability to find good property managers for your property.* Let's say that you found an incredible apartment bargain in a small city in Texas. You live in Chicago. Obviously, *you* are not going to be able to manage that building from Chicago.

Even if you can buy this property for 50% of its true value, *do NOT buy it until you know you can get a great local manager to manage it for you!* Without a great manager, the property will fall into disrepair, you'll lose tenants (or end up with a building full of bad ones), and your property will plummet in value.

Initially, your management company will be the *key player* on your real estate team. This person or company must be a specialist. After all, managing a senior citizen complex is far different from managing a strip shopping center with a mix of fast food restaurants and retail shopping.

You must find a *local* manager who has these skills. Don't rely on what a manager tells you he or she can do; go by what that manager is currently doing: units currently managed, in the area you're interested in, for the property type you're focused on.

Next you must consider the ability of the property to cash flow if it loses some of its tenants. I always teach my students to *hope for the best and be prepared for the worst.* If a worst-case scenario takes place, your property should still be able to support itself financially. If your property had a 25% vacancy rate, would it still provide you with a positive cash flow? If it had a 10% vacancy rate, would it still be cash flow positive? What is the cut-off point?

Now, ask the existing owners about the *highest vacancy rate they ever experienced.* Do the math. If that happened again, would the property still cash flow—or would you have to reach into your pocket each month to pay the bills?

At the beginning of your investing career, avoid properties that have only a few tenants paying the majority of the rent. These tenants make you very vulnerable.

Imagine you are buying a five-unit apartment building. Two of the units are three-bedrooms that rent for $1,500 a month each ($3,000 per month total). The other three apartments are one-bedroom units that rent for $650 per month each ($1,950 total each month). If only two of your five units are vacant, you could lose 60% of your monthly income! At that point, your investment would be bleeding red ink.

It would be much better to buy a five-unit building that had five two-bedroom units each renting for $1,200 per month ($6,000 per month total). Even if two units were vacant, you would still be collecting *$3,600 per month* (versus only $1,950 per month in the previous example).

Next, *analyze how difficult it might be to replace tenants.* For instance, is your building dependent on many tenants who work in the same factory down the street? You're looking for hidden risks.

I'm a pretty positive guy. In fact, I make it a rule to surround myself with positive, upbeat people and not ones that drag themselves down all the time—and take me with them!

Still, it's important to *stress test* your proposed investments by actively looking for flaws. A chain is only as strong as its weakest link, and the same holds true of deals. Better to find that link now, and know how you'll handle it, rather than have it drop into your lap later.

SECRETS OF GREAT WEALTH CREATION

Choose a property type that will have a *large number of qualified buyers*. When the time comes for you to sell your property and reap your rewards, you want to know that there will be other investors ready to pay a fair price for your property. The larger the pool of potential buyers, the faster you can sell and move your profits—*tax-deferred*—into another high-potential emerging market. This is one secret to great wealth creation in real estate investing.

Another secret is to move to bigger deals, as soon as you can.

Imagine you have a choice between two different properties in the same market, and you have $*100,000 cash.*

One property sells for $100,000 and the other is going for $1 million. If the market increases by 20% over the next 18 months, you'd have created $20,000 in equity in the property that you bought for $100,000. However, if you bought the property listed at $1 million, you would have created $200,000 in equity! Same market, same holding period, *ten times* difference in profit.

The first property would have had a 20% return over your holding period, based on the amount of cash you put down. Using the same amount of cash, you would have earned a *200% profit* with the second property! Again, same market, same size down payment, same holding period. This is why you want to start doing bigger deals as soon as possible, if you are truly serious about growing your wealth.

And yes, I'm going to show you, later in this book, how the same $100,000 can purchase the much larger property.

WHERE YOU SHOULD START

Investors ask me all the time, "Where should I start, Dave?" Obviously, few investors can start by investing in really large properties. The truth is, you start with the kind of properties that are in your comfort zone. Doing a small deal now is infinitely better than hoping to make the *Big Score* someday, but never getting around to it.

Notice that I said *start* with these types of properties. They are not your final destination.

During the first 3 years of my investing career, I bought a variety of smaller properties. I *gained experience, learned from my mistakes, and worked on expanding my comfort zone.*

As my experience and comfort zone grew, I moved up to bigger properties. I had a major breakthrough when I got over my fear of buying bigger buildings and purchased a 350-unit complex! To me, this was like owning a small town!

If you have the money and self-confidence, you can move into bigger deals even faster than I did. Some of my students have done over 100 units for their first deal! With the knowledge they acquired from my programs, they were able to create net-positive spendable income of several thousand dollars each month—from one deal!

One of my students worked on his comfort zone with big deals in Augusta, Georgia. Through my coaching, he got the knowledge he needed to do bigger deals. He overcame the fear many people have of large deals, and used one of my emerging markets property location techniques to identify and purchase a 110-unit property. This was his first deal! This property had a *positive cash flow, into his pocket,* of over $6,000 a month (*$72,000 per year*). On top of this was all the appreciation, down the road.

Best of all, *he got into this 110-unit apartment building with no money down.* He used the Equity Share technique I describe in Chapter 9 of this book. After just 18 months of holding the property, he found a buyer who purchased it for a *profit* of *$982,000!*

One of the greatest insights you will ever have as a real estate investor is this: *It takes just as much effort to do a $100,000 deal as it does to do a $1 million deal.* In fact, sometimes the $100,000 deal is more time-consuming than a $1 million deal. *Here's why:* Very few $100,000 buildings throw off enough positive cash flow for you to be able to hire a manager. If you own a $100,000 building, you will probably spend a lot of your time dealing with tenants and maintenance issues.

However, many $1 million buildings throw off enough cash for you to hire a professional manager. Many larger deals also have enough cash flow to hire a maintenance person to do all the repairs, paint vacant units, replace carpet, and so on. This frees up a tremendous amount of your time to find other great deals and multiply your wealth.

The big difference between doing small deals and large deals is not how much time they take to manage—it's that *you get paid a lot more money to do the bigger deals!*

THE SUPREME IMPORTANCE OF TIME MANAGEMENT

Of course you know that becoming rich in real estate does take *some* time and effort. But I have two pieces of very good news:

- The right systems can reduce that time to a minimum; and
- The actual time needed is small enough to be realistically done by a person with a full-time day job.

After all, I was a full-time landscaper when I got started. My most important requirement for a road toward financial freedom was that it not take too much time. The fact that you can simply plug in my systems will save you even more time.

Let's now look at some of the ways you'll get deals coming your way, even while you keep your current schedule.

HOW TO SAVE TIME AND MONEY WHEN INVESTING IN EMERGING MARKETS

The first is doing a *direct mail campaign.* This is simply sending mailing pieces directly to the owners of the kinds of properties in which you are most interested. You can get a list of owners from the assessor's office of the city in which you are interested. Ownership and tax records are public information.

The city assessor may require that you submit a written request and will then tell you how much they charge for the list. You can also call the assessor on the phone and find out exactly what they want you to say in your written request. Some cities have slightly different requirements. While you are on the phone with them, ask what the fee is for the list and to what address you should send the check. Within a couple of weeks, you should have your list.

Other cities will ask you to come down to City Hall, where you can review the list in person. Still others may say "We don't give out that information." In that case, you're talking with a clerk who probably is filling in during lunch hour. So you politely say, "Gee, I know this is publicly available information by law—maybe I'm calling it by the wrong name. Is there someone I can talk to there who might be able to give me a list of the types of files that ARE available?"

Your goal now is to talk with someone else, so however you want to word that, go for it. You may have to jump through some hoops to get this list, but every hoop should bring a smile to your face: That means not many other investors will have taken the time!

You may wonder why I recommend mailing right to the property owner, instead of going through a real estate broker. It's true that agents *can* be a great asset. A skilled agent will find you many good deals over time.

However, by going directly to the property owner, you can frequently save around 6% on commissions. Let's say you want to buy a $1 million property. A standard commission is 6%, or $60,000. The seller has to raise the price by $60,000 to cover this commission. If he or she instead sells to you directly, the seller can take about $60,000 out of the price of the property and still net the same amount of money.

Therefore, if the seller had been considering selling his or her property for $1 million to net $940,000 with an agent, he or she could possibly sell the property directly to you for $940,000 and end up with the same amount of net proceeds. *A few hours of work on your inexpensive little direct mail campaign has just saved you $60,000!*

There's another HUGE reason you must contact property owners directly: Agents concentrate on selling properties that are *already listed*. They want to move their existing inventory, and keep those sellers happy who have listed properties with them.

By sending letters directly to a large number of property owners in a city, there's a good chance you'll learn of a property NOT currently listed for sale. This could be one of the best deals in town—and ONLY YOU know about it, because you directly contacted the owner!

Another great source for lists of property owners are *mailing list brokers.* You can use Google or another search engine and enter the phrase "mailing list brokers." You will be amazed at the number of list brokers you find. Some brokers can quickly get the names and addresses of property owners in any city in America.

In some cases, you can order your mailing list online and have the list that same day or the next day. List brokers charge per name. A typical fee might about around $130 for the names and addresses of 1,000 property owners. The county assessor's office may be less expensive, but they may also be slower. Just make sure to ask the list broker how recently the data were compiled. You WILL get current data from the assessor's office; but the broker could potentially have stale information.

Just think of how easy it now is to contact property owners in any city in America. For $130 or so, you can get the names and addresses of 1,000 property owners.

Then buy 10 rolls of stamps and some envelopes and *you will soon have 1,000 property owners in that emerging market thinking about you and the fact that you are ready and willing to buy their properties!* You will find some great deals by doing direct mail campaigns.

Be as selective as you can with your mailing lists. If you only specify that you want a list of *property owners* in an area, you'll have people on that list who own raw land, single-family homes, office buildings, apartments, shopping centers—you name it.

If you are *only* interested in, say, properties with more than 25 rental units and with assessed values of more than $600,000, ask for such a list. You may have to ask a few brokers, but you're likely to get what you are after. This will save you much time and money because you won't be mailing to people with no interest whatsoever in the properties you want to buy.

If the list broker can't help you get your "dream list," then settle for something close to it. For example, your list broker might not be able to get you a list of the owners of 25+ unit buildings. However, he or she might be able to get you a list of the owners of 20+ unit buildings. This list will include the owners you want to reach. Go for it! Maybe the broker can get a list of owners of all properties assessed at more than $600,000. That's close enough, too.

SECRETS OF SUCCESSFUL DIRECT MAIL CAMPAIGNS

List brokers offer what they call *list segmentation*, or *selects*. These are selection criteria that further *narrow* and *target* your list. They will charge you a little extra for each segmentation, but it's money well spent.

If you want a list of homeowners in Georgia, the cost might be $130 per 1,000 names and addresses. If you wanted a segmentation of only homeowners in Atlanta, the cost might be $135 per 1,000 names ($5 for the extra computer sort). If you want a list of homeowners in Atlanta who own homes valued at more than $400,000, the price might be $140 for 1,000 names meeting such criteria. Each additional computer sort might cost $5 or $10. But each sort also gets you closer to the exact people you're trying to reach.

That not only means you're sending fewer letters and less cost, but you can tailor those letters to speak directly to the audience you're reaching.

A great way to segment your list is by *out-of-state owners*. From years of experience in doing mailings, I have found that I get a higher response from the mailings that I send to out-of-state owners. I have also found that these owners tend to be more amenable to doing creative deals.

What makes out-of-state owners such good prospects? Some of them have never found a good local management company. They don't know how to manage a *far away* property. They may be frustrated, or may want to sell the building and invest closer to where they live. They could have inherited the property from a relative who lived in the area. In that case, they may have no emotional attachment to the area, and may be very willing to sell it.

Another key reason why they're such good prospects is few if any other investors are contacting them. People take the easy route, and you've had to do some digging to get these names. The out-of-state owners aren't beaten down by dozens of offers to buy their preforeclosure property, for instance.

To be successful with your direct mail campaign, you must do it *consistently*. Few direct mail campaigns are winners right away. You might even do a mailing to 1,000 names and get no strong response. Do NOT give up! On your very next mailing, you might find a highly motivated property owner who will sell his or her $1 million apartment building to you for a great price!

Another key to success in your direct mail campaign is to *delegate it to someone else*. It's okay to stuff envelopes the very first time, to understand the entire process. But just as soon as you possibly can, find someone else to do it. You can find kids, high school students, people at the local senior center, or residents at a disabled center to do this type of work—gladly! I currently pay about 15 cents a letter. Your mileage may vary, but not by much.

If you rely on yourself to send out those letters each month (aim to send out between 500 and 1,000), you'll have less time for your deal making. Then, as soon as the deals start coming in, you'll get too busy, and will forget to do your mailings. Your pipeline of future deals has just dried up!

Many people are happy to take on other part-time work. Employ them to do all sorts of jobs, like signing and stuffing envelopes, taking them to the post office, and so on. You must be focused on *finding deals, creating cash flow, and cashing checks*. The sooner you delegate all other activities to someone else, the more money you'll make.

I know it feels wrong to pay others to do this work at first, when you have less money than any other resource. All I can tell you is it's a major milestone in your road to wealth: When you delegate, you've just moved from the bumpy country dirt road to the interstate.

Once you have your mailing system up and running, it takes little time and energy to mail to a new batch each month. Eventually some owner will contact you with a great deal. While your mailing person is sending out 500 to 1,000 or more letters each month, you should be spending your time answering phone calls and emails from potential sellers.

WORKING SUCCESSFULLY WITH AGENTS

Commercial real estate brokerage firms are another great source for deals in the market you've targeted. Agents at these firms specialize in selling *investment, commercial (apartments are considered commercial), and industrial properties.* They do not sell single-family homes. Many agents who sell single-family homes are part-timers. Most commercial agents dealing with apartments, offices, shopping centers, and industrial buildings are *full-time professionals.*

In most areas, commercial real estate brokers do not have multiple listings; there is no central directory showing all properties for sale. *For this reason, get to know agents at several different firms.* Some firms treat their listings as proprietary and don't inform agents outside of their office of these listings. The only way to learn of these listings is to work with an agent at that firm.

You need to be active in this network, because when agents get a listing, they offer it first to buyers, starting with the top of their list. If one of these Top Dogs does not make an offer on the property, the agent shows the listing to everyone else on the list.

The best way to get to the top of agents' lists is to buy a property from them. That's not the only way, though: Most agents realize that once an investor has purchased a property, he or she may not be able to buy another property for several years. Therefore, while existing clients are always shown properties first—they are NOT the only ones to learn about deals on the day they are listed.

To move to the top of agents' lists, *stay in constant contact with them.* When they send you a deal, *call them and give them feedback immediately.* If the deal does not meet your parameters, still call them!

This is very important. You may innocently think "I got this lead, but it doesn't meet my needs; I don't want to hurt the agent's feelings, so I'll just lay low and say nothing." Very bad move. While you're thinking that, the agent is thinking "What an ungrateful jerk! I sent him a deal and he doesn't lift a finger to say anything about the deal, or even just to say thanks. Forget that!"

If you expect to see more deals, then get back to the agent right away! You don't have to lie about the deal. If it's not what you're after, just *gently explain* the reasons to the agent. Do *not* say, "This deal is way overpriced!" or "I would never buy a property in that horrible neighborhood." Say "That one is out of my price range . . . I was looking to spend no more than $40,000 per unit," or "I'm hoping to find a deal on the South Side."

When you explain why you are not interested in a deal, you are *educating* the agent about what kind of deal you are looking for. Try to be complimentary about the listing. Let the agent know you think it is a good deal—but not for you. Then, *describe the exact kind of deal in which you are interested.*

When you give agents feedback like this, *do NOT correspond by e-mail.* Call them on the phone! Talk to them as one person to another, and *build a human bond.* Don't just be another anonymous e-mail address. This is the mark of a professional.

There will be many opportunities to e-mail your agents. They will e-mail you lots of listings (if you follow my advice!). You can communicate about many routine matters by e-mail. But when you're training an agent, it is important that you communicate by phone and really get to know each other.

It's through these calls that you will build rapport with agents. You will learn if they are married or single, how many children they have, what their hobbies are, and so on. As you get to know them better, you'll move higher up their list of prospects who are *the first* to be informed of new listings.

MORE DETAILS ON WORKING WITH AGENTS

Earlier in this chapter, I revealed ways to move up on agents' lists of preferred clients. Some may require that you sign an *Exclusive Buyer's Agency Agreement* stating that they will represent you in *all* transactions in that market for a certain period.

Do *not* confuse this document with a confidentiality agreement. The confidentiality agreement states that a particular broker or agent introduced you to a property and because of that introduction, you agree that he or she is owed a commission if you purchase it. Even if you purchase the property through another agent, you will owe that first agent a commission.

I sign such confidentiality agreements all the time. It's only fair that the broker who introduced you to a great deal earns a commission if you buy the property.

The Exclusive Buyer's Agency Agreement states that you will pay them a commission on any property that you buy in the market *regardless* of who introduces you to the property. I'm not too keen on signing this agreement. Think twice about signing such an agreement in a major market. Don't get yourself locked into such an exclusive agreement unless you are absolutely sure the agent will have access to a large number of high-quality listings as soon as they hit the market. Very few agents have such access.

Signing an Exclusive Buyer's Agency Agreement with a broker who gets most of his or her listings through other offices will put you at a major disadvantage; you will be seeing these listings after many other buyers have seen them. Chances are, the best deals will be taken by buyers who were exposed to the deal before you were. You will be seeing the left-over deals.

Remember that all brokers and agents like to show their listings *first* to their own best clients and prospects. If you are not on the "best prospects" list for several agents, you are not likely to see the best deals in that city. If you are primarily being represented by a Buyer's Agent, I can assure you that you're missing out on a lot of great deals.

Is there a time to consider signing an Exclusive Buyer's Agency Agreement? Yes, when the market is small and your agent has a lot of influence in that market. Under such circumstances, your agent's company may get 50% or more of all new listings. An aggressive agent at the top firm in a small city knows all the hot listings, and can *shake the trees* to find you great deals.

In bigger markets, I like to have two to five agents working for me. Sometimes I use two agents in the same office. Why? One agent may be great at getting listings on the north side of town. The other agent may be very well-connected in another part of town.

In a rapidly growing emerging market, get several agents to find you properties so you're exposed to multiple high-quality deals, as soon as possible.

FINDING GREAT INVESTMENT PROPERTIES ON THE INTERNET

The Internet can be another source of great deals for investment properties. Some websites specialize in listing and selling *income-producing properties*.

You are probably thinking, "Yeah, but don't you only see junk left-overs on the Internet?" It's true that some of them are overpriced or in areas where you wouldn't want to buy. But there *are* some great deals to be had on the Internet.

The Internet—that great equalizer—also *enables owners to sell their own properties directly to buyers*. These are some of the *best* deals you'll find anywhere.

In addition, residential agents (those who sell single-family homes) often also list their investment properties on the Internet. That is because they don't have a long list of prospects for such properties. The Internet enables them to expose their investment listings to thousands of potential buyers. In the "For Sale by Owner" listings and the ones by residential agents, you'll find some true gems.

Some junk investment properties listed on the Internet are put there by commercial brokers. They sometimes stick up a listing on the Internet when they cannot sell it by any other means. However, in some cases, they list it on the Internet to expose it to buyers all over the United States.

Pay close attention to investment listings posted by commercial brokers. You may not be interested in any of these listings. However, notice WHO is putting up a lot of listings. This will identify for you the *most active commercial brokers* in the area. For every property these highly active agents have put on the Internet, they may have several more (and better) deals that they're only showing to their best clients. Bingo! Get in touch with these active agents.

Here is your action plan for contacting them: Call them up and explain that you saw their property on the Internet but that the particular property you saw doesn't make sense for you. Then proceed to tell them the exact type of property in which you are most interested. *They might tell you on the spot that they have a property that meets your exact buying criteria!*

Using the Internet as your own personal bird dog can yield a consistent flow of high-quality deals.

Here is just one other example of my power prospecting techniques: Your courthouse posts eviction cases, with the name of the landlord who is suing a tenant or trying to evict a tenant. Needless to say, a number of these frustrated landlords may be motivated sellers!

Sandra Nesbitt of Hartford, Connecticut sent out her first set of letters to landlords she found this way. Her mailing was successful, to say the least: On her first deal she took over a property from a seller who had over $140,000 in equity! The seller just wanted out. Sandra refinanced the property and *pulled out $100,000 in cash.*

This wasn't a "no money down" deal: It was a "*$100,000 in your pocket for doing the deal*" deal! In addition to that $100,000 of cash in her pocket, she still receives a very handsome monthly check from the building's cash flow.

Using the same technique and the same letter that I provide my workshop students, she earned a profit of *$51,000* on her next deal and *$62,000* on the deal after that! On those three deals, Sandra made more than a quarter-million dollars of profit.

This direct-marketing stuff works! To get started finding great deals in emerging markets, you need to devote only ½ hour a day, 4 days a week to your marketing efforts. That's only 2 hours a week! If you are serious about your success, you can find 2 hours to devote to this highly profitable activity.

Some people don't believe me when I say "2 hours a week." What I'm referring to is just to *get started*. That's the beauty of it: While you have your day job, you need to devote only a couple hours a week to finding good deals. Now, once you find the deal, you'll be highly motivated to spend more time at odd moments making that deal happen. After all, using my deal analysis techniques, you'll have a pretty good idea of the cash that will soon be in your hot little hand!

HOW RESEARCH CAN HELP YOU DOMINATE AN EMERGING MARKET

The first step to dominating an emerging market is to make sure you are in one!

Real estate markets are made and broken through population growth and job creation. Some areas of Florida do not have much job creation. Still, real estate values are soaring because hundreds of thousands of retirees flood into those areas every year from the cold North. As these retirees move to the Sunshine State, they create jobs.

Though retirees usually do not work, they buy fast food and go to restaurants. Their homes need to be built. They buy cars from dealers, and later need those cars repaired. The biggest job creator of all is catering to the health needs of these seniors.

You must get employment data if you are to invest successfully in an emerging market. You can get it from the *Bureau of Labor Statistics*. That data will tell you how many jobs are coming into an area now, and how many came in over the past few years. These helpful government number crunchers also *forecast the number of jobs* that are likely to come into the area in the future. I hope your ears just perked up!

Examine the population and employment growth trends for an area over the past 5 years. Then look at predicted future job growth. You should be in a market where *jobs are predicted to increase significantly*. This is a true emerging market.

Next, contact the *Economic Development Committee* of your target city. Determine what they are doing to attract jobs and which employers are committed to coming to the area. The more, the better!

Invest in cities or towns that have announced the building or moving of a major new plant, factory, or corporate headquarters to their area. These are prime locations for investment.

As you continue to invest in that area, regularly take the pulse of the leadership. Has it remained the same or have new elections brought in antigrowth people? Such activists in government positions can be the *kiss of death for investment success.* Is the current political leadership still committed to growth? Are the new politicians and zoning officials serious about attracting jobs?

Don't judge them by what they say; instead, look at how many jobs they've brought in over the last year compared with prior years. Action is the only thing that counts.

As emerging real estate markets develop, the influx of new people, jobs, and buildings requires more infrastructure. As a city begins to expand on its growing edges, roads are built and widened. Then come new schools, fire and police stations, and water treatment facilities.

All this activity creates still more jobs and helps fuel further growth. It is an upward cycle.

It IS possible for a city to become *too aggressive* in its growth mandate. To lure business in, some cities offer 10- or 15-year tax breaks. These deals definitely can attract high-quality employers, but sometimes the city gives away too much: The city may not receive enough in revenues to pay for needed infrastructure, schools, and roads. Quality of life may stagnate, causing other employers to rethink moving to the area.

With some of the biggest new businesses not paying their fair share of taxes, the burden often shifts to taxpayers. Pretty soon, the tax cost for average citizens starts to creep up. Property and sales taxes go up.

If the city is not careful, taxes may creep up to the point where it's no longer attractive for people to move to that city, or even stay in it.

Keep track of the tax base, and make sure the city is not running up deficits. Follow the news in the cities where you are investing. You can often read the local newspaper online. If not, then pay a few dollars a year for a subscription, and write it off your taxes as a business expense.

It's money well spent to stay on top of your market cycle research.

Also research the *types of jobs* coming into an emerging market. Not all jobs are created equal! An area that creates 1,000 new jobs in fast food and discount warehouse stores is not equal to an area that attracts 1,000 new engineers. However, don't necessarily look down on lower-paying jobs. All jobs may not be equal, but all job growth is good.

Some companies are replacing higher-paid older workers who retire with lower-cost young employees. Sometimes high-paid union jobs are being replaced with lower-paid, nonunion jobs. To keep jobs, some unions are voluntarily agreeing to two-tier pay scales with new employees being paid much less than older employees.

These forces lead to the creation of many more lower-pay jobs. Many of these employees cannot afford to buy a house or condominium. They'll become our tenants.

When investing in emerging markets, look for a *local workforce that is made up of approximately 40% service-sector jobs*. This means that about 40% of the local employee population could consider renting in one of your buildings.

HOW TO FIND A HIGH-QUALITY MANAGEMENT COMPANY

The next step is to find an outstanding management company. Look for the Certified Property Managers—the designation I described earlier in this book. When interviewing CPMs, ask about their experience in the geographical area where you plan to invest. Speak with more than one property management company, because you'll gather intelligence from each company.

All markets have A, B, C, and D *areas*, and A, B, C, and D *properties*. A areas and properties are the best and D areas and properties are the worst. *You don't have to own A or even B properties to make a fortune in investment real estate.* In fact, some A and B properties are so over-priced that it's difficult to collect enough in rents to pay all your bills. Sometimes bread-and-butter, nonglamorous properties are your best investments.

Try to invest in A properties early in an emerging market. At this stage, such high-quality properties are still affordable.

Thirty years ago, you could purchase small ocean-front apartment buildings in Southern California for $30,000 per unit. Many small communities of Southern California were emerging markets at that time. Today, those same properties are selling for $1 million per unit!

As the emerging market starts to mature, turn your attention to B and C properties. You can make a fortune on such properties, as more people come to an area that is being discovered.

THE ALL-IMPORTANT PATH OF PROGRESS

Be sure to determine the *path of progress* for the city. The path of progress is where the majority of the new construction is taking place. Is the town growing fastest on the north side, the east side, or some other area? Ask the local property managers for their opinions on the path of progress. The path of progress becomes the A area in which to invest.

One of the most lucrative investment strategies of all is to *purchase B or C properties in an A area.* Huge numbers of people want to move to highly desirable A areas. However, very few can afford to rent in an A building, in an A area. As more people move in, they will pay higher rents in your B and C properties.

You should invest close to the path of progress for another reason: As an area goes from being undeveloped land to fully developed, prices of land and construction go way up. By loading up on properties on the outer edges of the path of progress, you're locking in a lot of profit.

As the path of progress engulfs your property, *you will experience high appreciation, quickly.* Then it's time to either refinance your property (to pull out hundreds of thousands of dollars for a new investment), or sell it and buy another property at *the new outer edge* of the path of progress. Why ride that profit wave only once, when you can surf it twice—or even more?!

Watch the market closely, though: The path of progress is not ALWAYS a great area in which to invest. When a market matures, the path of progress will dry up. Even though that outer land is cheap, no one will want to build upon it. When a market starts to turn, *it is the fringe areas of the path of progress that will be the first to experience a major slow-down.*

Stay in touch with your management company. Have them be your eyes and ears in that community. They will alert you to some of the greatest growth opportunities in that city. Also have them let you know *as soon as they see any sign* of a weakening market in the areas that were formerly on the path of progress.

HOW TO DETERMINE WHERE AND WHEN TO BUY

When buying properties in an emerging market, always keep an eye on the number of building permits that are being applied for and where the building is projected to take place.

The majority of new properties that come onto the market are A properties. They are new, clean, modern, and beautiful. Tenants consider these properties highly desirable. If two or three A properties are coming on the market within a mile of your property, it may be time to sell and move to a different location. It will be very difficult to compete with these newer A properties. They'll siphon off some of your best tenants, who are driven by the latest amenities.

The same is true for some B properties. They may be low-cost buildings, quickly erected by a builder. Although they may not have many amenities, the very fact that they're new may attract tenants from your building. In addition, because the properties were inexpensive to construct, the owners may be able to charge lower rents.

The more properties that come onto the market, the more saturated the market becomes. If developers build faster than tenants can absorb them, there will be an oversupply of rental units. This has been the downfall of many an emerging market. Always be on the lookout for overbuilding!

As rental rates fall, tenants who were living in B properties can now afford A units, and they will move there. Likewise, tenants who had formerly rented C properties will now find they can move up to a B rental. This realignment of tenancy is very dangerous for property owners.

You really should be out of such markets before this trading-up takes place.

Try to buy in a market where there is some sort of *restriction on supply*. Boston doesn't have any raw land to add new supply. Montgomery, Alabama is surrounded by flood plains, and it's difficult to get new multi-family construction permits there. In parts of California, building is severely restricted due to lack of water; builders sometimes wait years just to get a water permit. I like these kinds of markets!

How to Find the Money You Will Need

Next, you need to determine how much money you'll need. First, figure out what size property you want to buy. As I previously explained, it often takes no more time to invest in a big property than it does to deal with a small one. Large properties throw off so much free cash flow that you can afford to hire managers who will do all the work. Donald Trump has a point when he says, "If you're going to think, you might as well think big!"

I started out doing small three- to six-family buildings. I then made a big leap to a 211-unit complex. I realized that it took just as much effort to do the smaller deals as it did the bigger ones, but there was one big difference: the number of zeros at the end of the monthly cash flow checks. A small building might produce a monthly cash flow check of $1,000. Medium-size ones may yield monthly checks of around $10,000; and large ones can produce *$100,000 or more in monthly cash flow!* And that doesn't even count appreciation potential.

I bought my 211-unit property for just over $11 million, and sold it less than 2 years later for $14.4 million. That is a $3.4 million profit in about 2 years. Remember, I used to be a weed picker. Needless to say, such deals have made me a true believer in the power of investing in emerging markets.

If you are going to buy a $1 million property, then assume you'll need a down payment of 10% to 20%. The deal can still be no money down, though! That's because the down payment doesn't have to be your own money. Let's assume you need $100,000 to $200,000 to get going. We'll call this your *seed money*. You can get your seed money from a number of different sources, including: private lenders, hard money lenders, equity sharing partners, repair allowances, friends, relatives, banks, savings and loans, and owner financing. In Chapter 9, we'll take a closer look at your best financing options.

Using other people's money to build your real estate fortune is very smart. There is nothing wrong with using your own money, but the problem is that most of us have a limited amount of money when we first start out in real estate! The more quickly you can do a large number of deals, the faster you will build your real estate empire. For most of us, doing more deals requires using other people's money.

Continuously build your *war chest of cash* because you never know when you will find the deal of a lifetime. When that happens, you want to be able to spring to action quickly—before someone else snaps up this incredible deal. In real estate, those who hesitate will frequently lose.

I was contacted by Rose Morris, a graduate of one of my live events. *Rose is from Columbus, Ohio.* She found a tract of land that had already been subdivided and approved for 90 townhouses. The majority of the engineering had already been completed. This alone was a savings of tens of thousands of dollars—and a savings of 1 to 3 years of planning board meetings.

The three partners who owned the land, and who had planned to do the subdivision, were not getting along. The ill will between the partners was to the point where they just wanted to sell the land and get back what they had invested.

After a quick meeting with a builder, Rose learned that the townhouses could be built at a cost of about $44,000 each, and sold at starting prices of $89,900. That would be a total profit of *$3,200,000* on the development!

The highly motivated sellers were willing to sell the land to the person who could *most quickly come up with the needed cash.* The price of the land was $350,000. I agreed to partner with Rose and pay cash for the land. After a quick title search and due diligence, we closed the deal 10 days later and beat out two other investors.

Rose Morris is a great, honest, hard-working person. Yet, without my money, she could not have done this deal. Having connections to money, and being ready to go in an emerging market, is truly the key to rapidly building real estate riches. My partnership with Rose has been a true pleasure.

I'm looking forward to doing many more deals with her, and maybe with you, too!

IN THE NEXT CHAPTER

They say patience is a virtue. To tell you the truth, I've never been the patient type. I've always wanted to see results as fast as possible.

Are you the same way? I thought so. That's why I've prepared a little treat for you. In the next chapter, I'm going to show you my simple, straightforward, 100% tested and proven method for doing a single-family home deal, pronto.

Special Offer for Readers of this Book:
As mentioned on the cover, you can claim
bonuses worth more than $375.00 for free.
Simply go to: www.MarketCycleMastery.com
and type in the words "Reader Bonus" for details.

CHAPTER 5

How to Jump-Start Your Wealth Through Single-Family Investments

The reason you're reading this book is to get wealthy, fast. If you've read this far, you're well on your way to achieving that goal. But right now, I need to help you sidestep a major pitfall in your investing career: Intimidation.

I'm not talking about the bully type of intimidation, but instead of deal-size intimidation.

Don't feel like you have to do a big transaction right away. The key is to take action, get into the game, and get your *first* deal done as soon as possible, regardless of its size. It's a temptation to want to get to your end-game investing destination right now, especially if you're a take-action kind of person. But at this stage, your motivation can be more easily derailed by certain inevitable setbacks. That's because you haven't yet felt the thrill of that *fat paycheck* to keep you going. (But you WILL feel it soon!)

Sailors talk about getting their "sea legs," which make them able to navigate rough oceans without losing their lunch. I need to help you get your "real estate legs," which will do two things:

1. You will be comfortable with the entire emerging market investing process; and
2. You'll make some fast cash.

To do that, you might consider investing in some single-family homes right in your own backyard.

In the last chapter, I recommended that you start looking for emerging markets in your area, because you may be sitting on a pot of gold and not even realize it. I have the same advice when it comes to single-family homes.

I've done several hundred single-family rehabs in my career. I continue to buy them today, even though I'm a big fan of multi-family properties that can generate really big checks. I still continue to flip single-family houses and put a nice 10, 20, or 30 grand in my pocket for a few hours of work.

I could go on in great detail about many different ways to do a single-family investment. But I suspect you would appreciate having just the most straightforward route to doing your first deal. So I'll spare you the variations, and give you the express lane.

So let's walk through the steps you need to take to get that first deal under your belt.

STEP-BY-STEP TO YOUR FIRST PAYDAY

Get the Leads Flowing In

One of my very favorite ways of getting deals is to contact out-of-town owners. I have three good reasons:

1. Less Competition. The competition for these sellers by other investors is much less than with the more obvious foreclosure situations that make the papers every day in your town. These properties often look normal, and the sellers aren't there to answer the door when your competition knocks (they're out of town).

2. More Motivated Sellers. Imagine owning a property in another city or state. You get no benefit from it—only headaches. First there are the mortgage payments. Even if the property is paid off, you still must pay real estate tax every year.

Then there are the insurance headaches. Insurance is almost impossible to get on residential properties that are unoccupied for more than 6 months. Why would an insurance company take a risk on a property that's a likely target of vandals? Therefore, the seller lives in constant anxiety that he'll receive a call that the property burned down, was looted, or both.

To counteract these problems, a seller can always pay someone in town to cut the grass and make the place look occupied. That gets expensive over time.

Now consider that the owner may not know anyone in town. "I'd love to sell this property, but I just don't know who's a reputable real estate agent in that area. Even if I find one, I'm not wild about paying thousands in commissions. I gotta do something about this property someday..."

By the way, these owners don't have to be out of *state*; they can just be from another town in your state. If someone lives and works in another town, and rarely gets over to see a property located even 15 miles away, that property can be just as big a headache as if it were across the country.

I have to tell you a story. I once did a campaign to just such out-of-town owners. I got a call from an elderly gentleman from Florida. I asked him the right questions (which you'll discover in the following pages). He said he'd be willing to sell the house to me for much less than I was willing to offer. I always deal with integrity, so I said: "Sir, I have to tell you that the price you just quoted is actually way lower than what you could get for the property. I would not feel right buying it from you at that price." He replied: "Look son, I know what my house is worth. I'm just completely tired of dealing with it. I want out. If you're saying we don't have a deal, then I'll just sell it to someone else, okay?"

"No sir, we DO have a deal!" I quickly added.

I made over $130,000 profit on that house! All for the price of a first-class stamp, knowing where to send it, and what to say.

3. Flexible Time Commitment.   Approaching out-of-town owners is an easy, hands-off way of getting started in real estate investing. You'll be contacting these property owners through the mail, using letters I'll give you. Therefore, it's ideal for the busy person with a day job: All you need to do is plop down in front of your favorite TV show, sign a bunch of letters, and stuff them into envelopes. No need to be somewhere at a particular time. Even if you did just a handful of letters each evening, you *will* get deals!

As soon as you can, get your kids, relatives, neighbors, or people at the local elderly center to do your mailing work for you. The going rate in my area is only about 15 cents to have your letters signed, folded, hand-addressed, and stamped. Then have the person hand deliver the stamped letters TO YOU. That way, you know the stamps are getting put on your letters, and not on someone's electric bill!

Where to Find Out-of-Town Owners

This is where your local government comes in handy. All property tax and ownership information is a matter of public record. You merely have to visit the clerk's office in your city hall and ask if you can see the property tax records.

Each piece of property that is generating tax revenue will be listed. You'll have both the property address and the owner's address. What you're looking for are situations in which the owner's address is out of town. Simple as that!

Sometimes these records will have more detail, like the type of property, the amount of tax, and the assessed value. That can be nice to know, but it isn't as critical as the owner's address.

When you're asking for these records, this is where cities will differ: Some will say, "Here are the records. You can look at them as long as you wish, but you can't photocopy them." In that case, just hand-copy the names and addresses down.

Other cities will charge you per photocopied page. You might even come across a clerk who says: "We don't give that information out." In that case, you'll need to ask for the head of the department, because tax records are public information.

On the other end of the spectrum, you should also check on the Internet. Find your city and state on the web, and search around using terms like "tax records" and "public documents." Some cities have all those records up on the web! You can sit in your favorite chair at home and grab all this information. It doesn't get much easier than that.

What the Letters Should Say

Here's what the first letter should say:

Headline: "Prices in [Name of City] Have Never Been Higher. Is Now the Time to Sell? Don't Miss Out on this Incredible Market! Read On..."

[Property owner name]
[Address]
[City State Zip]
Dear [Property Owner Name]:

Prices in the [city] area have skyrocketed! Now may be the time for you to sell your out-of-town property and get maximum cash out. You deserve it!

The trick to becoming wealthy is to buy low and sell high. You were smart when you bought your property; will you be smart again and sell it at the right time?

Now is the time to sell, and I'm interested in buying. I'm a local investor who buys properties just like yours.

Have you had enough of being an out-of-town owner? Are you tired of paying ever-increasing real estate taxes, and worried about vandalism?

I'd like to rid you of your problems and buy your property.

Call me at [your number] to discuss what a fair-market price would be for your property. I can close quickly, or you can take as much time as you would like. Call me now!

Sincerely,

[Your name]

P.S. To get the maximum value for your out-of-town property, call me now at [your number].

Notice that I say *first* letter. That's because you shouldn't stop at one letter. Do you always make decisions to buy or sell after seeing only one commercial? Neither do I. It takes repeated impressions for most marketing messages to sink in.

The great news is that very few of your competitors will be marketing to these out-of-towners in the first place, and just about none of them will send more than one letter. You'll be all alone in soliciting these deals!

I don't have space in this book to reprint all the letters you should send. But I have them all for you at my website. Just go to www.MarketCy cleMastery.com and type in the search term "Home Letters."

Then, simply print them all at one time for a lead and mail the first one. Drop another in the mail every 3 days. You'll soon have sellers telling you: "You know, I saw several of your letters, and I finally decided just to give you a call and see what you could do for me."

Screening the Deals

This next step is easy. You'll simply be gathering information from leads that call. Just like a miner, panning for gold, you're going to be performing a simple motion that will separate the worthless rock from the valuable bullion.

First, most recipients of your letters will not need your services. Fine. Of the ones that do call, a certain number are just *tire kickers*. You can tell they're not motivated, because they'll not only have a "We're just thinking about it" attitude, but they'll grill you more.

The really motivated sellers have one thing on their mind: What can you do for me NOW? Remember my story earlier about the gentleman from Florida? He really didn't care if I was a Nobel Prize winner, mayor, or garbage collector. He just wanted to know: "Will you buy my house for this price?"

How to Answer the Calls

You have lots of options for how to follow up on leads; some of them are not good. Here's my list in order from least to most effective:

Voicemail or Answering Machine.   Sure it's fast, easy, and cheap. But are you looking for maximum profits? If so, it won't be with this piece of machinery. People don't like to talk with robots, and that goes for even some motivated sellers. In my experience, using voicemail or an answering machine to screen your prospects will result in 50% fewer leads.

You Answering the Phone.   This has the virtue of a live person connecting with the seller, but it will take its toll on you.

When you're starting out in real estate investing, you're probably holding down a day job, or are at least busy all day. If you must drop everything you're doing—night and day—to answer the phone, two things will happen:

People will catch you at awkward times throughout the day, and you will NOT be at your best to establish rapport with them; and you'll get burned out. You don't yet have a framed photocopy of that nice, fat check from your last deal. You only see the work and interruptions from potential sellers. This is a prescription for a very short real estate career.

Live Answering Service.   This is the very best, because you don't have to be tied to the phone day and night, and your call gets answered by a live person.

You simply give the answering service the script I have for you in the following section. Then the calls or e-mails you get will be from that service, telling you of a new, prescreened lead!

For a current list of answering services I recommend, go to www.Market CycleMastery.com and type into the search box "Answering Service."

What Do You Say When Someone Calls?   Here's a script I've used for years. It's very simple but effective. (My comments are in italics.)

Good [Morning/Afternoon/Evening], [your company name], how can I help you?

"Yes, I got a letter from you that says you will buy my house."

Thanks for calling. My name is Dave, what's yours?

It's more effective first to trade your name for theirs.

Write down name:_____

[Say first name], could I get your phone number, just in case we get disconnected?

You want to be able to call back if you do get disconnected, or the person has to go suddenly.

Write down the phone number:_____

[Say first name], in order for me to determine a price that I can pay you, I just have a few simply questions. First, what is the property address?

This is of course vital to establishing a value later.

Write down what the caller says:_____

How soon are you looking to move?

This is critical; it tells you how motivated the person is.

Write down what the caller says:_____

How much do you think your house is worth?

It gives you a starting point to know if this person is in dreamland or not.

Write down what the caller says:_____

How much are you asking for the house?

Here again, you'll get a sense of motivation if the person offers to take less than it's worth.

Write down what the caller says:_____

How much do you owe on the property?

You'll have a good sense of how much negotiating room there is. If the property has tons of debt on it, you won't be able to buy it for much under market value.

Write down what the caller says:_____

Are you willing to sell the property for what you owe on it?

You might think this is a crazy question, but plenty of sellers will actually say "okay." If someone says: "Now why in the world would I want to do that?" you reply, "I don't know. But I can tell you that some people are just happy to get out from under the burdens of out-of-town ownership."

Write down what the caller says:_____

[If it's an answering service] Okay, I'm going to forward this information to (your name), who will be calling you back shortly. Or, "Thanks for this information. . . I'm going to talk with my investment partner, and we'll get back to you very quickly."

Thanks for calling [your company name]!

At some point in the conversation, the person may say "Can you tell me more about yourself and what you can do for me?"

What you say is: "As I said in my letter, I'm not a real estate agent, but I'm an investor. My specialty is looking for situations in which I can provide a good service to homeowners by buying their homes, while at the same time making a reasonable profit when I sell those homes to someone else." Then you get back on track with the previous questions.

Remember, there's no reason for you to sweat this process. You're just looking for the motivated sellers that will glint at the bottom of the gold pan. Those people will be more than willing to answer these questions. All the rest get washed back into the stream.

Making Offers

Let's say you just hung up the phone with a motivated seller. You might figure the next step is to jump in your car and visit the property. Not so fast. Yes, it sounds like you could have a live one; but you don't yet know if you have a profitable deal. Now comes some easy analysis.

Go to www.zillow.com. After you pick your jaw up off the ground at the kind of detail they have on your house and neighbors, then type in the address of the property you're planning to make an offer on.

You'll get an estimate of the value of that property. No doubt you feel that they've estimated your house too low. Maybe so. After all, the thing was done for free over the internet in about 5 seconds!

People usually overvalue their property; they not only value a lot of sentimental aspects that the new buyer does not care about, but they also sink money into their homes for things that actually do not raise its appraised value. You put a big fence around your property, spent a ton decorating your home, and even added a fireplace and patio? That's nice, but it may not result in nearly the same bump in value as if you added a bathroom or created off-street parking.

Sorry, but valuations are done on narrow, heartless grounds for the most part. I've been a real estate agent and broker for years; that's just the way it is.

Now you want to find *comparable* houses. Professionals focus on the following key characteristics.

Proximity. It should be within one mile of your property. The closer, the better.

Size. It should have the same square footage as your property, +/−20%. Also, the number of bedrooms and bathrooms should be as close as possible.

How Recently It Sold. Ideally it sold within the last 6 months. You can go out to 12 to 18 months if there aren't many sales around you, but that's about the limit.

Neighborhood.   This is a little harder to gauge. It means whether the house is in the same school district, and whether it's considered the same area by people that live there. If the property is across a river or train tracks, the housing situation could be very different only 300 yards away. That's not comparable.

To Summarize.   Over time, you'll get your "real estate legs," as I mentioned earlier. For now, just do your best in estimating the house's value. Remember, what's the big risk you're taking if you are completely wrong? Ten bucks.

Now that you have an estimate of the value of your target property, you need to cut that value by a factor of 7, and then by at least another $5,000 in order to arrive at your offer.

Why? Because you're not going to be selling this house to a homeowner; that's too slow. You'll be finding another investor to sell it to.

Down the road, when you're doing lots of deals, by all means get involved in rehabbing homes and selling them to the end-user customers. I've done hundreds of them. But this chapter is about getting you a deal the very fastest, no-risk, straightforward way. You don't want to wait around while a homeowner goes to get financing, has problems and tells you to wait, then sees another house and backs out of your deal.

Instead, you want someone who can decide on the spot to buy your deal, and who can pay cash.

Because you'll be selling to another investor, that person needs to make a profit, too. You'll sell the deal to that other investor for roughly 7 of the estimated value. What's the "at least $5,000" for, you ask?

That's YOUR profit, for doing this quickie deal.

Let's look at some numbers.

You do your number crunching on comparables for your deal and conclude that an average price for similar properties is $140,000.

Now you multiply $140,000 by 70% (in other words 7) and you get $98,000. Now subtract your profit and you're at $93,000. I'd use $90,000 as a starting place with the seller.

Why not just start with your final offer of $93,000? Because that's an important negotiating point. I'm not trying to get you to haggle; I'm trying to make the seller FEEL GOOD. If all the flexibility is on the seller's side in coming down to your price, then that person may very well feel taken advantage of, or at least weak. Disgruntled sellers back out of deals.

If, on the other hand, both of you have met the other somewhere in the middle, then both of you can feel a little victorious.

How to Approach the Seller with Your Offer

Remember that you don't need to grovel, cajole, or negotiate hard. This person responded to your letter. Even so, you don't want to have a "take it or leave it" attitude, either. You would like to do the deal. That's why you say to the person:

"Mr. Smith, I've done some research on current prices in your area, and I've also taken into account what I am able to afford for this property. In order for me to be able to recoup my time, expenses, and risk, I'm not able to pay full retail price for your property. What I AM able to do is make you an offer for $90,000."

Then you SHUT UP.

The next person to talk loses.

I *mean* it: Do not justify your price; do not say anything at all. If you do, before you know it, you'll be lowering your price even before the seller has a chance to counter offer. This is a rookie mistake.

The seller will say one of two things:

1. "You've Got to be Kidding Me! I Can't Sell for That!"   Now you can talk. Say: "As I said, I'm not in a position to offer you full price; I realize you may not be able to sell it to me for what I asked. What *would* you be able to sell it to me for?" Then you shut up AGAIN.

Wait until the seller names a price and then start negotiating from there down to where you need to be. If you can't get there don't get emotional and rationalize why you can buy the deal for a higher price than you planned. Simply walk away.

The other response you may get from the seller is:

2. "Well, Okay, I Just Want Out of This Thing. How Fast can You Close?"
It's going to be one of these two responses.

It's at this point that you need to have an "either way is fine with me" feeling inside. If the seller agrees, that's great. If the seller does not, you move on to the next deal. There are plenty of out-of-towners besides this person.

Worst case, you've gotten some valuable negotiating experience under your belt. Best case, you're very close to padding your bank account with several thousand more dollars.

Tie Up the Property

Before you even think, "But Dave, I don't have enough money for a down payment on this house!" let me put your mind to rest: You don't need one. You're simply going to "tie up" the property right now with an offer. It's going to cost you $10. That's right. Ten bucks.

Here's the big picture: You've contacted the seller and this person is motivated. You've now arrived at a price that you think you can profitably buy the property for. The $10 is simply to solidify the agreement, because legally, you need to give *something of value* in order to enter into a contract.

"But Dave!" I hear you saying, "What if I can't sell the property! I just entered into a contract!" Yes, and I have bad news for you:

If something goes wrong, you'll lose your ten bucks.

Why would a seller ever agree to enter into an agreement with you for ten lousy bucks? Just think about the circumstances:

1. The seller was probably not even actively trying to sell the property before your letter appeared out of the blue;
2. You've made an offer for this property that has become a stone around the seller's neck;
3. You're going to be closing relatively soon on the property, so the seller is not taking any risk; if for some reason you don't buy it, the seller is free to offer it to someone else.

This is important: At the same time you agree on a price with the seller, you MUST get a signed offer! If you don't, then there's nothing stopping this excited seller from shopping the property around your town for a better price. You need to lock the person in, right then.

I'm not talking about a "purchase and sale agreement," which you no doubt signed when you bought your last family residence. That's a binding contract that you'll buy the house, or else you're in big trouble.

The *offer* is still a contract, but it's much more buyer friendly: It says the seller must sell to you, but if you don't buy, the seller gets to keep the entire ten bucks you put down.

For a copy of the offer I use, go to www.MarketCycleMastery.com and type in "Offer."

Find Buyers

Here's another easy step: You've just done what most real estate investor "wannabes" never get around to doing: You've found a property and tied it up at an excellent price. Now, you simply get the word out that you have this property, and stand back. You're likely to have several investors want to buy it from you!

Here's how to find them.

1. Put an ad in the paper. It simply says: Handyman Special. Must sell. Cheap. Cash. Call 555-555-5555.

2. You can go to www.craigslist.com and do the same thing. Craigslist is a great resource that started in San Francisco some years ago. It's now a worldwide, largely free bulletin board. Find the town on the craigslist site that's closest to you, and in minutes you can open a free account and have your ad showing.

3. Go to your local real estate investors club. Usually those clubs have a session at the beginning or end when investors can stand up and offer deals for sale, deals they want to find, money they're looking to borrow, and so on.

Wear a bright shirt or dress. Mention the deal and then at the end of the meeting, stand in the back. People will remember the person in the bright yellow outfit and approach you.

If there's not a meeting of the association for several weeks, call the association president. Ask if you can put an ad on the association's website, or otherwise get a message to the group before the next meeting. If the deal's good enough, the president might just buy it!

If you get one or more investors who are interested in the property, give them the address. Because you have a signed offer from the seller, it's not like they can cut you out of the transaction now.

If for some reason you don't uncover any buyers yet, you can do one of two things:

1. Ask the seller for more time. The seller's not in a big rush, and will probably say fine.

2. Walk away from the deal and lose your ten bucks.

Assign the Contract and Collect Your Money

Let's say you have found a buyer who's willing to buy it from you for 70% of its value, or even higher. Congratulations!

What you're going to do is *assign the contract*. You will be taking the original contract you had with the seller, and legally turning it over to the new buyer, for the profit that you've negotiated with the buyer. Now, when the actual time for closing arrives, it will be the new buyer (the investor you found) at the closing table with the seller. You don't even have to attend the closing; that's because you'll be busy.

You will be down at the bank, cashing your cashier's check for your profit, and deciding how you want to celebrate!

In this one chapter, I cannot answer every question that may be going through your head about doing your first single-family home deal. I could do a whole book just on these deals. Still, I'm here to help you: Just visit my site and get even more information for free. Just go to www.MarketCycleMastery.com and in the search box type: "Single-Family" and you'll see even more details.

This is the key thing I want you to get from this chapter: Your first deal is much closer than you might think. You simply have to take the easy steps I've outlined. Put one foot in front of the other, and pretty soon you've walked a long way. Take each of my real estate steps one after another, and pretty soon you'll be cashing checks for many thousands of dollars apiece.

IN THE NEXT CHAPTER

I have so many profit secrets to lay on you, I think I'm gonna bust! Here's why:

It's great news when you can invest in an emerging market. But as great as that is, you can do even better: If you invest in apartments in an emerging market, the combination can make you be *SET FOR LIFE!*

The power of emerging markets, coupled with the power of multi-family investing done the *hands-off way*, is just astonishing! Turn the page and I'll show you why.

CHAPTER 6

MULTI-FAMILY INVESTING: YOU CAN MAKE MILLIONS, MY HANDS-OFF WAY

I have invested in *just about every type* of commercial and residential property, and still do. My investment of choice is *multi-family properties* (also known as apartments).

In this chapter you'll discover why the savviest investors include multi-family properties in their portfolios. I'll prove to you that investing in apartments is truly one of the most rapid methods in existence to explode your wealth—*if you invest in the right (i.e., MY) way.*

I'm not like other so-called gurus who find the need to tear down other forms of investing in order to make theirs look better. I freely admit that it's possible to make lots of money in several different types of real estate: apartments, single-family homes, commercial properties, and so on.

Still, apartments are my favorite method for making the most money the fastest. (If it weren't, I wouldn't do so much of it!)

Fortunately, real estate investing isn't an either/or proposition: You don't have to decide to invest EITHER one way OR the other. Over time, you can do what I've done, and profit from many types of properties.

Here's the bottom line on multi-family investing: The very fact that it's misunderstood makes it a fantastic investing opportunity. It's almost like there's a "Danger—Keep OUT" sign on the apartment investing door. Then a few brave souls peek in that door to see the smart investors sitting there counting their money!

Yes, you can lose money investing in apartments. You can also lose money in any other investment under the sun. So the trick becomes investing using proven, hands-off systems the way the pros do.

Let's take a closer look at the many unique advantages multi-family properties offer.

CASH FLOW IS KING

The cash flow you receive from multi-family properties is what will truly help you achieve financial freedom. When you buy a multi-family property for a good price in a great market, it's possible to start benefiting from that property the very first month, through positive cash flow.

By *positive monthly cash flow*, I mean money you'll get every month that goes beyond what you need to pay the mortgage, taxes, insurance, and other expenses. You can spend this money *any* way you like.

If you use that excess money wisely (for example to buy more properties, fix up your existing ones and raise rents, or to rapidly pay down your mortgage), your monthly positive cash flow will increase that much more.

Many of my students find that their positive monthly cash flow from multi-family properties soon *equals or exceeds* the money they get from their regular 9 to 5 jobs.

When you start making more money from your multi-family properties than from your regular job, you'll ask yourself if you even want to continue punching that time clock. Do you want to be a full-time employee and part-time real estate investor, or quit your job and become a *full-time investor?* It's a nice question to face, because it means you're making a bunch of money!

Imagine how it's going to feel, *being* THE MAN (or WOMAN!) instead of *working for* THE MAN! I can tell you from first-hand experience that it feels fantastic!

Investing in multi-family housing is about more than just making money. The money helps you achieve financial freedom *and* peace of mind. That cash flow is also going to allow you to have what I call *The Attitude.* That's when you know you can:

Do what you want,

When you want,

Where you want, and

With whom you want!

That is true freedom.

POSITIVE CASH FLOW IN ACTION

Single-family deals have their attractions, in terms of creating chunks of money when a property is sold. But let's compare the cash flow potential of single- and multi-family deals.

In my experience, the average single-family property cash flows at $200 per month.

Let's say you wanted to replace a $40,000 a year salary. To replace this salary, you would need to own 17 single-family houses, at $200 per month average cash flow. It would take a while to accumulate your first 17 houses.

Assuming you can get 17 single-family rentals—how much time will it take YOU to manage them? Remember that very few professional property managers will take on single-family houses. Even if they did the management, they would charge you extra for it (compared to managing apartment buildings).

In addition, factor in your driving time. It is impossible to get 17 single-family homes on one street in the average American city or town. Instead of going to nearby locations to manage your rentals, it's likely you will be driving all over town to visit these 17 properties.

 In my experience, the average apartment in a multi-family property cash flows at *$75 per unit*. This does not sound like much, but let's take a closer look.

If you have a few vacancies in an apartment building, you can often still make money or at least break even. If you have a vacancy in a rental house, you have NO income from that house. Yet you still have to pay all of the expenses, like mortgage, taxes, insurance, maintenance, and so on.

In most cities, if you invested in a $600,000 apartment building (often possible with no money down, by the way), you could produce much more rent from that building than from $600,000 invested in rental houses.

This means you can pay down your mortgage much more rapidly when you own apartments. Thus, you increase your equity faster. Your mortgage shrinks rapidly and rents continue to go up if you buy in an emerging market. In many cases, that $75 a month positive cash flow can grow to $150 a month, $250, and much more—for each unit!

Some investors who buy great properties in rapidly appreciating markets are able to pay off most or all of their mortgages. Imagine if the rent is $700 per month per apartment, and you are netting $500 per month from that! This DOES happen to some people.

But let's be conservative. If you only make $75 per month positive cash flow from each apartment, you would need to own 45 units to replace a

$40,000 a year salary. That sounds like a lot, but remember that you can purchase a 45-unit property in one location.

No more driving here and there to visit 17 different single-family homes. You drive to one building. Everything is there. In fact, you don't even drive there much, because your property manager is doing the work, paid for by part of the rents.

I know it sounds like a big leap to buy a 45-unit building. *That's why you're reading this book; I've shown my students step-by-step how to do it, and I'll show you, too!*

Just think: The cash flow from *one apartment building that YOU don't even manage* could liberate you from your job. You will be a free person. Your time is your own. You can live the life you want to live.

ECONOMIES OF SCALE

Continuing with our comparison, if you own 17 single-family properties, think about all the maintenance you'll be required to do. You'll have *17 roofs* that need to be repaired or replaced sometime in the future. This might be sooner, or later, but it WILL have to be done.

In a 45-unit apartment building, you may have roofs that need to be repaired or replaced on one to three buildings. It is much less expensive to repair or replace just a few big roofs in one location than 17 smaller roofs in 17 different locations.

You'll have *17 lawns* that need grass cut, fertilizer applied, sprinklers maintained, weeds pulled, flowers planted, shrubs trimmed. Yikes! I used to be a landscaper—I know how much work this is—and how much you'll have to pay to have it done on 17 different properties.

In the 45-unit property you'll have one or two big lawns and a few shrubs, even if you have several adjacent buildings. A gardener coming once a week can do this work in a few hours. That's another huge cost savings with apartment building investing.

I could give you many more examples, but you get the point. *Economies of scale greatly favor multi-family properties.* Labor and maintenance costs for single-family rentals are much higher than they are for apartment buildings. Bottom line: You have much lower profits when you invest in single-family properties than you have when you invest in multi-family ones.

START INVESTING PART TIME

You might have been a little intimidated by my discussion of owning a 45-unit building. I encourage my students to *think big*. As you will discover, it's often just as easy to do a big deal as it is to do a smaller one.

Believe it or not, in some cases, *it's easier to get financing for a big deal than for a small one!* That is because the bigger property produces much more rent and has relatively lower expenses (per tenant). Banks feel reassured that there will be more profit, making it easier for you to pay the mortgage.

Another advantage of multi-family properties is that you can start investing in them on a part-time basis. After all, you won't be managing them—you'll have a professional management company do that. This is not so with single-family homes, where most investors end up doing much of the management work themselves.

Do NOT make the mistake of trying to save a few dollars and manage your apartment building yourself! If you do, you will not be in the investment business; you'll instead find yourself in the *tenant business.* That means that you are taking phone calls, showing vacancies, doing maintenance work, cleaning, running credit checks, collecting rents, paying bills, and so on.

If you go that route you will burn out. You'll then join the ranks of amateurs who say "Apartments? I tried that! What a joke! I'll never invest in apartments again!"

You know what else will happen? Those same losers who were in the tenant business will get out by selling their properties at a discount to people like me (and soon you), at a steep discount!

Imagine if the failed landlord said the same thing about airplane travel: "Planes? What a stupid way to travel! I tried becoming a pilot once, and it was a nightmare! Got caught in a thunderstorm one time and almost died. I'll never fly again!"

The dummy never thought about hiring a professional to fly him. It's called *buying a seat on an airplane.*

In the real estate world, you simply hire a property management company the same way. Let them do the flying, while you sit back in first class! (Plus, with apartments, you don't have the ridiculous airport security restrictions to worry about! ☺)

The way I look at it, you should be in this business to *create freedom and wealth*, not to create just another job for yourself!

WHO PAYS FOR THE PROPERTY MANAGER?

Let your local property manager do all the heavy lifting. Let them do the maintenance, tenant screening, renting, evictions (yes, it happens), and all the other tasks involved in managing properties. They have systems for getting this work done quickly and cost effectively.

I'm often asked, *"How can I afford to hire a management company?"* It's simple. You don't pay for the property manager—your tenants do.

Frequently, professional apartment managers can do such an outstanding job that they *pay for themselves*. They add so much to the property that you're able to raise the rents. Great apartment managers can also find you outstanding tenants who can pay a little more in rent.

Managers also have *discount relationships* with plumbers, electricians, roofers, carpet companies, and others you will need. They can frequently save you 5% to 10% on professional services and purchases. These discounts alone can pay for a great property manager!

For a rough estimate, a manager for a property that's over 20 units will typically cost between 6% to 8% of gross collected rents. A property under 20 units will cost between 8% to 10% of gross collected rent.

Shop around and try to get a good deal. However, when you hire a property manager, it is much better to pay a little more and get a true professional. Do NOT go cheap and end up with someone who neglects your property, defers maintenance, and puts bad tenants in your building. In a real sense, a poor manager costs you money, and managing it yourself will cost you money; but a great property manager will make you money.

When you set the compensation for property managers, always set it based on COLLECTED RENT. This gives the manager a true incentive to work hard to collect that rent. Some management companies ask that you pay a minimum fee to have them manage your property. Be wary of such agreements! If you agree to pay them a minimum fee, then they have much less incentive to collect every rent check.

How to Get Lower Risk and Larger Returns

Single-family properties are okay short-term investments, but risky long-term ones. As I said earlier, the average return from a single-family house is $200 per month, and the average mortgage payment is $800 a month on that property.

If you lose your tenant for 1 month, you're going to have to come out of your own pocket to make that mortgage payment. That's 800 dollars. Another way to look at it is you've just lost 4 months of profit. If you can't find a tenant after 2 months, you'll have to make a second payment and you're now down 8 months of profits. Add 1 more month of vacancy, and you just lost your profits on that building for an entire year.

Compare that to owning a 10-unit building. If you lose a tenant, you still have nine tenants giving you rent, making the mortgage payments, and giving you cash flow. If you have 20 units and lose three tenants, the tenants are still making your mortgage payments and you still enjoy cash flow. The more tenants you have under one roof, the less risk you have in your investment.

TWO WAYS TO EXPLODE YOUR WEALTH WITH MULTI-FAMILY PROPERTIES

When buying multi-family properties, search for properties that provide special *value-added* components. I call these *Value Plays*. They are major opportunities for smart investors.

The irony is that your Value Play is the seller's *problem property*. That's because the seller just didn't know how to buy right and manage right.

Here are the most common Value Plays (with causes in parentheses):

- *Burned-Out Landlords* (too cheap or dumb to hire professional managers)
- *Bad Management* (either do-it-yourself management, or hired a lousy manager at a "great price")
- *Low Rents* (didn't know how to increase value and raise rents)
- *High Vacancy* (didn't know how to market)
- *High Expenses* (didn't know how to negotiate lower prices; and didn't have a good property manager to do it)
- *Properties in Need of Repair* (low rents = poor income = "saving money" by deferring repairs = lower rents and occupancy)
- *Crashing Market* (bought at a too-high price)

In Chapter 7 I discuss Value Plays in greater depth. Finding properties with these value-added components is like finding diamonds in the rough. With a little cutting and polishing, you will become very wealthy!

FINDING THE BEST USE OF YOUR PROFITS

I've seen many investors in multi-family properties make huge sums of money and then spend that money on sports cars, speed boats, luxury homes, expensive travel, and fancy jewelry.

That's okay, in moderation. A much wiser choice is to put all or most of your new profits to work for you, to create even more wealth.

Here are my two favorite strategies for taking profits from a property:

1. Refinance your property. Take some money out and invest it in another high-potential wealth builder in an emerging market; or
2. Sell the property and do a 1031 Tax-Deferred Exchange. You will pay NO taxes on those gains in the year you do this (even if you have made $1 million or more in profits!) and you can invest all the money you received in another high-potential wealth-building property in another emerging market.

If you choose to refinance, you should always keep some equity in the property. That enables you to continue to receive nice *positive cash flow*. If you refinance too much, you then raise your monthly mortgage payments to the point that you have very little safety margin, should you need it.

I always want to think and plan *conservatively*. Some popular real estate gurus encourage their students to take on massive amounts of debt and buy into markets that have already experienced high appreciation. I don't. I take more of a Warren Buffett approach to generating huge wealth in real estate.

Warren Buffett is probably the most successful stock investor of all time—he's the second richest man in the world, behind Bill Gates. Starting with very little, Buffett acquired his tremendous wealth through buying value stocks *at a discount*.

I take the same approach to investing in real estate. I like to buy high-value properties at a significant discount, and then let my profits run. You can also do this if you understand how to profit from real estate cycles. That's because there are tremendous opportunities in hundreds of cities all across America.

When you refinance, leave 20% to 25% equity in your property.

If you have purchased some of the "get rich in real estate" courses that are advertised on late-night infomercials, you have probably heard of *pyramiding*. This involves your taking 100% of the equity out of a property and using it to buy another property. Then you take 100% of the equity out of that second property and buy a third property. The idea is that you do this over and over again to rapidly build a large portfolio of properties.

This is a risky investment strategy. Not *if*, but *WHEN* one or two properties don't perform, your entire portfolio is at risk. You've mortgaged them all to the hilt, meaning all the cash flow is going to pay the debt. Now the cash flow drops, but the debt does not. Things quickly start to unravel.

If you want to use all of your equity to buy another property, I suggest you do a 1031 Tax-Deferred Exchange, which we examined in Chapter 3. This will enable you to take 100% of your equity out of a property, pay no current taxes on any of it, and roll all of that into a new property. The new, bigger property can be conservatively financed, so you're not magnifying your risk.

HOW TO DO FEWER DEALS AND MAKE MORE MONEY

Yet another comparison: The average profit to *quick turn* a single-family house is $20,000, in my experience. (*Quick turning* a property is when you buy it at a good price, and sell it right away to another investor.)

I know—$20,000 seems impressive until you hear that (again in my experience) the average quick-turn profit on a medium-sized apartment building is $200,000!

Doing one apartment deal is not much more work than the single-family home deal. Yet you may get as much as 10 times the profit!

I admit that apartment deals at first appear much more daunting than buying a small house. But I need to say it again: That's why they are such good values! The competition is ridiculous with single-family homes, while all those investors shy away from apartments, because of ignorance and fear.

Take away the ignorance and fear, by plugging in proven systems and mentoring, and all you're left with is less competition, bigger deals, and faster profits.

HOW TO CLOSE MORE DEALS WITH CREATIVE FINANCING

It is much more difficult to do creative financing on single-family homes than it is with apartment buildings.

When you're negotiating with a single-family homeowner, you're talking about the single biggest investment that person has ever made. Homeowners are usually very emotionally attached to their houses. To you it's just an investment. To them, it is a beloved home.

Due to this emotional attachment, many homeowners want to extract unrealistic value from their houses. This can make it much harder for the numbers to pencil out for you as an investor.

Because you're most likely dealing with a homeowner who's in need of some fast cash, there is little room for creative financing, like an additional mortgage, where they'll get their money over time. They just want out—and the faster, the better.

On the other hand, when you're negotiating with the owner of an investment property, there is little emotional attachment. Few apartment building owners live in the building they own. It's not a cozy place with memories; it's simply an investment.

Investors just care about the numbers. If they work and it's a win/win situation, usually investors will do the deal.

They're also more open to creative financing, because that's probably how they got into the deal in the first place! In addition, they may be using creative financing to acquire their next deal. They know the important role creative financing plays in getting deals done in the investment community.

Creative financing is especially common on smaller multi-family deals, under 100 units. Multi-family buildings over 100 units receive more attention from banks, which find such lending profitable.

MULTI-FAMILY PROPERTIES HAVE ONE OTHER MAJOR ADVANTAGE

People need a place to live.

In the spectrum of basic human needs, *shelter* is right up there with food. I like investing in such a profoundly necessary service.

Clearly there are millions of businesses in the United States, and owning those commercial properties can be good investments. I own some myself. But businesses have many more choices than people as to where they can locate.

They can be housed in office buildings, but they can also be run from the basement of someone's home. This is especially true with Internet businesses.

Major corporations might have their own, custom-built facilities. On the other hand, pick up any newspaper on any day, and you'll see where corporations downsize, or combine operations, or move factories overseas. That means properties—even giant ones—suddenly becoming empty.

There is also less need for warehouse space. In previous years, companies stockpiled months or even years worth of raw materials and inventory. Many of these companies got rid of warehouse space when they turned to "just in time" delivery of inventory, a technique that Japanese car manufacturers made popular.

With Wall Street scrutinizing companies for ever-higher profits each quarter, even healthy businesses often shed real estate as a way of improving the bottom line.

Contrast that with apartments:

- Everyone needs shelter.
- Population trends are in favor of apartments. The U. S. population recently broke the 300-million mark. And even with all the criticisms that people like to level against America, it appears that we're still the residential address of choice for much of the world.
- People are living longer, and family size is slowly shrinking. That means more people are living on their own or in nontraditional ways.

There's another very critical factor in favor of apartments: *It's the back-up housing choice of most people.* Sure, most people would love to live in a nice house. But,

1. Young people move out of their parents' homes and usually move into apartments;
2. People graduate from college and move to apartments;
3. Immigrants come to the United States—legally or otherwise—and often move into apartments (even if they move in with relatives, those relatives often live in apartments!);
4. Workers staffing new factories will first show up in town and move into nearby apartments on shorter-term leases, until they eventually find homes;
5. Great numbers of people who encounter financial difficulty will move out of homes and into apartments. This may occur because they could no longer afford the big home, or due to divorce, or whatever. But the fall-back housing choice is an apartment.

This critical role of apartments is a feature not duplicated by commercial properties, single-family homes, or any other type of real estate except perhaps hotels. (Hotel investing is an entirely different animal, though! They can be profitable, but involve restaurants, convention space, rooms, and retail space. It's a high-risk, high-capital-investment, cut-throat business that's beyond the scope of this book.)

From all the factors I've previously outlined, apartments can clearly be excellent investments. But I don't want you to get the feeling that they're a *sure thing"* Of course it's possible for too many apartments to be built in a town, or for an area to fall into recession due to job losses.

That's all the more reason for you to follow my advice! This book is all about following job growth and other key indicators, and avoiding weak markets.

Consider the factors that we've covered in this book so far:

1. Investing in the right part of the market cycle;
2. Identifying and investing in an emerging market; and
3. Investing in the housing-of-choice (apartments) at the right price.

Following any one of these principles can make you a bundle of money. But put them together, and you can create an avalanche of money into your bank account, making you filthy rich in a hurry.

IN THE NEXT CHAPTER

I'm not done showing you amazingly powerful profit techniques! In the next chapter, we'll talk about *Value Plays*.

They are instant profit generators—I'm not kidding. And better yet, they're found all across the United States.

You'll see what I mean when I show you how one person's trash truly can become another person's treasure.

CHAPTER 7

How to Find Diamonds in the Rough

We've discussed how to combine market cycles, emerging markets, and multi-family properties into a super-powerful profit machine. I have even more goodies to share with you.

There's another power tool you can add to the collection I'm building for you. I briefly referred to it earlier. It's the *Value Play*.

In the physical world, the United States is known for its great natural resources of oil and farmland. But in the real estate world, the United States has many thousands of *diamonds in the rough*, scattered in every state. They're the Value Plays. Finding real diamonds takes a good deal of luck. Finding multi-family Value Plays only takes the knowledge and skill I'm about to hand to you.

THE WEALTH-BUILDING POWER OF VALUE PLAYS

Every Value Play is a profit opportunity for a smart real estate investor. Ironically, to the sellers of properties, these same components are perceived as problems!

In most cases, they are problems due to some form of mismanagement. Because the current owner is unaware of his or her own mismanagement—or does not want to admit to it—it's much easier for that person to just call them *problems*.

When these problems cause a crisis of cash flow or stress for the owner, eventually the only option in the seller's mind is to get out of the property.

This creates a tremendous opportunity for astute buyers. It means that if we can recognize certain specific situations, we can create something truly amazing: *We can create instant equity.*

And just like emerging markets, you can use this tool over and over again to pretty much print money.

Not only will you become extremely wealthy, but you'll be providing a true service of fairly priced, quality housing for many people. You'll do well, and at the same time you're doing good.

The most common types of Value Plays are:

- Burned-Out Landlords
- Bad Management
- Properties that Need Repair
- High Vacancies
- Low Rents

Let's look at each of these Value Plays, and how you can benefit from them:

How to Find—and Profit from—Burned-Out Landlords

Some of the *easiest* money you'll ever make is from apartments you acquire from burned-out landlords. Often they are people who jumped into being landlords on a whim, after hearing about how much money they could make from apartments. They never really took the time to discover how to manage their properties properly (that is, through management companies). In many cases, they did not invest in their own education and professional development.

Imagine you opened a bakery. You have a beautiful store, and lots of great equipment. You have all the flour and other ingredients you need. Now imagine that you have no recipes.

Even with your great store, equipment, and ingredients, you would still most likely fail, despite working hard.

Real estate investing works the same way. It's not enough to have the building and tenants. You must know how to hire an outstanding manager who will skillfully run the property. It's the equivalent of hiring an award-winning baker.

Burned-out landlords think they are in the tenant business. They take an approach to the business that is both exhausting and counterproductive.

These amateur landlords try to manage the buildings themselves, deal with the tenants themselves, and—to save money in their downward spiral of property performance—sometimes even do repairs and cleaning themselves! This is a prescription for disaster.

Burned-out landlords are not happy people. In fact, they shouldn't even be called *landlords*, because they're lords over nothing. The land, building, and tenants direct *them*. Because they are trying to do so much themselves (often while holding down another job), the average new property owner burns out in 2½ years!

By cruising through different neighborhoods, I've found some landlords who were burned to a crisp. You don't even have to go very far out of your way. As you drive to a friend or relative's house, study the apartment buildings along the streets you travel.

Are there any apartment buildings in obvious need of repair? It's likely you've just found a burned-out landlord. That's a landlord who is not taking the time to keep his or her asset in good shape.

Do you see overgrown landscaping, shaggy lawns, or grass dead from lack of water? Are there worn-out looking cars parked everywhere, perhaps even on lawns or sidewalks? You've found a burned-out landlord. Is the paint peeling or cracked, windows broken, or trash piled up? Are tenants working on their cars or doing oil changes in plain view of passers-by? Are dogs and cats having a run of the place? Does the roof have loose shingles, or is it in obvious need of repair?

All of these are signs of burned-out landlords who are too stressed-out to maintain their properties.

Here's how the downward spiral continues: When a landlord stops taking care of his or her property, many tenants pack their bags and leave. Usually the best tenants—those with good jobs and money in the bank—leave first. The landlord is then left with bad tenants and empty units.

Now the building is in disrepair, with a number of empty units, and unsavory remaining tenants. The empty apartments become harder to rent. The landlord lowers his or her standards just to fill the units—and the problems worsen.

What kind of people move *in* to such a building? Ones who are used to living in substandard conditions, and desperate people who have no other choice.

Unfortunately, these are often the kinds of tenants who cause most of the damage to a property. Unless *the owner* changes his or her ways, the death spiral will just continue.

The only relief many landlords can see is to sell the building. Often they'll price the property significantly below market—just to get out. After all, even *they* realize that the property will attract few, if any, sellers.

This spells *major opportunity* for you. Just as the current owner was re-active and suffered a downward spiral, you can use what you discover in this book to be *proactive*, and enjoy an upward cycle of ever-higher profits.

Marginal tenants take more of your time and energy than good tenants. You have to chase marginal ones for the rent; good tenants mail it in and sometimes mail it in early! Marginal tenants tend to cause more damage to property. In contrast, good tenants will sometimes improve a property (such as replace the carpeting, upgrade the medicine cabinet, or put on a beautiful coat of paint) without even telling you.

A Secret Hunting Ground for Finding Burned-Out Landlords

Another great method for finding burned-out landlords is to go where landlords go when they need to evict their tenants. In most areas, this is Housing Court, Small Claims Court, or District Court.

Eviction is very stressful, both on the tenant and the landlord. The most frequent cause of eviction is nonpayment of rent. In some cases, you will find landlords who are owed 6 months of rent from a single tenant! Why did they wait so long to evict the tenant? They wanted to avoid the stress and expense of going to court.

A landlord who is not receiving rent from one, two, or more tenants is often very motivated to sell. His or her dream of easy living has turned into a hell of monthly mortgage payments and daily maintenance calls from tenants.

The public courts have provided me with some of my very best deals. In addition, when you deal directly with such a highly motivated seller, you don't have to pay a real estate commission. The burned-out landlord might sell you his or her property for $50,000 or $100,000 below market value. You might save another $50,000 in real estate commissions. Talk about a *Value Play, and instant equity!*

Keep in mind that while you're making good money, you're also doing the burned-out landlord a favor by taking the headache property off his or her hands. Some of these stressed-out landlords are compromising their physical and mental health by holding on to properties they cannot manage. Getting out of the property gives them a clean start. In addition, when you buy the property from them, you may save some of them from foreclosure and from ruining their credit.

VARIATION ON A THEME: THE LANDLORD WHO HAS JUST HAD ENOUGH

Sometimes landlords have owned property for many years and have just had enough. They simply want out of the business. The property may not even be run down. They may have okay tenants. But because they've been trying to do everything themselves, they are burned-out.

Who can blame them that they want out, so that they can finally leave their toilet plunger at home and go on a vacation?

To get the sale done quickly, they lower the price. Another great purchase opportunity for you!

Though you may not get a rock-bottom price from this type of burned-out landlord, I've found that these "enough is enough" landlords often allow me to structure deals with them that offer me very favorable terms.

Because many of the enough-is-enough landlords have been in toilet-unclogging business for many years, a number of them own their properties *free and clear*, with no more mortgage payments to make.

Whenever I'm negotiating with a landlord who owns his or her property free and clear, I can usually get owner financing for the entire mortgage amount. This saves me a huge amount of money, both because I often get a slightly lower interest rate, and because I do not have to pay fees to a mortgage broker. Plus, we can do the deal quickly!

Here are two fascinating facts about owners who have paid off their mortgages:

1. Landlords who own property free and clear are accustomed to receiving a large amount of cash flow each month from their property. Because they do not have to pay a mortgage, cash flow is maximized; and

2. When they do sell, they're probably going to receive a large profit and therefore have a very large tax bill!

Here's how to get a great deal: You make the owner an irresistible offer: "How would you like to still receive a large monthly check, but not have the hassle of dealing with tenants and maintenance?"

You then explain to the seller that the huge monthly check will come from you—the buyer.

You then make the owner a second irresistible offer: "How would you like to minimize your tax bill?" You then explain the benefits of an installment sale, in which the owner will only be taxed by the government on the part of the purchase price that he or she receives each year from the sale of the property. Furthermore, the tax could be as low as 15% on long-term capital gains.

Instead of being hit with a huge tax bill and being forced to pay a gigantic lump sum, the seller will be able to space smaller payments out over time. In addition, because inflation erodes the power of the dollar by about 3% each year, he or she will be paying the tax bill with cheaper dollars in the future!

A Case Study in How to Deal Successfully with a Burned-Out Landlord

Kristy and *Kevin Frew* of Flint, Michigan found themselves in Buyer's Market Stage I. Because of the closings of auto manufacturing plants in their area, Flint had been losing jobs and population for a long time.

Flint was also suffering from a *brain drain*. Some of the brightest people were leaving for better jobs elsewhere.

Due to all these factors, Flint had suffered a stagnant economy for almost 10 years. Many houses and multi-family properties were boarded up. Some were simply abandoned.

Even in this bleak atmosphere, Flint had several positives going for it: City Hall had visionary leaders who created a master plan to revitalize the downtown area and also make it family-friendly. Flint employed aggressive marketing and mounted an economic campaign to attract desirable businesses to the area. The economic campaign started to kick in as businesses began returning to Flint.

Having done their homework along with possessing the knowledge of the previous facts, the Frews set a goal after leaving my boot camp to own a multi-unit property of at least 40 units before the end of the current year. My event took place in May, so they had only 7 months to reach their goal.

Using the systems they acquired in my program, the Frews found a 52-unit building with a burned-out landlord. The building was actually in great shape. It had higher-than-market occupancy (94% full, versus 88% for the market). It also had nice hardwood floors. Overall, the building was in fine shape and did not suffer from deferred maintenance. But terrible water!

The seller had owned the property for a number of years and had just "had enough." She wanted to be out of the landlord business, so she structured a deal with the Frews that enabled them to get into the property with no money down!

The property was on the market for $1,700,000. Using the negotiation techniques I gave them at my event, the Frews bought the property for only $1,550,000. They saved $150,000 because of the systems they had from my 3-day event!

The Frews secured 80% financing from a local lender. They negotiated with the seller for additional savings of $77,500. They then got another 11% of the purchase price through a private-money loan, and took out a credit line on a single-family property they owned for the remaining 4%.

While other investors were fleeing Flint, the Frews bought a solid property from a motivated seller for below its asking price, and created instant equity of $227,500, without taking any money out of their bank account!

This deal contained several powerful *Value Plays:* First, they were dealing with a burned-out landlord. Second, the rents were low by $15 to $25 per unit per month! When you multiply this by 52 units, you can see that the Frews will have much better monthly rental income than did the previous owner.

Not likely!

The third Value Play was the likelihood of Flint going from a Buyer's Market Phase I to a Buyer's Market Phase II. This now seems to be happening, but it will depend on job growth. The sooner this transition occurs, the better it will be for the Frews.

Last time I checked, positive cash flow was *$37,000 per year* for the Frews. This is just the current benefit from just one property, for which they took no money out of pocket to buy. They're now raising the rents and expect their cash flow to jump to $59,000 per year. Not bad.

There is one additional bonus that the Frews got from this deal: Because Kevin was a real estate agent, he collected a commission of *$32,300* at the closing! Thus their first-year income from this one property was more than $69,000.

Over the years, the tenants will pay down the mortgage, and the Frews will enjoy even greater cash flow. When the mortgage is paid off, it's likely that rents will be well over $1,000 per unit. That will be a minimum of *$52,000* in *monthly* rental income.

Even after paying taxes and some maintenance costs, there should be plenty left over for the Frews to live in high style.

Using my system, the Frews have truly found *one deal to retirement!*

How to Avoid Management Nightmares

When investing in multi-family properties, the key player on your team is the management company.

Getting a great management company to handle your properties is an absolute must. In Chapter 4, I explained how to find high-quality management companies using the Institute For Real Estate Management's website. You can also find great management companies through referrals from commercial brokers and from other *experienced* investors at your real estate investment club (do NOT listen to bleary-eyed, angry, burned-out landlords!).

Remember that your management company controls your cash flow. Without proper cash flow, you're out of business. But with a skilled management company, you can be going gangbusters. A good management company more than pays for itself with the increased cash flow it brings in.

Management companies are usually paid based on the amount of rent they collect. Given this fact, you would think that their primary goal would be to collect as many rents as possible, fill vacancies, and keep tenant turnover to a minimum.

However, this is not so in many cases. That's because some property management companies are mismanaged!

Any time you hire a new management company to either take over an existing property or start managing a new one you've purchased, you must watch over them very carefully—especially during their first few months on the job. (Hang on—I'll show you how.)

By your careful study of the performance of the management company and by staying in constant contact with them, they will know you're an owner who cares about his or her properties and expects results. You'll be in another class from the many owners who buy a property, hand it to the management company, and forget about it!

The management company hears very little from these absentee owners. But as with most other areas in life, the squeaky wheel gets the grease. If you don't squeak a little (in a polite way, of course), you will not get the attention you and your property deserve.

Your ultimate goal is to keep your contact with the management company to a minimum. However, *to start with*, you will need to have more frequent contact. You must assess whether they are doing the kind of job you want them to do.

If everything goes fine with your management company, there will be less and less need to contact them. You'll ultimately be in the position where you're reading one report a month (an executive summary, with an income and expense section). Once it has proven itself, a skilled management company can make your property perform with little intervention on your part.

If they know you are watching them, *they are much more likely to perform at a higher level.* If they think you're not interested, they will focus their time and attention on the owners who *are* squeaking.

I discovered a powerful lesson a long time ago: "What is accounted for, gets done." Make sure the management company knows you are holding them accountable. Do this in a friendly way. Even when you are disappointed, do not yell at them. Doing so will accomplish very little and may do more harm than good.

Instead, offer helpful suggestions and guidance. If they still cannot perform the job with your guidance, it's best to look for a more skilled property management company.

RED FLAGS IN DEALING WITH A PROPERTY MANAGEMENT COMPANY

Over the years, I have discovered the need to recognize a number of red flags in dealing with property management companies. Ignore them at your own risk!

For starters, I have six red flags that—when you see them—should make you jump out of your chair, rush to the phone, and demand an explanation from the management company. (And if you don't get an answer that satisfies you, it may be time for a change.) Here they are:

Red Flag #1: Higher than Average Vacancy

If your property has a higher vacancy than the average for its area, your management company is not getting the job done. Ask for a traffic report (how many people stopped in to look at vacant apartments) and the conversion rate (how many of these prospects they converted to tenants).

When you start measuring their activities, good property managers tend to respond rapidly. Also, get the phone numbers of potential tenants that didn't rent. Ask a few of them what they didn't like about the property. Was it the unit? If so, what needs to be changed—the carpet, paint, or something else?

In some cases, people who did not rent will tell you they were treated rudely by the management company. Perhaps the management company showed up 20 minutes late to show the apartment. Maybe they rushed the tenant through, or made a critical comment about the prospective tenant. None of these is a good sign! A management company that mistreats prospective tenants is taking money out of your pocket.

Good management companies will keep your apartment filled at *higher than average occupancy levels*—as long as you allow them to keep the property looking good.

After you provide positive feedback and helpful hints to the management company, they should be able to rent units more quickly and rent them to higher-caliber tenants. If this is still not the case, examine the ads they are running to attract tenants. Are they boring? Do they persuasively describe the amenities and benefits your apartments offer?

Is the management company running the ads in the best local newspapers or on the best websites? Give the management company feedback on how to write better ads and suggestions on better newspapers or websites in which to run them.

If the management company still cannot fill the units with good tenants, it may be time to quote Donald Trump and say, "You're fired!" Then, find another management company that can fill your units and maximize your monthly profits.

Red Flag #2: Sudden Increase in Notices to Vacate

A sudden increase in notices to vacate usually means that the property is being mismanaged. Pay particular attention to 3-day notices to pay rent or quit (which the management company issues to late payers).

Good, happy tenants almost always pay their rent on time. They don't want to pay late fees! When more than a few tenants pay their rent late, it often means you have unhappy tenants. *Find out why they are unhappy, and do all you can to correct it.*

Often, tenants are unhappy because management has stopped responding to tenant requests and deferred maintenance has started to spread throughout the property. How would you feel if you had a stopped-up sink and management took several days to send out a plumber? What if you had to wait several days to get your air conditioning fixed in the middle of summer? Who wouldn't be mad if a refrigerator stopped working, and food spoiled before management replaced or fixed the refrigerator?

When tenants have a problem, your management company should solve that problem as soon as possible. They should respond promptly to phone calls. A company that can only be reached through an answering service or voicemail is often a nonresponsive one. Try to work with a management company that has a real person answering calls from 8am to 5pm each day.

After hours, it is understandable that they might rely on an answering service. However, that service should get *directly* in touch with the managers (even if it means waking them up) if there is a fire, flood, or another emergency. Lives could be in danger, and your investment certainly is.

Whenever a maintenance request is submitted to your management company, it should be completed within 72 hours if the maintenance is a nonemergency. Emergencies should be completed within 24 hours—or sooner!

For example, if a unit does not have heat in the middle of a cold winter, the management company should send out a repairman immediately. If a pipe breaks and floods an apartment, a plumber should be sent immediately. There are dozens of other similar emergencies that can potentially arise.

Though these emergencies are rare—they must be dealt with immediately. Judges and juries have little sympathy for the landlord who dallies on handling emergencies. "Blaming it on the management company" is a weak excuse that does not carry much weight in our legal system. "If the management company was so bad," you will be told, "you should not have hired them."

The fact that you hired an incompetent management company—or did not supervise them properly—could mean that *you* are liable if a tenant is harmed. Likewise, if your insurance company determines that you hired a substandard management company or did not properly supervise them, it may refuse to defend you or to pay any judgment against you.

Now for the good news. If you hire a great management company and properly supervise them, they will know to immediately respond to any emergencies in your buildings. *The management company will maximize your rents and will minimize your headaches.* The tenants will know that management cares about them. They will stay and be happy to pay rent increases for the privilege of living in the beautiful apartment that they call home. And when a vacancy occurs, it will be quickly filled through word of mouth.

Red Flag #3: Taking too Long for "Make Readies"

Making a vacant unit ready for a next tenant should take no longer than 3 to 5 days per unit. If the units are not quickly ready for new tenants to move in, *your cash flow could be severely affected.* The longer units are vacant, the less you receive in rents. Bad management companies take much too long to get a unit ready to rent or lease.

You should never show a unit that is not 100% ready to a potential new tenant. Good tenants will not take a unit that's in bad shape. The applicants who *will* take a unit in such poor condition are desperate tenants that you do NOT want.

Therefore, insist that your management company get vacant units in *show condition* in 3 to 5 days. If they can't do so or don't want to, find a better management company.

Red Flag #4: Not Completing Deferred Maintenance

Expect to pay about 10% of your gross rents for property maintenance. Remember, it is actually your tenants who are paying it. Also, the cost of property maintenance is tax deductible, because it lowers your net rental receipts.

It doesn't get too much better than this: An expense that someone else pays (your tenants) and that you can use to lower your taxes! This is one reason why multi-family housing is a far superior investment to the stock market.

Maintenance is a cost of doing business. If your management company is not keeping up with maintenance on your property, you will suffer two major consequences:

1. It will be harder to rent to good tenants, because they do not want to live in a run-down property. Good tenants have options. They earn a nice living, have good credit, and many landlords want to rent to them.
2. It will cost you more in the long run to do repairs, because many maintenance problems get worse over time.

For example, let's say that you have peeling paint on the outside of your building. Catch it early and a spot-painting job can probably fix it. Let it drag on and the exterior of the building may have to be extensively sanded, sandblasted, or otherwise prepared for painting. You may need a base coat and one or two top coats. Instead of a minor expense of spot painting, now it's a major expense.

Be sure to visit you property at least once every 4 to 6 months, or have someone you trust carefully examine the property. When you do your inspection, *do not let the management company know you are coming.*

Surprise inspections will allow you to see exactly how your property is being managed. You'll be able to take all the time you need to inspect the property, without being rushed through by the management company.

Red Flag #5: Being Charged for Repairs that Aren't Being Done

A common management company scam is to charge owners for repairs that were never done.

Some management companies think that because you're a long-distance owner, they can get away with this. For example, one of their reports may tell you that $3,212 worth of carpeting was installed in vacant units. In fact, they might have only paid $1,500 for the carpet work. Who keeps the difference? The dishonest management company.

Good management companies won't do this, because they know their good reputations will make them more money than thievery would. But even if you get the best of references, you often don't really know with whom you're actually dealing. I like to protect myself at all times, just as restaurant owners must ensure their booze and steaks are not being pilfered.

 Any time there is a repair that needs to be completed, I have the management company take a picture of the repair with a local newspaper next to it. This tells me when the picture was taken. When the repair is complete, I have a picture of the completed repair with that day's newspaper in the photo. This way, I know the repair was actually done and I'm not charged for the same repair twice.

As simple as it seems, this advice could save you tens of thousands of dollars as the owner of a multi-family property.

If the repair is over $500, I ask the management company to *get two bids*. If the repair is over $1,000, I want *three bids.* They can either fax or e-mail me the bids so I can respond almost instantly. After receiving and reviewing the bids, I call the other companies just to make sure that they are actually legitimate companies that are in business. I don't want the management company to send in phony "competitive bids" so that a friend or family member can get the job at an inflated price.

Let me tell you about a bad experience I had, which I hope you'll *never* have to go through. I once hired a management company that would get one contractor to give three bids for a job. He would provide his bid and then he would make up letterhead for two fictitious companies. His bid would miraculously be lowest of the three. This bid was incredibly inflated so that he had lots of extra money to pay the management company a kickback.

This cost me a lot of money until I developed the system I previously shared with you.

One management company charged an investor friend of mine for snow plowing on days that it didn't snow. After receiving the bills, he checked with the weather bureau in that area! It had snowed days before, but the roads were clear on those days he was charged.

Tricky management companies know dozens of ways of inflating bills or getting kickbacks from the vendors they use. If you employ my system, you will never have to worry about such unethical practices.

Red Flag # 6: The Permanently Vacant Apartment

When looking at your monthly rent roll, check to see if there is one particular apartment that always seems to be vacant. Perhaps there is actually a tenant in that apartment who's paying cash—under the table to the management company!

If the apartment building is within driving distance, simply drive over and look in the apartment. If it's out of driving range, or you want to save time, simply call the tenants in the neighboring unit and ask them if the apartment next door is indeed vacant. *Need to know who lives there + Phone #'s*

Please understand that these property management nightmares don't happen often. When they occur, I want them to happen to someone else, and not to you! You're taking the time to discover the right way to run your money-generating apartments. You therefore deserve to know my tools and simple methods for keeping management companies on their toes.

Don't let the prospect of having an unethical management company prevent you from making the great deal of money that's waiting for you in multi-family investing! Once you have my systems in place, all my safeguards and techniques really take very little of your time.

HOW TO ACQUIRE 100 UNITS WITH YOUR FIRST DEAL

I know it seems almost impossible to many first-time investors, but using my techniques, you can even acquire a 100-unit apartment building as your very first deal! My student from Augusta, Georgia is one example.

Before my bootcamp, Justin had the common first-time investor concerns about dealing with tenants and big numbers. Going through my system, I showed Justin and my other students how to eliminate those fears by following several easy, safe steps. Justin left my training all pumped up to do his first apartment deal.

Justin used my technique of simply *cruising neighborhoods* in his area, to look for properties that need some TLC (tender, loving care). He quickly spotted a 100-unit complex that was a major diamond in the rough.

Justin stopped by the management office and asked if he could have the owner's name and phone number, so he could talk about buying the complex. Remember, Justin had never owned even a small apartment building before!

Justin felt the fear but he took action anyway. *Lady Luck shines down on those who are determined to make their way in this world.* Lady Luck shined down on Justin that day. But if he had not mustered the courage to ask for the owner's phone number, he'd never have had a deal.

The owner happened to be on the property that very day—and he was interested in selling! After using my power negotiating techniques, Justin bought this large apartment complex for a great price.

He had only one minor detail in his way...

...*He didn't have any money!*

Justin wasn't about to let that technicality prevent him from buying this property! That's because I showed Justin how to do *equity sharing*, a technique you can use to get into properties with no money down. Justin realized that all he had to do was find a deal that made sense and *the money would come.*

In Justin's case, the money came from his attorney. His attorney reviewed the deal, saw it was a good one, and that it had the potential to become a great one. After seeing this, the attorney agreed to supply the 20% down that was needed to complete the financing.

For his 20% down payment, the attorney received 20% of the net positive monthly cash flow and would get 20% of the net profits when the building was eventually sold. That meant the attorney got $1,200 of the monthly cash flow while Justin got $4,800.

This property is currently under agreement to be resold. The *profit* is *$980,000* after a holding period of only 2 years!

How long do you have to work to earn $980,000? Many people have to work 10 to 20 years—sometimes at a job they despise—to earn this much money. After paying about 30% of their income in taxes and spending the rest on food, housing, a car, and medical care, most people don't have much left after 20 years of hard work.

Justin applied some straightforward techniques and made $980,000 in 2 years from a multi-family investment. Poor Justin gets only 80% of that (a mere *$784,000*), but he can console himself that he didn't put any of his own money down! (Remember also that the tax on real estate is much lower than the tax on wages you earn.)

The attorney is quite happy with his $196,000 profit, and wants Justin to do more deals!

Of course, every student of mine doesn't have that same success story, but I do have file folders bulging with students across the country who have plugged in the same systems and gotten wonderful results.

Properties that Need Repair: Polishing Those Diamonds

Some of the most profitable Value Plays are properties that need repair. If you find a property in need of repair, only buy it if you can:

1. Get it at a substantial discount, OR
2. Easily complete the repairs and sell at a premium, OR
3. Easily complete the repairs and refinance out some of the equity you just created.

For every dollar you spend polishing your property, you should expect to get several dollars back. For example, you can sometimes buy a run-down looking apartment building and then paint it, re-landscape it with nice trees and beautiful flowers, put in new carpets, and attract higher-quality tenants who will pay more in rent. Simple polishing like this can raise the rents and increase the curb appeal of your property dramatically. If you wisely spend $50,000 on repairs, you might very well be able to sell your building for $150,000 extra (a 3 to 1 return).

Given these economics, *why don't all owners polish their diamonds?*

In my dealings with hundreds of investors, I can tell you why: Many of them have too much greed and too little vision. They take as much cash flow as possible out of a property and then blow it on fancy cars, expensive vacations, and the like. They simply don't see that if they reinvest those dollars into the right property improvements, they can multiply their profits. They'd be able to buy much fancier cars later—but they want gratification right now.

When you start out, the only good reasons to take large amounts of cash flow out of a property are to fix up that property, or to buy another outstanding property.

Property problems start out as deferred *maintenance*. When that maintenance does not get done, it turns into deferred *repairs*. Repairs are much more expensive than maintenance! Repairs are to be avoided or minimized if at all possible.

Repairs for multi-family properties are usually figured on a per unit price. For instance, *cosmetic repairs* will typically run between *$1,000* and *$3,000* per unit. Cosmetic repairs can include paint, carpet, and appliances.

Performing cosmetic repairs on a 50-unit property can run as high as $150,000 ($3,000 × 50). Typically you will finance those repairs with a Repair Allowance (which I cover in detail later in this book) so you won't have to come out of pocket to get them done.

If your repairs cost more than *$5,000* per unit, you're getting into *serious ones*. Just as a medical doctor distinguishes between minor injuries and serious ones, you must make the same distinction. Serious repairs not only cost a lot more, but you must contend with tenant occupancy issues if the repairs drag on too long.

If you need to make serious repairs, you must make sure that you have adequate cash flow to support you through the entire repair process and through the re-tenanting of the building.

For example, if you have to take off the old roof (due to termite damage, wood rot, fire, or other causes), there is a high likelihood that tenants with no roof over their heads may move. The city will probably require you to empty those units. Plus, you must give them advance notice of such disruptive repairs. Once your major repairs are finished, you'll have to rent those vacant units.

Having to do serious repairs, combined with losing tenants, is a double whammy that can temporarily destroy cash flow. When you run out of money, you have no other choice than to sell—usually at a discount or even at a loss.

The best solution is avoidance: Simply don't buy *buildings that need major repairs*—unless you have very deep pockets. Once you own a building, do not defer maintenance. Keep your building well-maintained and chances are that you will never have to do major repairs. In the world of multi-family investing, an ounce of prevention is worth a pound of gold in your pocket.

A REPOSITIONING SUCCESS STORY

Rehabbing a property is sometimes called *repositioning*. For example, your property might formerly have been positioned as a B- property. With your improvements and upgrades, you might be able to turn it into an A- property.

Important note: It is usually not financially feasible to turn a B- property into an A+ property. You would have to spend a fortune—and you might not get all of that money back when you sold the property. However, transforming it from a B- to an A- property would not cost nearly as much, and could significantly boost its resale value.

Many repositioning projects have occupancy rates lower than 85%. Due to this relatively low occupancy rate, most lending institutions and banks will consider your property to be *unstable*. As a rule of thumb, you need *at least 85% occupancy for at least 3 months for your property to be considered stable*. Lending institutions vary in their standards and some require higher occupancy or longer periods before they will finance your loan.

If your building has less than 85% occupancy, it could still get financing through what is called *mezzanine financing*. This is just a fancy name for short-term financing. It involves both higher closing costs and higher interest rates, but sometimes it's worth it.

Mezzanine financing can get you the money you need to polish your diamond, and make a small fortune by then increasing rents. And as you know, higher rents mean a higher selling price.

Here is a repositioning success story that shows the power of mezzanine financing. *Oliver Mann* purchased a 45-unit property in Birmingham, Alabama. The seller was a bank and the property needed some repairs. The bank sold the property for *$1,250,000* and agreed to finance $1,000,000.

Oliver had a small issue: He was broke. He needed $250,000 for the down payment and even more for the repairs.

Because he went to my boot camp and had my systems, Oliver was not deterred. He knew this was an outstanding deal, and he knew how to find *financial partners*.

He found partners that would put up *$450,000* for a *33% equity stake* in the deal. Now Oliver had his $250,000 down payment, plus another $200,000 to make needed repairs.

Six months later the rehab project came in $75,000 under budget. Oliver and his partners are enjoying $3,000 a month in spendable cash. Instead of spending $200,000 on repairs, they only spent around $125,000. Their total cash invested in the building was now about *$375,000*.

The property is now worth approximately *$2.1 million*, with a mortgage that's a bit less than $1 million. The gross equity is about $1.1 million. After factoring in their $375,000 invested in the property, they now have a *net equity* of about *$725,000*!

Oliver Mann started investing in apartments while dead-flat broke. Fortunately, *lack of money is rarely an impediment to success if you have the right systems.*

SOLVING THE PROBLEM OF HIGH VACANCY... ONCE AND FOR ALL!

Many investors are afraid of properties with high levels of vacancies. You should not be. When you are buying a property with high vacancies, view this not as a problem but as an opportunity.

High vacancies are a problem for the seller—but not for you. Perhaps the seller never took the time to hire professional management. *You* will not make that mistake! The seller maybe never supervised the management company properly. You won't make that mistake, either.

Like any other business, attracting customers (in your case, tenants) requires *marketing*.

Owners who suffer from high vacancies do not use creative marketing. Most use only one or two techniques to fill vacant apartments.

The most common method is to put an ad in the classified section of the local newspaper and pray that the phone rings. That's the mark of a real amateur.

I've found and developed *106 different ways to attract new tenants*. At any given time, your management company should be employing at least 10 of these methods, even if you have just one vacancy.

Most of these vacancy-filling strategies are *free* or *low cost*. For example, you could have the maintenance man drop off a flyer to every tenant in the building. The flyer describes the vacant unit, and offers a referral fee to the tenant, who refers a prospect, who later rents the unit.

Most people would like to have a friend, family member, or coworker living close by. If the tenant has a young child, and a friend or family member moves into the vacant unit, the tenant may have a great baby-sitter in the building. Other tenants will have their own motives for wanting a friend to move in. In almost every case, it's better to have friends living in the building than strangers moving in.

Keep in mind that everyone will be motivated by the $50 to $100 referral fee you pay! This is nothing, compared to the cost and time taken by advertising the vacant rental in the newspaper. Point out to tenants that if they refer several people to you over the course of a year, they could make several hundred dollars! You will be amazed at how many great referrals you get.

Because existing tenants know that you're going to screen anyone they recommend, most will only recommend quality people. No one wants to have the landlord and other tenants knocking on the door asking, "Why did you refer that loser into this building?" Tenants most often provide referrals of people who they respect. That's why the referrals you get from tenants are typically higher quality than the applicants you get from newspaper ads.

Another effective strategy for attracting tenants to your building is to send a postcard to all tenants of apartment properties similar to yours. These people have already shown a desire to live in a property like yours. Some of them may be ready to leave their current properties: They may be unhappy with management, or might want to live in a different-size unit. There could be dozens of other reasons.

Whatever their reason, some may want to move. Because your property is in the area, you have a good chance of drawing them in as new tenants.

On your postcard, mention the amenities your property has. If you can, list amenities that the other property does not have. These might be microwave ovens, free or low-cost cable TV, garages instead of carports, pets allowed, pets NOT allowed, and so on. Just one of these features might be enough to make the person come over to your property.

Another creative strategy is to *give* something of value to attract new tenants. Instead of just supplying an apartment with a microwave oven, consider giving the tenant a new microwave oven! It might cost you 100 bucks. If you fill that vacancy 1 month faster than you would have without the microwave, *you've just saved 1 month's rent*, which is a lot more than $100. You also create word-of-mouth buzz that might fill other units of yours.

You can also give away a free month's rent. Here's how to do it, though: Give the free month of rent *after* the tenant has lived in your building for 6 months. If the new tenant moves in during December, give them next June's rent for free. This way, you deter the scam artists who hop from free rent to free rent. Instead, you reward the longer-term tenant.

You can even stipulate that the free month's rent is only for tenants who also pay their rent on time each month. For quality tenants, these rules are easy to follow.

Share these strategies with your management company. Yes, it's the management company's responsibility to fill your property with great tenants. However, even some good companies are not highly skilled at filling vacancies.

When you are interviewing management companies, ask them what their marketing plan will be to fill vacant units. If they have a sophisticated and in-depth marketing plan that employs multiple ways of attracting prospects and converting them to tenants, you have a *keeper!*

More on High-Vacancy Properties

Buying a high-vacancy property can be a major bargain—IF you negotiate correctly.

Your purchase price *must always* be based on the *Net Operating Income* (NOI)of the property. The NOI is the annual income, minus annual expenses. It does not include the mortgage.

Some owners try to sell their properties based on *what the income could be if it were fully rented*. This is called a Pro Forma and is somewhere between a guess and a prayer.

Never buy based on seller estimates! Here's why:

1. You never know if the income will *ever* reach the estimated level stated in the seller financials. Never mind all the rosy excuses and stories from the seller on why the vacancies are only temporary. The fact is, those units are vacant.

2. *Why reward an owner for managing his property poorly? You* deserve the reward for taking over a distressed property and bringing it back to life. The current owner does not deserve that reward just for having a fantasy about what the rents *could* be.

High-vacancy apartments are such a great value play because all you have to do to increase the value of the property is to fill the units. In some cases, you don't even have to fix up the properties! I say "all you have to do" on purpose, because it simply involves tested and proven marketing methods.

HOW THE PROFIT MULTIPLIER WORKS

As I explained earlier in this book, *for every dollar you receive in additional rents, the value of your property will increase by an average of 10 dollars.* That's one powerful argument for buying multi-family units that are suffering from temporary vacancies, filling them up, and watching the value of your property soar!

Let's take a look at the economic benefits of getting rid of just one vacancy: If you rent one additional apartment for only $600 a month, multiply that by 12 and you see that you just increased the income of your property by $7,200 for the year.

As a rough rule of thumb, apartments are valued at 10 times their NOI (net operating income). So the $7,200 additional dollars coming in from that one property will increase *the value of your property by $72,000! Look at all your potential economic value just from renting out one single vacant apartment!*

Now think what happens when you buy a property with 10 vacancies and you put my 100+ tenant-filling techniques to work!

Of course, there will be higher expenses in a full property. But your profits will grow much faster than your expenses, if you follow my professional approach.

HOW TO GET A STEADY PAY RAISE

Finding properties with *low rents* is another great Value Play. Raising rents does not usually require any extra manpower or expense. Plus keep in mind that *you* will not be raising the rents—your management company will.

Many owners do not raise rents because they're afraid that one or two tenants might move out. This is usually an unjustified fear. Is a tenant going to go to all the trouble to find a new apartment, pack everything up, and go through the hassle of moving just because the rent has been raised a few dollars?

It costs hundreds of dollars to move, not to mention the time and energy involved. Most tenants don't want to do it. They would have to get their mail and utilities changed. Plus, people hate the unknown—and they would not know what their new neighbors are like.

For most tenants, it's much easier to just pay the rent increase and stay where they are.

Other landlords don't want to raise rents because they don't want to hear a new round of repair requests coming from tenants. If you've been following my advice, there shouldn't be anything busted in their apartments in the first place! But if something new pops up, by all means have the repairs done. They'll only increase the value of your building.

If some requests are ridiculous ("I want brand-new carpeting" when the carpet is in fine shape), have the management company tell the tenant that such optional improvements cannot be made. Most tenants are reasonable and will understand.

Landlords who are afraid to raise rents are weak—and weak landlords have skinny kids!

When you own a multi-family building, you should continuously raise the rents. After all, inflation is going up, as are salaries and hourly wages. Most of your tenants will be earning more each year. Therefore, they can afford to pay a bit more. Even in a stagnant market, tenants expect rent increases. Don't disappoint them!

In a down market, you can do a *nuisance increase*. That means raising the rents by $10 to $20 per month. It's not enough to upset tenants or motivate them to move. From the tenant's viewpoint, it's just a small nuisance. However, it helps you to pay your expenses and overhead—which may be increasing.

Regular rent increases raise the value of your property. If you have 50 units and increase the rents by $20 per month for every tenant, you've just increased your monthly cash flow by $1,000. Multiply that by 12 months and you've increased your income by *$12,000*. Due to the rent multiplier effect, you just increased the value of your property—in a stagnant market—by approximately *$120,000*! Do not neglect to raise rents.

In an emerging market, make sure you increase your rent right up to the market level, or just a bit below. Remember that in these types of markets, both rents and property values rise quickly. Huge amounts of money, jobs, and tenants are flowing into an emerging market.

In some emerging markets, I have increased rents by as much as $150 in 1 month! Multiply this by 50 units, times 12 months, and times the rent multiplier of 10, and you can see how exciting it is to invest in emerging markets! With the stroke of a pen, it's possible to give yourself a *$7,500 per month* raise!

What happens when tenants receive a rent increase notice? Some wonder "What took so long?" A few may shop around for another apartment. When they do, they soon discover that the market rent is just about where you have set your rent. (If you're keeping on top of market rents, that is.)

It may seem harsh that I'm such an advocate of raising rents. After all, we're talking about doing so to families trying to make ends meet. But please consider what I preached earlier in this book: *You need to treat your tenants like gold*—respond to their maintenance requests promptly, and make sure they have a clean, pleasant place to live. Those are all the expenses and risk that I take on. But the other side of the coin is the tenants' responsibility: To pay a fair market rent on time, and to respect my apartment property and the rights of other tenants. In my opinion, it's not only a fair trade, but quality apartment owners are performing a valuable service to the community.

Always deliver solid value for the apartments you provide. This is the key to keeping tenants loyal and happy. Charge at about the median level for your apartments, provide a great place to live, and you'll be all set.

THE ART OF THE RENT INCREASE

When you take over a property that has low rents—or when you're making a substantial rent increase for existing tenants—it's vitally important that you do the rent increase in a certain way, so as to *reduce* the number of tenants who might think of moving.

First, consider *how* you'll notify the tenants of the rent increase. This is usually done with a letter, but it's what is *in* that letter that counts.

You justify the rent increase on rational grounds. If tenants think you're raising the rents for no reason at all, they'll be unhappy. Some will look for other housing. One way to justify the increase is to point out your increasing expenses. Every year you probably pay more for handymen, carpet, paint, and other expenses.

Every tenant knows that inflation is a fact of life. Tenants see prices increase throughout the year in almost every other aspect of their lives (just look at gasoline!). Your rent increase will simply be seen as a normal and expected continuation of this trend.

Make sure your letter sounds sincere and a bit apologetic. Do *not* show any pleasure in raising the rents.

A letter that's cold and matter-of-fact will cause higher tenant turnover. A sincere, kind, and rational letter will result in little more than shrugged shoulders.

In keeping with your part of the bargain, make sure the landscaping and common areas are in good shape. When tenants get the rent increase notice, they start taking a closer look at the building and surrounding areas!

Make sure there is no peeling paint, all mailboxes are in working order, the grass is green, and all shrubs are cut and neatly trimmed. See to it that all trash is picked up and that laundry rooms are clean and in great working order.

If you're taking over a property, always make the necessary changes *before* you ask for an increase in rents. If you raise rents too early—before you do deferred maintenance—tenants will see you as simply greedy, and some will consider moving.

Instead, your first duty is to have a survey done of every unit and every tenant. Find out what repairs need to be done to each unit, and do them. Often you'll find that tenants have had problems or needed repairs for months or even a year! *When you finally correct that condition, they will be extremely grateful, and will have no problem paying a rent increase.*

THE ECONOMIC POWER OF FORCED APPRECIATION

As you have seen, just by bringing in one new tenant to fill a vacancy, you significantly increase the value of your building. When you *combine* this with a rent increase, you raise your equity in the property.

You in effect have *forced the appreciation in value of your property* through your intelligent actions! You don't even have to wait for the surrounding real estate market to go up.

It's just one more reason why I like multi-family investing so much: It gives you maximum opportunity to employ forced appreciation.

If you force appreciation on a rental house, you increase the monthly income by a factor of 1. If you force appreciation on a 50-unit apartment building, you increase monthly income by much more.

When you combine the

- rising appreciation of a Buyer's Market Phase I, with
- an emerging market, with
- the multiplier power of raising the rents and other Value Plays,

. . . you've got a *wealth rocket* that's about to shoot to the moon!

One factor you must consider when you use a combination of Value Plays is that some tenants may be on 1-year leases. When you purchase a property, you acquire the obligation to honor these leases; they do not end just because ownership was transferred.

If you buy the property in January and the leases expire in June, in most cases you cannot have a rent increase until June. Often, leases expire at different times because tenants have entered into leases at different times during the year.

Some of the leases may expire during the month you buy the building! You can raise those rates as soon as these leases expire. Other tenants will probably be on month-to-month agreements. You can raise their rents simply by sending a 30-day notice.

When you do a thorough prepurchase analysis of all leases, you'll know exactly when you can raise rents, and by how much. When done right, there will be very few surprises when you purchase the property.

If you employ these strategies and treat your tenants with respect—as I do—you will make more money than you ever imagined possible. I'm looking forward to hearing *your* success stories!

IN THE NEXT CHAPTER

Imagine having a multi-millionaire make all the big mistakes before you do—and then tell you exactly how to avoid them. Well, that's what the next chapter is all about.

I went from having under $800 in the bank to being set for life—all in under 4 years. Imagine how much faster you will make *your* millions, when you know not only where the profit potential is (the previous chapters), but where the landmines are, and how to avoid them (the next chapter)!

THE 10 BIGGEST MISTAKES INVESTORS MAKE IN EMERGING MARKETS, AND HOW TO AVOID THEM

In the chapters leading up to this one, I hope you've had a taste of the unbelievable profit potential of real estate investing done right.

By *done right*, I refer to investing in the right part of the market cycle, in the right (emerging) markets, and through the right kind of property (multi-family). I am living proof that these principles are worth literally millions of dollars.

But just as a coin has two sides, there's another side to real estate investing: Doing things wrong.

I've made a whole bunch of money—but I've also made almost every mistake there is to make! I know just about all the other real estate gurus, and have heard countless stories of blown deals, missed opportunities, and lessons learned.

This chapter by itself is easily worth hundreds of thousands of dollars, if you apply its wisdom. I've distilled the many possible investing mistakes into the 10 biggest ones. More importantly, I show you how to sidestep these landmines and make money faster and more confidently than even I did.

Let's now explore the dark side of investing, and how to stay on the right path:

MISTAKE #1: THINKING ANY INVESTMENT IS A GOOD INVESTMENT

You're in an emerging market. There are great opportunities all around you and you're like a kid in a candy store. It's easy to conclude that because you are in a full-blown, honest-to-goodness emerging market, that every investment is going to be a winner. "After all," you think to yourself, "A rising tide lifts all boats!"

Well, some boats are shipwrecks that even the highest tide can't float.

Yes, the chances of buying a good deal in an emerging market are far greater than in any other market phase. But there are also market forces that you must be very careful of, or else you will be buying a disaster waiting to happen.

As I mentioned earlier, there are four different types of properties, and four different types of areas in a given city. Both the properties and areas get a letter grade of A, B, C, and D. A is good, D is bad. (I will cover this in much more detail in Chapter 10.)

Buying a B property in a C area, where the path of progress is going the other way, is not a good idea. Given that the path of progress is going the other way—ever farther from this property—the neighborhood will be in decline. In fact, far from being where the action is, your proposed investment is going to struggle just to break even.

As that happens, your B property will no longer attract B tenants, because of the neighborhood. People don't want to live below their economic level; they're usually looking to live above it. Your B property will soon be filled with C tenants who are moving up!

Before long, your nice B property will turn into a C. Because of this downward evolution, the price you can expect for your C property will be less than what you would have received when it was a B property.

Your goal should be to buy C properties in A or B areas, or B properties in A areas. Then, by applying my systems, you can get that property to blossom into that higher area, with better-quality tenants paying more rent. This is where you get the highest appreciation.

Carefully consider your unit mix as well. That is the proportion of one-, two-, and three-bedroom units in a particular property. For instance, a property might have a unit mix of 14 one-bedroom units, 42 two-bedroom units, and 14 three-bedroom units.

Buying a unit mix of all efficiencies or a large number of three or more bedrooms can also turn out to be a deal to avoid. (Efficiency apartments are small one-bedroom units, where the bedroom, living room, and kitchenette are all in one room.) Efficiencies attract a very transient tenant base. There tends to be high turnover and high maintenance expenses.

If you know this going in, and you make sure you're compensated for this extra risk with a lower purchase price, then you might be okay. If you don't have experience with efficiencies, and invest based on regular buying parameters—not knowing the extra management risk involved—you're in for a nasty surprise.

On the other end of the unit mix scale, buying properties with many three-bedroom units can be a problem. Larger families will rent these units. Larger families mean more kids. That in turn means more maintenance issues, and the prospect of teenage kids loitering around the property. It may be difficult to rent to new tenants, because some people get nervous when they see gangs of kids hanging around.

If you didn't have someone with lots of scars advising you on the matter, you might think "Lots of three-bedroom units means more rent per unit, which will give me bigger cash flow. . . Hey, that's great!"

I'm here to tell you otherwise.

When buying in an emerging market, be sure to do all of your due diligence. Analyze each deal thoroughly, be sure you know why you are buying, and make sure the numbers work. Follow the steps in this book each time you purchase, and you'll be well on your way to exploding your wealth in emerging markets.

MISTAKE #2: INVESTING WHERE THERE'S NO REAL EMPLOYMENT BASE

One of the key elements in an emerging market is population growth. You definitely want to see evidence that people are migrating into an area, and creating demand in that area. That translates into vacant units getting filled up.

You must be careful, though: It's possible to have an increasing population in an area without an adequate employment base.

If a city is still stagnant and has not attracted major corporations to that area, any increased population will be coming from two main sources: immigration and *echo boomers.*

Pick up the paper these days and you don't have to read far to find a story related somehow to illegal immigrants. They tend to congregate in certain areas—usually in the same areas where legal immigrants from their country also live. Just because there's an influx of people does not mean there is an equal influx of jobs. Just like the famous movie line, "Show me the money," you should be thinking, "Show me the jobs." Keep an eye on current job creation and employment outlook.

Echo Boomers are the babies of the Baby Boomers. They are 20- to 34-year-olds, and are reaching the prime age group for renting. The problem is, they tend to stay with their parents longer than in previous generations! That may or may not be nice from a family perspective, but it's not good for us investors: We want them out there, renting apartments!

If this key demographic segment is strong in an area, the absorption rate of apartment units is likely to be lackluster. That can help to keep a market stagnant, and not help to drive it into the emerging phase.

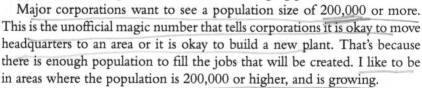

Major corporations want to see a population size of 200,000 or more. This is the unofficial magic number that tells corporations it is okay to move headquarters to an area or it is okay to build a new plant. That's because there is enough population to fill the jobs that will be created. I like to be in areas where the population is 200,000 or higher, and is growing.

MISTAKE #3: BEING TOO LATE TO THE PARTY

When an investment becomes so popular that everyone knows about it, it's not time to get IN—it's actually time to get OUT!

A very common investment mistake is entering a market way too late to make any significant gains. These people think they may be buying in an emerging market, but it had finished emerging long ago.

Amateurs want to have it both ways: They want the *big score* that comes from major growth, but they also want the comfort of knowing that people already have made lots of money in that market. The reality is they can have one, or the other, but not both at the same time.

If you're buying in the midst of lots of good investment results in a given market, you can still make a little money. There is a much bigger risk that the market will soon turn, and you'll get stuck in a flat or decreasing market.

When a market enters its emerging phase, hardly anyone knows about it. The market has been stagnant for a long time, and properties have been on the market seemingly forever.

The market has a local reputation as a nonperfomer. When you buy into this market, you'll get the opposite of comforting social support: Your friends will think you're crazy, and the locals will think you're just dumb. But they'll be very happy to *unload* their properties on you.

Markets need to be hot for quite a while in order for their heat to penetrate all the layers of ignorance, fear, and past mistakes. By the time the once-hot market has thoroughly warmed up all investors, that market is on its way down again.

That should be okay as far as you're concerned. You know (from this book) that there's always another market—somewhere in the country—at just the right stage to explode, and explode your wealth right along with it.

MISTAKE #4: NEGLECTING TO GO INTO EVERY UNIT

What you don't know CAN hurt you!

You've just put a great property under agreement, but it has an awful lot of units. The owner says that a full property inspection would take 2 or 3 days, and he can't guarantee that he can get you into all of the units during that period.

He strongly suggests that you do what's called a *survey*: You only go into every second or third unit, to get a feeling for the overall condition of the property.

The owner might even tell you that he's been investing for years, and does surveys himself when he invests. He may imply that only wet-behind-the-ears types bother to go into every unit. This sounds pretty good to you. Hey, not only will the property inspection not take so long, but you won't be charged as much by the property inspector.

This is a very dangerous practice!

The units you do not get into are usually the ones that need the most amount of work. They house the deadbeat tenants, or have some other defect that the owner would much rather you not know about.

When you're doing your property inspection, *this is your only chance* to be compensated for something that:

- is wrong with the property;
- the owner did not disclose to you; and
- you did not know existed.

Go into every unit! Yes, it takes more time. Yes, it costs more for the property inspector to schlep into every unit. But it's about the cheapest investment insurance you can possibly buy.

It is common to see things the owner did not tell you about. Then you can go back to the owner and seek either:

1. Repairs to be done;
2. Money back at the closing to do these repairs; or

3. A reduction in price as compensation for work that needs to be done on the property.

All three of these are good news to you, and great news to be discovered before the closing.

Sometimes owners are just as surprised as buyers after learning of these problems, because they didn't know that they existed either.

The last thing you want to have happen is you take over a property and notify tenants of that fact; then immediately the tenants start putting in all kinds of repair requests, in the hope that the new management will do all the repairs that the old management had neglected.

Rather than have all these repairs cut into your cash flow, make sure that you get the current owner to eat them, while you still have leverage before the deal closes.

MISTAKE #5: GETTING MIRED IN POLLUTION PROBLEMS

When you're buying a multi-family property, not only must it be structurally sound and generate cash flow, but it's also good if it is not a ticking environmental time bomb.

If you buy a property that's polluted in some way, and you don't discover it until you own it, you may just have bought a true nightmare.

Even though you may try to go after the seller for neglecting to disclose key facts, the government may go after you—the current owner—to have the mess cleaned up, at great expense.

There are different types of pollutants that affect multi-family properties. If you buy a property with asbestos, you run the risk of the asbestos becoming airborne and getting into the lungs of your tenants. Asbestos breaks down into tiny particles that look like fishhooks. Once inside the lungs, they never come out. Asbestos poisoning causes emphysema, cancer, and a giant hole in your bank account.

You must have the soil analyzed to be sure that nothing has contaminated it. There are many man-made environmental hazards that can contaminate soil. If your property is close to a gas station, there may have been seepage from the underground gas tanks, over many decades.

If you're buying a property that is close to warehouse storage (even the new mini-warehouses), you don't know what was stored there. Many people store hazardous materials and conveniently forget to tell local authorities. If it gets released from the containers and into the soil, you may have a problem.

There could be hazardous items buried right in your own property. The most important of these are underground oil tanks. If there is an underground tank on your property, you must require the seller to remove it before you purchase the property! If you don't, your buyer will require it of you.

The problem with underground oil tanks is they corrode and start to leak into the soil. It can go on for decades. If this is discovered while you're the owner, you'll have to clean all of the contaminated soil out of the property. You'll actually be lucky if just the soil is contaminated. If that oil gets into an underground water source, then you will be responsible for any area that was contaminated from your tank. This gets extremely expensive. I know this from first-hand experience. It happened to me!

Check to see where is the nearest dry cleaners, and if one was ever present on or near your property. The majority of dry cleaning sites are contaminated with the toxic chemicals used in the dry cleaning process. This cleanup can be very costly.

Sometimes contractors bury items on properties as they are being built. A developer may see an opportunity to dispose of construction materials from another job by burying it in the ground of other properties that he or she owns. Always ask if there are any known construction materials buried on the site. You should mainly be concerned about asphalt shingles, because they are made with oil.

Another issue that you must contend with is toxic mold. This mold by itself is not a big issue and can be remedied easily. The real issue with toxic mold is where it is exactly, and what's causing it.

If you have toxic mold next to a ventilation system and it gets into that system, you're going to have a lot of sick people in your building. Your primary goal is to determine what is causing the toxic mold, and whether it can be cured. If it can be cured, have the seller cure it. You shouldn't have further problems.

Have it inspected by a certified mold inspector and have him or her certify that the situation has been remediated.

If you can't determine the cause of the mold, or can't remedy the cause, don't buy the property. You will have a very difficult time reselling it. Not only will your sales price suffer, but you'll personally suffer from all the potential tenant and board of health problems that might occur.

I had a 92-unit apartment building under agreement in Oklahoma City. We discovered toxic mold during the due diligence period. The mold was in the basement units and was being caused by a higher than normal water table. To remediate the problem, the owner would need to install special drains surrounding the exterior of the basement of all eight buildings. Even then, there was no guarantee that this would work.

He elected not to do the work. He wanted to wait for a buyer who would either take the building *as is*, or who was stupid enough to not do a thorough property inspection. We were neither, and passed on the property.

Of course, you must also test the water to make sure it's clean. Without good, clean water, you're not in business.

The lending institution usually requires that a "Phase I Environmental Study" be done to protect its interest in the property. This study will cover most of the problems that I just described.

If they find something that is out of the ordinary, they will require that a "Phase II Environmental Study" be done. This is a more intense look at the property and its surroundings.

MISTAKE #6: OVERPAYING FOR A PROPERTY

We are going to cover this extensively in Chapter 10, but let's cover the basics here.

There are certain key ratios you must consider when analyzing a property.

The first number is the capitalization rate, or *cap rate*. Every income-producing property in every market has a cap rate. In a normal market, cap rates range from 7 to 12. The lower the number, the more expensive the property. New construction usually sells at the lowest cap rate. Properties in bad areas or that are in need of repair will sell at higher cap rates.

Look at it this way: If you had an investment with little risk, you would expect a lower return. The riskier the investment, the higher the return you require, in order to compensate you for the risk. The cap rate works in the same manner.

If you buy a property that is in need of repair at a low cap rate, when you try to sell that property, you won't get as much money for it, compared to your profits if you had bought it at the right cap rate.

Comparable properties will help you to determine the right cap rate. Compare the property that you're buying with similar properties that have sold recently in the market. This will tell you what investors are willing to pay for *this* type of property, in *this* market, at *this* time. *You* can get comparable property information from a local commercial broker, or the archives of the financial newspaper in that area.

Another number to focus on is the *debt–service ratio*. This number tells you how many times your income covers your debt. Most lending institutions will not finance you unless your income covers your debt by 1.2 times. The closer this ratio gets to 1.0, the closer your property is getting to a break-even point. That means you have a higher risk of being in a negative cash flow situation.

If you buy a property with a debt–service ratio less than 1.2, you're paying too much for the property. There is a good chance you will not be able to secure conventional (i.e., bank) financing to close the deal.

Also look at your *cash-on-cash return*. *This is the amount of money you'll get back* by the end of your first year, compared to the money you actually took out of your pocket to get into the deal.

A normal cash-on-cash return is 10% to 20%, depending on what phase of the market you're in. This means that you are getting a 10% to 20% return on your money, not including appreciation or principal pay down. You certainly can't get this level of return at your local bank or from a certificate of deposit!

As with the debt–service ratio, the closer you get to 0% with cash-on-cash return, the closer your property is getting to a *negative cash flow position*, and the more you are *overpaying* for the property. Smart, conservative investors like their cash-on-cash returns to be around 15%. There are markets and times, though, when it's okay to settle for less, and other markets where you should require much more.

MISTAKE #7: TYING UP ALL YOUR MONEY IN ONLY ONE MARKET

When you begin to invest in emerging markets, focus on one particular market, do a thorough analysis, take the time to make the right connections, nurture those connections, and start doing deals.

Avoid the temptation to jump from market to market, looking for the very best situation. That's a prescription for being really busy, and getting no deals done.

There's the opposite risk, though: Other investors find a market and then park themselves there. Yes, they're doing deals and making good money. Because of that, they get comfortable in the market. Too comfortable.

You need to be diversified in other markets, so that you can make the maximum amount of gains in the shortest time.

Two common problems can happen if you have all your eggs in one basket:

1. Markets occasionally shift very quickly. Examples are New York City after 9/11; New Orleans after Katrina; and Southern California after earthquakes/forest fires/mudslides.

2. You're in a market and doing very well. You've collected lots of units, your cash flow is strong, and your market starts to take the normal turn in the business cycle. Your brain tells you what's going on and that you should be moving your money into another market. But your emotions allow you to get complacent. You like this market too much! Maybe you'll just ride this cycle out. Besides, you've got so much equity that you're fat and happy. It would take a major shift in the market before you came close to being in the red on one of your properties.

What you're doing is giving up a great opportunity to grow more wealth for you and your family. By not moving your money, you're virtually guaranteeing the loss of some equity as your market goes through the cycle.

This is equity that could be in another market, doubling or tripling itself, while your current market makes its way through the cycle.

Diversify that portfolio!

MISTAKE #8: IGNORING OVERBUILDING

Jobs are what brings a market back to life. But it's always oversupply that eventually stalls a market and triggers the beginning of the end of an emerging market.

At the beginning stages of an emerging market (in the Buyer's Market Phase II), the only building that is going on is speculative. These builders are hoping that rents and demand will rise to a level where they can make a profit on their new construction.

During the previous phase—the Buyer's Market Phase I—there was virtually no new construction. So much supply was on the market that the last thing the market needed was more construction. Even if a builder did decide to build, it was very difficult to get favorable financing: Most banks at this stage had portfolios full of projects from builders who had gone under.

In the early state of a Buyer's Market Phase II, rents are not high enough to warrant new construction. Most new construction does not pay for itself, so any plans to build are put on hold until market forces change.

As rents rise and absorption takes place, finally the market gets to the point where new construction does pay for itself. It is now profitable to build. This point is called *equilibrium*. It's what separates the Buyer's Market Phase II from the Seller's Market Phase I.

When the market reaches equilibrium, new construction permits begin to spike, and a lot of new projects are scheduled. This new inventory usually takes 1 to 3 years to enter the market, given the time it takes to get permits and build the projects.

Demand becomes higher as job growth continues to climb and population swells. Builders continue to build but eventually job growth stagnates. Even so, all those projects in the pipeline continue to pour units onto the market.

Now the absorption rate of these new units slows, as demand further weakens.

Many investors make the mistake of *not watching the absorption rate* as they plan their building. Even more common is that they see the market softening, but their project is already somewhere in the pipeline. They remember the recent profits, and just hope they can hurry up and get in on the market before it changes too much. A lot of them don't make it.

The most successful investors make decisions based on hard numbers and hard-headed analysis, and not wishful thinking.

MISTAKE #9: SELLING TOO LATE

This is also an affliction of emotional, nostalgic investors. They bought an investment at the right time and each year enjoyed more equity. Monthly cash flow also grew nicely. Now they're emotionally attached to the investment, as if it's become the family pet. And who's so cruel as to sell Fido!

But the market is changing. Jobs are beginning to stagnate. Population growth is flattening, even if a few other indicators are positive.

Then it happens.

You start to see a couple more units vacant than usual. Not as many new tenants are taking out applications. It's taking longer to fill your vacancies. That means net operating income (NOI) is down, given the lower rent collections.

Lower NOI means your property is now *losing value.* Your once-proud Prince is slowly starting to look more like a Frog.

Okay, so it's now time to sell—time to take your money and find another investment in another emerging market. But there's a problem: There aren't as many buyers out there as there used to be.

Other owners are also seeing the change, and have been affected by lower NOI. They want out, too! There are now even more properties on the market.

The smart investors are long gone. Because of this, there are fewer buyers in the market.

Speculators once bought properties with no cash flow in this market, relying on the Greater Fool Theory to sell their properties at higher prices. Only now, they have become the Greater Fool. They are now desperate to sell, because each month they have to come out of pocket to meet all the expenses.

The cycle then gets uglier by the day.

Just last year there were investors coming out of the woodwork to buy! Appreciation was going gangbusters, and properties on the market for less than a week could get full asking price, or more.

When you buy in a Buyer's Market Phase II, all the way into a Seller's Market Phase I, your investment is like a *cash cow*. Each month it goes out and grazes, and you can then milk it for big buckets of cash.

As you hold that investment into a Seller's Market Phase II, that cow begins to turn into a pig! It gets bigger and fatter. And we know what happens to pigs—they get slaughtered!

The wise investor pulls his money out of a market at the beginning of a Seller's Market Phase II. Yes, there still is profit potential in the market. There better be, for you to have a group of eager buyers! It's time for you to call it quits, and move to another market that is just beginning its upswing.

MISTAKE #10: PAYING TOO MUCH IN TAXES

U. S. Judge Learned Hand once said: "There is nothing sinister in so arranging one's affairs as to keep taxes as low as possible."

I agree! Give to Uncle Sam his due, but not any more!

After you've accumulated a few properties—or even one large one—if a qualified accountant is not doing your taxes, you're making a mistake. Get an accountant who specializes in real estate.

A good real estate accountant is a key member of your team. The tax laws are simply too complicated for you to waste your time trying to stay on top of them. A good real estate accountant knows the tax laws that will affect you, and the rules you can benefit from.

A good real estate accountant will save you many thousands of dollars. I remember early on when I switched from one accountant to another. I was concerned because my taxes weren't being done in a timely manner. Because I had grown so big so fast, my accountant used to look at my pile and kept pushing it off to the side, doing all the easy clients first. Each year he would file extension after extension, even though I had long since gotten all my information to him!

I started to get the feeling that I was more of a burden than a client, though I liked this guy. He was a former IRS auditor and knew a great deal about tax law.

I got a referral from another investor to an accountant who had many real estate clients. They all held him in very high regard. I made the switch. With one stroke of a pen, he got me a $14,372 refund! I then liked him even more!

When interviewing accountants, ask them how many real estate investors they are working with, and what are the sizes of their portfolios. If they're working with a lot, that is obviously a good sign. If they only have a few real estate investor clients, move on to someone more experienced. Also, get names and phone numbers of those investor/references, so you can call them to confirm the reference.

I talk elsewhere in this book about the 1031 Tax-Deferred Exchange. It's a fantastically powerful method of exploding your real estate portfolio with no current taxation.

If you own real estate investments and are not harnessing the power of 1031 exchanges, you are giving up potentially millions of dollars of profit. I'd call that one of the Top 10 Mistakes!

The combination of a good real estate attorney and 1031 exchanges will create more money in the first place, and keep more of it in your pocket, away from the tax man!

After you've made some nice profits in real estate, it's easy to forget some of the fundamentals that got you there. That's why I urge you to review this chapter regularly. That way, you won't get successful, then complacent, and then make the same mistake twice.

IN THE NEXT CHAPTER

We've covered a lot of ground in discussing what makes a great market and a great property. I've explained how to find these deals. Now it's time to talk about how to finance them.

The fantastic news is that there are many ways to invest in real estate, even if you have little or no money, and bad credit. Turn the page to find out how.

CHAPTER 9

HOW TO FIND ALL THE MONEY YOU NEED TO DO YOUR DEALS

"Remember that credit is money."

—Benjamin Franklin

If you're just getting started in real estate investing, you may not have money to invest. Certainly that was the case with me and most of my students.

In fact, money is probably the reason you're considering real estate investing: You're tired of living from paycheck to paycheck, struggling with budgets that never seem to work out, and always trying to figure out how to get the good things in life.

If that's the case, you'll especially like this chapter, because I can free you—once and for all—from the belief that you can't get the money you need to invest in real estate.

First things first: Let's talk about the things that hold good people back.

FOUR MYTHS THAT WILL KEEP YOU POOR (IF YOU BELIEVE THEM!)

Do you know how they train elephants? When the elephant is a baby, it's not strong enough to break a stout rope. So the trainer ties the elephant to a post planted firmly in the ground.

The young elephant's natural desire is to be free, so it pulls and tugs at the rope constantly. It tries everything, but it fails to budge the post.

Eventually it gives up trying.

By the time the elephant is full grown, it can easily snap the rope. But it still sees the same rope and the same post and does not bother to try.

Humans, with their much larger brains, are worse off than the elephants! Why? Because they often don't even try to test the limits of their strength. No, they're too smart for that. Instead, they listen to older and *wiser* people that tell them:

- "It's no use."
- "Don't bother."
- "I tried that and it didn't work; what makes you think it will work for you?"
- "You'll never pull it off; after all, you're (too old/young/dumb/uneducated/etc.) to make it work."

Some of those older and wiser people are just trying to look out for you. But others are losers who deep down do not want to see someone else succeed.

You need to surround yourself with people that have a *can do* attitude. You need to have examples of success around you—people who will pull you *up* to their level, rather than drag you *down* to their level.

But watch out for another trap! I can hear somebody's thoughts right now: "But Dave, I don't have anyone like that around me! I have negative people nearby, and there's nothing I can do about it. I guess that means I'm destined to stay where I am...."

Wrong! It would be nice to be surrounded by enthusiastic, successful people. But if that's not the case, you only need to do two things to get started on the right foot:

1. Don't listen to the naysayers. Avoid them when you can (you know who they are!), and don't ask for their opinions. If you simply can't avoid them, then nod politely, and let them empty their big bags of hot air. Don't bother to argue with them, because they have built a fortress around their failure, and you really don't want to get inside that fortress anyway.

2. If you can't surround yourself with positive people, just start with one person. I have good news for you: I'll be that first one! Keep listening to what I have to say. I'll keep your spirits up and keep you pointed in the right direction.

Let's look more closely at four myths—or elephant ropes—that don't need to hold you back any longer.

Myth #1: "You need money to make money."

A lot of people think that you need a pile of money to get started in multi-family investing. The good news is this is simply not true.

If that were the case, there would be no self-made millionaires like me and a number of my friends.

There are at least 27 ways to finance real estate investments with no money down. I know, because at one time or another, I've done just about all of these 27 ways. (I'll tell you about a fascinating one, later on.)

Sure, when you do have a lot of money, it's easy to put it to work and make more money. But I developed my Four-Step Financing System, which will give you all the money you'll need to get yourself started on a lifetime of wealth.

More on that in a minute, but let's look at the other myths first:

Myth #2: "I have bad credit. No one will loan to me."

Boy do I love real estate!

One reason is because your bad credit or my (former) bad credit does not have to hold you or me back from doing tremendous deals.

As you'll see a little later when we talk about *hard money*, experienced real estate lenders don't care if you just stepped off a spaceship from Mars. What they care about is the property you want them to lend money on. If it's a good enough property, with plenty of security for their loan, then they will do loans all day to Little Green Men.

Myth #3: "'No money down' investing is just a scam peddled by those late-night infomercial guys to ignorant, gullible investor wannabes."

It's true that the term *no money down* has become synonymous with late-night infomercial gurus. But *no money down* isn't just for beginning investors.

Consider this: Prosperous investors may be earning piles of cash from their investments. They may even have bank accounts bulging like overinflated balloons. But every smart investor—even when super successful—always tries to get into a deal with as little money down as possible. That's because the more deals you can control with the least amount of money, the wealthier you'll become.

If you were in charge of real estate investments at a Fortune 500 company, and suddenly decided to do nothing but all-cash investing, you'd suddenly find yourself thrown out on your ear. Major institutions practically invented the concept of putting little or no money down when buying property. So join the club, with your head held high, and start making some serious money.

Myth #4: "Banks are where the money is, so that's where I'll get my loan."

The famous bank robber, Willy Sutton, was asked why he robbed banks. He said "Because that's where the money is."

Willy maybe was right about where the most *actual* currency was stored—but not about where most of the *wealth* is. Real estate investors think of banks as only one of many, many sources for deal financing.

When you stop thinking of gray-suited, conservative bankers as your only financing alternative, a whole world of possibilities opens up. As you'll see a little later, that other world is eager to loan money to real estate investors, if you know how to approach them.

FIVE REASONS WHY YOU'LL BE ON EASY STREET WHEN YOU HAVE ALL THE MONEY YOU NEED FOR INVESTING

1. You Can Do Deals Even When You Have No Money and Bad Credit.

There are lots of things you can't do when you're broke and have lousy credit. But you CAN do real estate deals, believe it or not!

To tell you the truth, I'm glad that most people don't understand this. If they did, millions more investors would be competing for deals!

You can do deals when you have no money because you don't have to invest in every deal. Instead, you can profit from being a match-maker.

Ebay is worth a few billion today, not because it buys all that junk that's put up for auction! No, it makes its money by matching sellers and buyers.

It's the same thing with many real estate transactions: You can profit from putting together people who:

- Need to sell;
- Want to buy or rent a property; and
- Want a better return on their investments.

When you're broke, just putting the first two groups together will make you money. But as soon as you have a steady stream of private money to invest, you'll put your real estate business into fifth gear.

2. You Can Do More Deals.

Once your marketing machine is working right, your phone will be ringing with calls from sellers of properties of all types. It would be a real shame to pass up a great deal, just because it's larger than you have funds to handle.

Larger deals often mean larger profits—for the same amount of work. Naturally, you have to buy right, after analyzing the numbers. But when you have plenty of investing capital at your disposal a whole new horizon opens to you of doing deals you simply could not touch before.

3. You Can Do Bigger Deals.

Most investors start buying deals between $500,000 and $3 million. On the other hand, most banks and other conventional lenders prefer to lend on deals whose purchase price is $3 million or more. This is because banks earn their money as a percentage of the purchase price. If they lend on a deal that has a purchase price of $10 million they make a lot more money than from lending on a deal with a purchase price of $500,000—and it takes the same amount of effort.

If you could make a lot more money with the same amount of effort, what deal would you look to do?

Hold that thought: Here again, when you decide that you only want to do big deals because they take the same amount of effort and you get paid a whole lot more, your wealth is going to explode!

4. You Can Do Deals Faster.

When investors have to wade through the paperwork of conventional lenders, deals take time. So many people must scrutinize the deal, get appraisals, wait for committees to approve the loan—the list goes on.

When you have private money at your disposal, you can literally do two or three deals in the time it takes another investor to sweat together one deal.

5. You Can Negotiate Better.

You'll have the money NOW.

Think back to the last time you bought something big. You probably did your research and comparison shopped. You took your time deciding which version you wanted to get. But when you made your decision, you wanted it NOW! And the company that could supply it NOW became very attractive.

It's the same when you're buying real estate. Sellers start out as *tire kickers*, casually thinking about selling their property some day. Then, as they say, time and circumstances change all sellers' minds. Now they NEED to sell.

Let's say you are competing against other investors for the deal. Those other investors are working to arrange bank financing, and hope that it comes through in the next 30 days. You, on the other hand, have the money ready to go, and can simply write a check.

You are going to be able to negotiate a MUCH better deal—maybe worth tens of thousands of dollars more to you—by being able to satisfy those sellers right now.

You come across like you don't need the deal.

Having the cash available means you do more deals, and they'll be higher quality. That in turn means you begin to take on a certain confidence when you approach the next deal.

Not only are you now making good money as an investor; you know that behind every deal is another, and yet another.

So, when the seller starts negotiating hard with you, it won't be a situation in which you NEED that deal. You'll be confidently negotiating, and that confidence will show.

Horses can sense a confident rider, and sellers will sense your confidence, too. That can only help your bargaining position.

THE MIRACLE OF LEVERAGE

With the proper use of leverage, you'll be able to create enormous wealth for yourself, in the same time that others merely make a few dollars.

Leverage is simply using other peoples' money to do your deals.

Let's say you had $20,000 to invest and you put all of it down (20% down) on a $100,000 property that's giving you $500 a month positive cash flow.

Instead, what if you could only put 10% down and buy two properties for $100,000 each? Now you have two properties with cash flows of $500 each, and two properties appreciating each day, creating more wealth for you.

What if you had those two properties and now were able to buy two other properties with a value of $500,000 each, and a cash flow of $2,500, with no money down. Now you've got over $6,000 a month in total equity, and property worth $1,200,000.

That's the difference between investors who think they need to put 20% down on each property and investors that look at each deal very creatively, thinking of ways they can get in with the least amount of money possible.

This is good news for beginning investors because, either out of having no money or the desire to create great wealth very quickly, they now have available many different methods to do deals with little or no money down.

I'm NOT saying that the more leverage, the better. Leverage is like a lever. It's a tool. It can be used right, and misused. Whether you're buying for all cash, or none of your own cash, there's one extremely important rule you must follow, and it's right up front in the next section.

THE FOUR-STEP SYSTEM FOR FINANCING ALL YOUR DEALS

Step One: Big Secret: Buy RIGHT

The numbers need to work.

If you are paying way too much for a property, all kinds of things happen—all of them bad:

- You won't get conventional lenders for the property, because they know you paid too much;
- You need to raise more money than you otherwise would;
- Possibly some private lenders will loan you money, not knowing what they're getting themselves into. But sooner or later they'll find out it's not as safe a deal as they thought;
- You now have little or no cushion against a market down turn.

Let's now look at what happens when you do buy RIGHT:

- You need less money to finance the deal;
- You have more of a safety cushion, because you can afford to sell at a lower price and still make a profit;
- Professional lenders gain respect for you as the person who brings them solid deals;

- You'll get better deals on loans when there's more equity in the deal, because there is less risk for the lender;
- You can now possibly get a second or even third mortgage on a property, to hold it longer or cash you out, or both.

Buying right is the foundation of any real estate transaction. So how DO you do it?

There are three components to buying right:

Education.   You don't need a ton of education; you need to be doing what you're doing right now—learning from an expert. Contrast that with other people, who blindly dive into real estate because they saw their cousin Ralph do it.

If you want to get to your (real estate) destination fast, you need to take the roads that were paved by experts before you. Sure, you can go over land, and blaze your own trail with machetes; why would you want to?

I applaud you for taking the time to find out what good deals look like, when the next one comes knocking.

Deal Flow.   This is absolutely the most critical aspect of buying right. If you have plenty of deals coming your way, you can pick and choose the best ones. Your back is not against the wall. If you don't jump at the first ones, you'll soon get a sense of the prices in your market.

There's another hidden benefit: Even if you don't want to buy some of these deals to lease or rehab, you can simply flip some of them to other investors who are starving for deals.

I consider deal flow to be so critical, that I did two things:

1. I made it the focus of intensive study for YEARS. I went to over two dozen real estate seminars to find out the latest techniques others were using. I spent well over $110,000 on my own education from consultants and gurus in many different fields, like direct mail, publicity, advertising, and copywriting.

I'm not suggesting that you have to do the same! It's already done FOR you. That's the second thing I did:

2. I put everything I discovered into a box. It's my *Complete Marketing System.* I encourage you to take it for a no-risk, completely guaranteed test drive, by going to www.MarketCycleMastery.com; and in the search box, type in the keywords "Marketing System." It will save you literally years of figuring this stuff out on your own, not to mention tens of thousands of dollars in tuition, fees, and lost profits.   *what is this?*

Analysis.   Even if you've read up on what makes a good deal, and gone to some seminars, you still want to run the deal through some analysis software.

It doesn't matter how experienced a pilot is—the person STILL goes through a checklist before taking off. That's because it's too easy to forget a step. In fact, the more experienced you are, the more likely you'll just casually forget to do something, because you've done it a million times before, and the deals begin to blur together.

Let your software be your checklist and guide as to just how good a deal you really have.

Step Two: Reduce the Amount of Outside Financing Needed

Let the current owner be your lender of FIRST resort!

In the many hundreds of deals I've done, I can tell you that a great many sellers don't NEED the money. And when they do need some of it, they often don't need all. In fact, some don't want it!

Let me explain. Sure, there are some great deals when the seller must sell. It might be due to job relocation, divorce, or many other reasons. But here's the great news in the form of myths:

Myth: "Owners, of course, want all their money now."   Do not ASSUME that the seller needs all the money! You know what *assume* means in the military, don't you? ASSUME means we're about to make an "ASS out of yoU and ME."

It's much better to ask sellers if they would be willing to *take back paper* in the form of a second mortgage that is secured by the property.

Even if the owner does not own the entire property free and clear, he or she still may consider seller financing. This means you would get the primary financing from another source, usually a lending institution, and the owner would provide you with some of the remainder amount due for the property.

A typical second mortgage would be written with an interest rate that is 1% to 2% higher than what the lending institutions are getting at the time. They are usually calculated with a payback period of 25 years, with a balloon of 5 years. That means you'll pay the first 5 years as if the loan is going to last 25 years, and then the whole thing becomes due after 5 years.

When sellers give you the remainder of what's owed on the property, they are providing you with means to create 100% financing. If the property cash flows properly, this is a good thing. Other times they may give you 10% or 20% of the purchase price, which would help you to reduce the amount that would have to come out of your pocket to buy the property.

Why would a seller possibly want to do that? Because it can reduce taxes. You only pay taxes on proceeds that you actually get from the sale of a property. Spreading the proceeds out over monthly payments for 20 or 25 years is a great way to reduce a property's tax burden.

Another incentive you can offer is to pay slightly more for the property. The seller may very much like that higher sales price, and be willing to wait for a sizable portion of the money in order to get the somewhat higher price.

Here's another reason: You'll be surprised how many owners own their properties free and clear and have no mortgages. Some of these owners like the monthly cash flow that they are getting from the property but no longer want the management responsibilities. These owners are likely to finance the property for you so they can continue to get that monthly cash flow (from you).

Myth: "The seller knows about owner financing, and didn't bring it up, so I shouldn't bother." One thing's for certain: You will NOT get seller financing if you don't ask for it! I can't even remember the scores of deals I've done, and millions of dollars I've financed, the easy way—from sellers— simply by asking for it.

Do NOT assume that just because sellers don't mention owner financing, they don't want it!

They may not know how it works. You could be dealing with someone who was just willed an out-of-state property that's the first piece of real estate he or she's ever owned!

Just bring up the topic in a matter of fact way, and go from there.

Myth: "The best deal you can get is to put 5% down." I've gotten money BACK at closing! I've been PAID to do real estate deals, up front.

You may run into a situation in which a property needs work, but there's a lot of equity in it. Sometimes you can structure a deal in which the current owner takes out a small mortgage on the property, and then sells the whole thing to you.

The owner may get a piece of the loan proceeds, and the other piece goes to you.

The owner doesn't care, because he or she won't be the owner any longer. And you've just put money in your pocket.

How to Profit from Repair Allowances. A repair allowance is a great way to get into a property with little or no money down. It also allows you to finance into a loan the repair costs of a property, so you don't have to come out of pocket for the repairs.

How to Get a Repair allowance. There are three ways to get one:

1. Have the seller drop the purchase price by the amount of the repairs. This isn't the best option because you will have to pay for those repairs out of your pocket.

2. Ask the seller to give you the amount that's necessary to do the repairs (the repair allowance) at the closing. By doing that, you have just financed the repair costs into the deal.

If the purchase price remains the same and the seller is giving you a repair allowance, then your ratios and cash flow will remain the same.

3. You can minimize the amount of money you put into the deal by asking the seller to increase the purchase price by the amount of the repairs. They then give you that money at closing in the form of a repair allowance.

Remember: If you do this, you must first recheck your ratios to make sure that you're still getting the return and cash flow that you require. If the numbers work, you do it!

You may discover repairs that need to be done to the property and the seller will not give you a concession for those repairs. If you find yourself with a great deal—even if you have to pay for those repairs yourself—you might just want to take the property *as is*.

Key Principles

1. You should always try to put as little money into the deals as possible. That's so you can control as many properties as you can, with the least amount of money. This will make you wealthier, faster.

2. Not all banks will be okay with repair allowances, so you should only work with the ones that do. Some banks will require the repair allowance to be held in an escrow account and the money be disbursed as the work is being done. Other banks will allow the buyer to receive the full amount at closing.

I like to work with banks that do allow me to have the full amount at closing. For a current list of these banks, just go to www.MarketCycleMastery .com and type in the search box the keyword "Banks." Perhaps I'll use some of that money for the down payment on another property!

Common Objection.   A common objection that you might get from sellers is that they don't want to pay taxes on the amount of money that you're increasing the purchase price by.

Your answer to that objection is they don't pay capital gains on the higher amount because they are giving the money to the buyer and it is treated as an expense and reduces their overall *tax basis*.

In rare cases, some sellers still don't understand it, or are just plain stubborn. Then you've got to refer them to their accountant to have the accountant explain how the process works.

Equity Sharing with the Current Owner.   You may come across an owner who wants to give up the responsibility of owning the property, but doesn't want to give up all of the cash flow or appreciation potential. In that case, you have a perfect candidate for equity sharing with the current owner.

Here's how this works:

Let's say you are buying the property for $1,000,000. The owner has a mortgage for $650,000.

The owner refinances the property for $800,000 and gets $150,000 cash back. (The difference between the current mortgage of $650,000 and what he or she just refinanced it for: $800,000.)

Before the refinance, you determine if the property is in a Limited Liability Company (LLC). If it is not, the property is transferred into an LLC, with you now being included as a member.

The owner will retain a 20% equity position in the property since he or she's still waiting for the remaining $200,000 in equity that is still in the property upon the sale.

What just happened?

The owner is free from the responsibility of managing the asset. You've now taken that over. The owner will get 20% ($200,000) of the equity upon sale of the deal, plus 20% of the cash flow.

You benefit by getting an 80% share of the property for no money down, and having an experienced member on your team: After all, the owner knows this property well.

This is just one technique out of dozens that are available to finance properties. If you haven't already, you should get my Special Report, "27

Ways to Invest in Real Estate With No Money Down." It's available for free by going to www.MarketCycleMastery.com and typing in this keyword: "27 Ways."

Step Three: Use Other People's Money

Let's review where you are: You've just identified a property at a great price, and let's assume you've worked with the seller to provide some (maybe all!) of the financing. Now what's your best move?

Use other peoples' money to finance the rest. Why use your own money, when other people will be more than willing to let you use theirs—once you know how to approach them?

Many names on your personal address list can also become your private lenders. One of the very best sources of money for real estate is in the IRA accounts millions of people have.

Myth: "But Dave, I read my IRA agreement very carefully and it does not allow real estate as an investment!" That is not only a myth, it should be a crime.

Here's the *Dirty Little Secret* Wall Street does NOT want you to know:

Your IRA—and the government—is perfectly fine with your holding real estate in it. But Wall Street is NOT, so they simply left real estate off the *permitted investments* section of their IRA applications.

Why? One word: *Profit.*

You see, they can make a fortune off you when you invest your IRA money in one of their bloated, overmanaged, fee-heavy mutual funds. They're okay with your taking their stockbrokers' advice about buying and selling stocks in your IRA (fat commission checks). They'll even allow you to park your dough in a money market account, where—that's right—they skim the cream of their profits off the top, before handing you the rest.

But they conveniently leave out any mention of YOUR RIGHT to invest in real estate through your IRA, because they haven't figured out how to make a buck (or two or a thousand) off your real estate investments.

There's something wrong with this picture: The government makes them tell me that there's sugar in a pack of bubble gum, but there's no disclosure law that forces investment companies to tell me everything that my IRA can contain.

Enough bad news. Here's the good news: You can fix this situation quickly, by getting a TRUE self-directed IRA. They're out there, if you know where to look. I do know where to look and I'll give you a continuously updated list of the good providers I've found. Just go to www.MarketCycleMastery.com and type in the keyword "IRA List."

What makes these companies different is that they are pure IRA specialists. They make their money on just their reasonable set up and maintenance fees. They don't play games by telling you that you have a *no-fee* IRA on the one hand, and gouging you with mutual fund fees or stock commissions on the other. Because they do not manage the investments within the IRA, they are unbiased. In fact, they don't care what you put in there, as long as it's legal.

As to what's legal, these companies are true experts at what can and cannot be done in an IRA.

Here's How to Approach People to Become Private Lenders. It's very simple: Just ask people you know with money if they would like a better return than they are getting in their IRA retirement account, savings account, or CDs (certificates of deposit). Tell them that not only can they potentially get a substantially higher rate of return, but their investments are secured by real estate.

When they sound intrigued, tell them that you are looking for private investors to borrow money from in order to purchase real estate. Let them know that the money is secured by the real estate in the form of a mortgage. Let them know the return that you will pay them (anywhere from 8% to 15% depending on current market conditions; you always try to pay the lowest!) and explain to them what you know about the property and how you know it.

This is where education comes in—again: They will not want to loan you money if they don't think you know what you are doing. You must be able to explain to them exactly what you plan on doing, and how you plan on doing it. This is actually a presentation.

You should practice this presentation until you've gotten it down cold.

"But Dave, I don't have a presentation!"

That's where I'm going to fix you up yet again: Just go to my website at www.MarketCycleMastery.com, where you can download an entire presentation. Just type in the keyword: "Presentation."

You need to know every objection they might come up with, and be prepared to answer them. Fortunately, they're the same questions, over and over. Once you have my presentation, and have practiced it on a family member or friend, you'll be completely confident about approaching people in casual settings.

First, they'll need to understand how Wall Street has snookered them for years about what can be held in an IRA. Then they'll need to understand that their investment is not guaranteed, but it's secured by real estate. (Hey, it's not guaranteed in a mutual fund, either.)

Trust me on this: Soon, you'll have more money from friends than you know what to do with.

Once you do a few successful deals, those friends who invested with you will brag to their other friends about the return on the money they got by investing with you.

Then those friends will want a piece of the action and everyone will be coming after YOU: "Hey, when can you invest more of my money just like that deal you just did!"

Don't worry—you'll get used to it.

Attracting Strangers as Investors.   If you just don't want to approach your friends and family, there's another whole world of investors looking for good alternatives to CDs and mutual funds.

There are two ways to approach them.

The first is the *big time* formal way, by issuing a security known as a *private placement* or a *Reg D offering*. This is definitely not a do-it-yourself project. It involves hiring a securities attorney and other advisors, and preparing a formal document. If you get to the stage of wanting to raise a great deal of money frequently (think along the lines of 8 figures, two or three times a year), then this route is for you. Otherwise, it is more trouble than it's worth.

The second way is to attract these investors locally. Right in your town there are attorneys, doctors, dentists, and small business owners with some-where between $10,000 and $500,000 of investable assets. If you brought them a deal in their home town, where they could make 8% to 15%, secured by the property, you WILL get some takers.

After all, this isn't some faceless mutual fund run by some silk-suited dandies on Wall Street. It's a property they've probably seen since childhood and may drive past every day.

Exactly how do you find these people and start up a conversation? You network through your attorney, doctor, Chamber of Commerce, and many other places. A friend of mine has actually reduced this whole process to a science. He holds *investor lunches*, where he gathers 10 or 15 people in a room and talks to them about the type of real estate he currently buys. My buddy—and his investor students—literally have more money than they know what to do with from this technique.

If you want to discover the ins and outs of attracting strangers to loan you all the money you need for investments, I recommend that you go to this link: www.MarketCycleMastery.com and type in the keyword "Private Money."

***Think Outside the* Loan Box; *Think* Equity Share.** A great way to find private investors for your deals is through equity sharing. This is how it works:

1. Find a great deal that generates cash flow;
2. Get a private investor (friend, family member, your attorney, doctor, etc.) to give you 20% for the down payment. In return for that 20% down payment the investor gets 20% of the net monthly cash flow and 20% of the profit when the property is sold; and,
3. You get 80% of the net monthly cash flow and 80% of the net profit when it is sold. *question of out of state income tax + estate taxes in different states*

This a good deal for both you and the private investor. You're the one who found and put the deal together. You get the lion's share of the profits. But the private investor gets a much bigger return on his or her money than would normally be available in a mutual fund or a certificate of deposit.

Depending on the deal, some investors may want quite a high interest rate. If other options are not available and the deal still cash flows properly with the higher interest rate, then give them what they want.

The most common concern from private investors in this arrangement is how the loan will be secured. It is secured by a mortgage on the property. That means if you default, the private investor will retain title to the property (though they may have to go through the foreclosure process to get it).

This also means that because the mortgage will be recorded, you will not be able to sell the property without the private investor being paid. This is the second most common concern and it's better to address it before it is asked.

Hard Money Lenders. Hard money lenders are the mercenaries of the real estate investing business. I know that sounds harsh, but I don't mean it as completely negative. They are like mercenaries because they are completely emotionless about the investment opportunity: It either passes their test of a good deal, or it doesn't.

Hard money lenders really fill a need for the very fact that they are emotionless. They don't care if you just landed on the shores of the United States and have no money. They don't care about your credit rating, or whether you make a *good impression*.

All they care about is the deal—and how much they're getting paid.

You bring them a deal. They don't need a lot of documentation, because they'll send their own appraiser and property inspector out. They can move quickly and have cash in your hands in as little as 4 days.

They don't care about your credit rating, because if you default on the loan, they grab the property.

Why wouldn't everybody use hard money lenders?

There's the little matter of cost. You'll be paying between 6% and 15%, PLUS 2 to 8 points on the loan (1 point is 1% of the loan value, paid up front).

"But Dave!" you say, "No way I'll pay that interest rate! They're robbing me!"

No doubt about it: You'll pay dearly to have a hard money lender finance your deal. But what if you have no alternatives? Paying high rates that eat into your profit is better than having no deal and no profit.

Hard money lenders are a convenient tool that you should consider, after first exploring other, cheaper forms of financing.

Where do you find hard money lenders?

There are a bunch of them on the Internet. Just type in *hard money lenders* and stand back.

Another good source is your local investing club. If you stand up at the beginning of the meeting, when people usually describe their deals to each other, just ask if there are any lenders in the room. Most likely, a few will approach you during the break.

Another Financing Tool: Broker Participation. It's amazing to me how many residential and commercial real estate brokers don't own multi-family properties. They are exposed to all kinds of good deals. They help other people become wealthy by finding them people who want to sell their properties.

While they are earning commissions on their properties, brokers really have a secret desire: To do what you're doing! That's right, they want to be a real estate investor, but they have not gotten over that fear of taking the first step. Or, possibly, they don't want the responsibility of running an investment long term.

Whatever the reason, when you find a good deal and you're short on funds to make it happen, offer the real estate broker an equity position for using his or her commission as part of the deal.

There have been more times than I can count when I've made a low offer on a piece of property and had the seller accept it. Then the real estate broker said: "The seller agreed to *that* offer? If I had known he would take that price, I'd have bought it myself!"

Step Four: Use Your Own Money or Credit

You should now be seeing that there are plenty of ways to finance your deals before ever thinking of going down to the bank yourself.

But when you get busy enough with deals, you may reach a point where some of your own funds are needed. Even so, you don't necessarily need to withdraw cash from your savings to do the deal.

Instead, you can do any of the following.

Get a Line of Credit.   If you currently own a piece of property, whether it be another investment property or your own home, chances are you have equity that's sitting there idle. It could instead be working to make you money.

Go down to the bank where you keep your savings and checking account and ask the customer service rep what their process is for obtaining an equity line. Usually you have to fill out a simple application, wait a couple of days, and your equity line is approved. Here are two pitfalls with credit lines:

1. Be sure to obtain an equity line that only charges you fees when you have withdrawn money. A good equity line works like a checking account. You get a checkbook and withdraw money only when you want it. You don't want an equity line in which the bank deposits the sum of the equity line in an account and you start paying interest on the money right away.

2. It's important that you are disciplined with your equity line. Use it *only* for real estate investments, and pay it back *as soon as* the investments are sold.

Some people fall into the trap of knowing that they have this money at their disposal and using it for items other than real estate. Or, they sell or refinance their property and don't pay their equity line back and so continue to make monthly payments.

Don't Ignore Credit Cards.   If you've been cultivating your credit, you probably get three to four credit card offers per week in the mail.

I don't recommend that you try to build a real estate empire through credit card borrowing. But I'd be lying if I said I never used them. In fact,

I maxed out my cards at first, until I did a few deals and the cash started rolling in.

I was disciplined about repaying the card balances, so I never paid that much of their ridiculously high interest rates.

It's just another tool for you to consider, after exploring all the others previously described.

The Sky's the Limit with Creative Financing.   Do you have a parcel of land you're looking to develop? Is it full of trees? Do you even know what's beneath the surface?

Sell off those trees, sell the mineral rights, or give someone else the ability to explore for that oil, and you may have just paid for your purchase.

When I was just starting out and had no money, I looked for deals in which I could partner with people who *did* have money. I'd do the research and the leg-work, they'd fund the deal, and we would split the profits.

I found a parcel of land that was going up for auction. A friend of mine was a real estate agent and I knew he had close contact with Jane, the developer. I knew this agent had some money, and I knew Jane had a *lot* of money and experience with developments. This property was in a great location, and I thought the three of us could develop it.

I explained the situation to my friend and asked him to present it to Jane. A couple of days later, he told me that Jane wasn't interested. Because he didn't seem all that interested, and I didn't have the cash, I dropped the deal and moved on.

A month later, my friend was supposed to show up at a birthday party, but was not to be found. I called his house. His mother answered and said he was at an auction. I immediately realized the auction was taking place for that parcel of land I had identified. I assumed he was there with another of his builder clients, who was bidding on the land, while my friend would get the new house listings.

When I saw him later that day, I asked if his client was the high bidder for the land. He said no. I thought "Oh, too bad; an opportunity lost." Then a funny feeling came over me and I asked him, "Who *was* the high bidder?"

He told me it was Jane!

Both my "friend" and Jane had visited the property after I proposed it to them. When they got there, they discovered there were two huge mounds of a special type of sand that must be used for septic system installations.

The value of the sand was *just over two million dollars!* Jane bought the property for $385,000! Nobody at the auction knew about the value of the sand except the agent and Jane.

I found out later that the agent and Jane were partners on the deal, which meant my friend had gone behind my back and cut me out of the deal.

Money does strange things to people.

That was the first million—and first "friend"—that I lost in real estate investing. I am happy to say I haven't lost any other money or any other friends since!

The moral of that story: Take a good look at the land to see if there are other ways to profit than just the development. You might just run into a million (or two-million) dollar deal!

IN THE NEXT CHAPTER

Remember Step One of my Four-Step System? It's to *Buy Right*. That's such a critical part of your real estate investing strategy that it merits its own entire chapter, so read on...

How to "X-Ray" Your Deals the Fast and Easy Way, So You're Buying Right in ANY Market

"Power and speed be hands and feet."

—Ralph Waldo Emerson

When you learn the language of a multi-family real estate investor, you'll understand that properties are classified into four different types: A, B, C, and D. Just like the letter grades that you got in school, A is good and D is bad.

A Properties: The Cream of the Crop

An A property has usually been constructed within the last 10 years. It is typically tenanted by younger professionals and commands the highest rent in the area.

These properties come with all the amenities: pool, full workout room, tennis courts, clubhouse, and so on. In fact, at this top end, developers compete with each other for the latest amenities: "High-speed internet in every unit!" "Security system in every unit!" "Ocean views!" The list goes on.

Most institutional investors (i.e., pension funds, corporations) like to invest in A-class properties because they are very low maintenance and have low-risk tenants.

Tenants who live in A properties are probably there temporarily:

- They've been relocated, and are looking for a home;
- They're young doctors on their way up; or
- They may be newly married DINKs (Dual Income No Kids).

Whatever the circumstances, they have the money and want comfortable living. When they move out, it's either because they're buying a condo or single-family home, or because they're relocating again.

B Properties: Still High-End

B properties have been built within the last 20 years. They aren't as new as the A's. They can't command the rents that A properties get, but the rents are still quite high.

Tenants that typically rent B type properties are white-collar workers, with a mixture of higher-paid blue-collar workers.

C Properties: Gold that Looks like Lead

C properties have been built within the last 30 years. They are typically tenanted by blue-collar workers. You might also see government-sponsored tenants with Section 8 vouchers in C-type properties.

You can usually tell a C property by viewing its outside. The architecture will be representative of the era in which it was built.

You can also tell a C property by the types of vehicles in the parking lot. You may see a higher than normal ratio of pickup trucks and cars that are 10 or more years old.

Another clue that you're looking at a C property is that most vehicles are gone during the day. That's a good sign. It means people are working for a living.

C properties usually come with some amount of deferred maintenance. That's good! It means we'll be able to fix this deferred maintenance and charge higher rents.

When we do this, in effect we are instantly creating appreciation through one of my *Value Plays*. (See Chapter 7.)

Here's Where You Can Make a Fortune

The tenants in C properties will probably never be in a position to buy a single-family home. After taxes, rent, and food, there isn't much income left over to save for a house.

Because of this, if you treat them right, they will stay with you forever!

Even though A properties are nicer, you will usually find the higher occupancy rates in the C properties. That's because they are the lowest-cost housing that's still decent.

You'll find lots of hard-working people in these properties. They may have been *downsized* from their jobs, newly single after a divorce, or have some other story to tell.

The C property is their fall-back position, and they'll work hard to keep from falling farther back.

This combination of solid tenant, good occupancy, and appreciation potential from improved maintenance are all reasons why I really like to invest in C properties.

D PROPERTIES: EVERYTHING ELSE

D properties are usually found in the worst areas of town. They usually suffer from some sort of functional obsolescence because they were built 40 or more years ago.

D properties are inhabited by a tough group of tenants. You can usually buy them at a deep discount and acquire a pretty good cash flow from them; that's because of the functional obsolescence, the type of tenant, and the area of town these properties are in.

But the cash flow comes at a price!

These properties are management intensive. You must hire a management company that has a successful track record managing—not just any type of property—but *this type* of property. If you hire a management company that does not have such a track record, you're in for trouble.

Trust me on this: If you do not have a strict and tough (but fair) management company, the inmates will quickly begin running the asylum, and it will cost you a lot of money in lost cash flow to get it back.

Think about it: Why do these people live in the lowest-quality housing? No doubt many of them are the "salt of the earth" and are wonderful people just down on their luck. But many of them do not work, and aren't even trying to get work. Others are recently out of prison. Still others are operating—shall we say—*unusual pharmacies* out of their units.

You get a whole broad cross-section of people in D properties. Unfortunately, it doesn't take many bad characters to drive off the decent people. Then all you're left with are bad characters and other people without the will or means to get out.

These are not the type of properties that you want to start off investing in. There is a great deal of money to be made in B and C properties. Cut your teeth there.

After you become experienced, if you feel the need to buy a D property (there is never really a good excuse to do so, except for an absurd amount of profit to be made), you will have good solid foundation to do it successfully.

How to Grade Areas as A, B, C, or D

Just like property types, *areas of a city* also are graded by letter type. Again, they go in descending order: A is good, B is next best, C comes next . . . and you don't want to collect your rents at night in a D area!

A Areas

Your A areas are where the upper levels of the socio-economic ladder reside. The high-end properties are here. This is also where you will most likely find the *path of progress* in the city.

The path of progress is where the new construction is heading. It's where old properties are being rehabbed and restored to their previous beauty.

In this area, houses are bought and scraped off to make room for completely new residences. Land that long ago might have housed the downtrodden is now being revitalized and regentrified.   *Kirkwood*

B Areas

B areas are typically where blue-collar workers live. You can tell a blue-collar area by the types of businesses in the area. These will cater to blue-collar needs and desires, like bowling alleys, nail salons, movie rental stores, pizza shops, and so on.

B areas are filled with a combination of the working class and government-subsidized housing. Some of the tenants with government housing do not work and have their entire rent paid by the government. Others work and contribute to the rent, while the government pays whatever else is needed to meet the rent. "Section 8" is one of the forms of government subsidy, but there are many others, too.

If you allow government-subsided tenants to live in your buildings, I suggest you make it a requirement that they have a job. This does two things: It shows you that they are fairly responsible, and it also keeps the wear and tear of your units to a minimum. Think about it: If they are home all day, they'll be causing much more wear and tear than normal!

C Areas

C areas are filled with restaurants and businesses that support C-type tenants. You'll see old strip malls in need of repair. A small percentage of the business space will not be occupied. This was once a thriving area that has been neglected, because the path of progress went the other direction. Now the city typically does little to promote A or B housing or businesses to stay.

D Areas

It's very easy to tell the D areas of a city: They are areas most in need of repairs. You will see businesses with bars on their windows, even when they're open for business!

The gas station attendants stay behind bullet-proof glass, using a metal drawer to collect the money for gas and candy.

There are usually high vacancy rates in the apartment complexes, where the windows also sometimes have bars. That's an insurance company's nightmare, by the way (if people get trapped)!

There are usually a lot of cars on blocks in the street—and in front yards—waiting to get worked on.

Just as with D properties, you really don't want to invest in the D areas unless you *really* know what you're doing. When you have the experience and resources to know that you have a screaming good bargain—and can risk a lot of money and time to bring it to fruition—then have at it. Until then, there are many easier methods to make a lot of money.

Your goal is to buy a B property in an A area.

This combination gets you into a good property in a great area. It will allow you to get higher-than-normal B rents, with the potential of the rents going even higher, even faster.

Is it possible to make money from a C property in a D area, and other such combinations? Sure. But if you're asking me what's the best combination, look for the Bs in an A area.

Now that we've talked about properties and areas in general, it's time to get the calculator out.

You may be tempted to skip over this section because you think it might be too difficult or boring. Here's the thing: That cheapo calculator is like a buried-treasure metal detector to me. That's because with just a few easy buttons to push, it will quickly tell me if I'm looking at a lump of clay or a golden nugget. Come on, it's easy! I'll show you how...

SIX EASY PIECES: THE SIX CALCULATIONS YOU CAN MAKE IN MINUTES TO RATE ANY PROPERTY

If you love numbers, I'm sure you could find a couple hundred different calculations to make before buying a property. Well, I don't love numbers. Fortunately, it hasn't stopped me from making many millions of dollars in real estate.

That's because you only need a handful of key numbers in order to evaluate any deal.

Why so few? Remember, we're not looking for *squeakers*, or deals that just barely will make a profit. If they are that borderline, then there's not enough of a safety net for me.

I'm looking for the deals that have loads of profit potential, and you should be, too. That way, if the numbers are a little off, it's no big deal.

Easy Piece #1: Understanding the Cap Rate

Determining the value of a multi-family property is different from determining the value of a single-family property.

With single-family properties, we usually use the *Comparable Method* of appraisal. That means we compare the property we are looking to buy with others in the area. Don't bother considering the property a *comp*, or comparable one, unless:

- It's a similar size and style;
- It sold within the last 6 months; and
- It's within a mile or so from our property.

We don't do that with multi-family properties. Instead, we use the *Income Method*. That means we determine the value of the property by the income that it produces.

Unlike many single-family homes, an apartment is an investment. Therefore, it's critical to know what that investment is earning you.

The capitialization rate (cap rate) is simply the rate of return that you expect to get for your investment.

In a normal market, most investors would like to see a rate of return of 10%. The thing to remember about cap rates is, the higher the number, the cheaper the property.

I know, this is somewhat counterintuitive. But think of it this way:

Q: What is the investment vehicle with the least amount of risk?

A: The United States Treasury Bill.

Q: What is the rate of return on the United States Treasury Bills?

A: Real low—maybe 2% or 3%.

Q: Why is it so low?

A: Because United States Treasury Bills are backed by the same folks that make our dollar bills. Because there is no default risk to speak of, they are the safest investments available. Because there's so little risk, there's so little return.

If investors put their money in something that is riskier, then they require a higher return to compensate for that risk.

It's the same principle when investing in multi-family housing:

- The higher the risk,
- the cheaper the property,
- the higher the return potential, and
- the higher the cap rate.

On the other hand:

- The lower the risk,
- the more expensive the property is,
- the lower the return potential, and
- the lower the cap rate.

So when you see a property that is selling for a very low cap rate, say a 7 Cap, then that property is probably a very good one, in good repair, in a good neighborhood, and with good tenants. It's probably an A property.

If you have a property that needs a lot of repair, is not in a good area of town, and with tenants that make you nervous, then this is a D property. You should want to be compensated for this management-intensive, high-risk property. You should be buying this at a 12 Cap or higher.

Let me ask you a question: If you were analyzing a property and determined that it was selling at a 14 Cap Rate, what would you do?

Most people would think this property has got to be a dog in a war zone. They will most likely go on to the next property. Though that might be true, there is another explanation that might instead be true: The property might be a great BARGAIN!

You've heard the expression, "Don't judge a book by its cover"?

The same holds true for multi-family properties. Numbers beat looks. If you run the numbers on a property, and they don't work, then there's no point in wasting time going to see the property. It might be pretty, but you can't take *pretty* to the bank.

Other times, you'll see a property that doesn't look promising at all. But that's when you might just want to stop and dig a little deeper (assuming it's not in a D area).

That frog just might be a prince! What if it was a B property selling at a 14 cap rate? Whoa baby! Jump in your car and get the signature!

I know what you're thinking:

"Dave, why would anyone sell a solid B property for a 14 Cap Rate?"

Answer: I don't know. In fact, I stopped asking *why* a long time ago.

Sellers do the darndest things. I've made hundreds of thousands of dollars on single deals in which the owner left a huge amount of equity on the table—with no explanation. He just left it there for Old Dave to be in the right place, at the right time, and profit handsomely from it.

Usually what happens is they've just had enough and want out of the property. At that point, for them, the quicker the sale, the better.

That's why I always have a reserve fund waiting on hand when these deals come up. When I get asked the question, "How fast can you close?" I always respond, "How fast would you like to close?" These are some of the best deals.

When such a deal presents itself to you (and it will, if you're out there enough), don't spend too much time wondering why. Just do the deal, and reap the rewards!

How to Calculate a Cap Rate. The cap rate is determined by the following formula:

$$\text{Capitalization Rate} = \frac{\text{Net Operating Income}}{\text{Value of Property}}$$

...or stated another way...

$$\text{Value of Property} = \frac{\text{Net Operating Income}}{\text{Capitalization Rate}}$$

Here is an interesting fact: When selling a property at a 10 Cap, for every dollar you increase your Net Operating Income, you increase the value of your property by 10 dollars.

If I gave you 10 dollars for every 1 dollar you give me, how many dollars would you give me?

As many as you could, of course! That's why you always want to focus on increasing your Net Operating Income.

The Two Moving Parts that Increase Your Net Operating Income.   Boosting your Net Operating Income can only be done in the following ways: by increasing your revenues, decreasing your expenses, or both.

The rate of speed that you build your wealth will be determined by those factors.

But all things are NOT created equal! Of those moving parts, I focus much more on increasing revenues.

Why? Because there is no fixed limit on the amount you can increase income by. But you can only decrease your expenses to zero. And of course, you can't even do that, because if you're going to have a decent property, it's going to incur constant expenses.

By all means, look for ways to decrease expenses. In fact, in my home study materials I give dozens of ways to do just that, while maintaining a fine property. But while you're working on the expenses, really work on increasing those revenues.

"Inefficient" markets = Your Gain.   Go to your friendly local stock broker and ask him or her to buy you 100 shares of IBM stock. At that moment, pretty much anywhere in the world, if people are buying IBM stock, it will be for the price your broker gets you.

That's the definition of an *efficient* market. Everyone's in the same boat, with the same information.

That's not so with apartments—and that's good news!

Yes, investors do have a stock market of sorts with properties. They may have different terms than A, B, C, and D. But knowledgeable investors know what cap rates are appropriate for what types of properties in what types of areas.

The wonderful thing about apartment investing is that exceptions do occur. (Again, I don't care why they occur; I just know that they DO.)

That means you may be in a market where you can typically buy a B property for a 9 Cap Rate. But you come across a B property in this market that's selling for a 14 Cap. Think about breaking out the champagne, because you could turn around and resell that property for a nice profit, *the day after you buy it.*

It's as if your grandmother gave you IBM stock for $50 a share, and today it's going for $75 a share. Instant profit, with no work.

These are situations you will be looking for—they are not common, but they're out there! How do I know? I've bought them, and so have my students!

Stick with me, and before long, you'll be finding them, too.

Easy Piece #2: How to Use the Gross Rent Multiplier

Want a quick and easy way to determine if a property makes sense? Use the *gross rent multiplier.* The gross rent multiplier measures the number of times the gross rents equal the value of the property.

$$\text{Gross Rent Multiplier} = \frac{\text{Value of Property}}{\text{Gross Rents}}$$

This means if you bought a property with a gross rent multiplier of 5, you would get the entire purchase price that you paid for the property back in 5 years!

When we're buying in the beginning stages of an emerging market, we typically get into properties with very low gross rent multipliers (GRMs). Anything below 5 is usually a good deal. (But before you start buying deals based solely on GRMs, read on.)

As the market starts to appreciate, the GRMs start getting higher and higher. Before you know it, you're selling your property at a GRM of 8 or higher! This is great, because if rents have been steady or growing, and the GRM is going up, the property value will *really* skyrocket.

Though the GRM gives you a quick snapshot of a property, it *is* only a snapshot. It should not be the only criterion you use to determine the attractiveness of the deal; that's because it has one major flaw—can you figure out what it is?

Look back on the equation. The gross rent multiplier does not take into consideration the expenses of a property. It looks at GROSS rents. But what if expenses were extremely high for a particular property? This usually means there is some sort of problem with the property. But if you were only using the GRM in your evaluation, you would have missed this costly error.

Use the GRM for what it's worth. It's one handy dimension to look at when you're deciding whether to invest in a property.

Easy Piece #3: How to Do a Cash-on-Cash Return

Would you like a ratio that can stand alone in determining whether to buy a property? I've got one for you. It's the *cash-on-cash return*.

The cash-on-cash return will tell you how long it will take to get back every dollar you invested to purchase the property.

When you're an investor, you want to get our money back as soon as possible. That way, you can go out and get another property under your control. This starts to snowball, and you'll soon grow both your income and your equity.

When determining your cash-on-cash return, first calculate your net cash flow from the property. Calculate this by subtracting your yearly expenses from your yearly income. If you remember, this is the formula we use to get the NOI. Then take it one step further and deduct the debt service.

Debt service is just commercial real estate lingo for the mortgage amount. When you subtract debt service from net operating income, you get net cash flow.

We divide that net cash flow by the acquisition cost of the property. The acquisition cost is any money that you had to take out of your pocket to buy the property. If you're putting money down on the property, you add this to your closing cost and you'll get your total acquisition cost.

Your closing cost will be the items that you paid for at the closing: property survey, property title (though these two could be a seller expense if you write them into the contract like that), loan points, attorney fees, property inspection, and so on. Total these up and you have your total closing cost.

Here's the easy calculation for cash-on-cash return:

$$\text{Cash-on-Cash Return} = \frac{\text{Net Cash Flow(NOI} - \text{Debt Service)}}{\text{Acquisition Costs}}$$

In markets that are emerging rapidly, you should be happy with a cash-on-cash return of 10% or more. In other markets that are not performing so well, or markets in your own backyard, you should expect a 15% to 20% cash-on-cash return.

If you're buying a property with no money down, you still may have out-of-pocket closing expenses. But if you did buy a property truly with zero money down and had the seller pay all your closing costs, you would not be able to calculate your cash-on-cash return. That's because your return would mathematically be infinity! Now that's my kind of deal!

A word of advice: Not all no-money-down deals are good deals. If you are buying a 100-unit complex for no money down, and the property is at a break-even or slightly cash flowing, this is not a good deal. Any number of problems could arise that would have you sticking your hand in your pocket each month to carry that property. From experience, I can tell you that on some months, you'll be sticking your hand deeply into your pocket!

Think of cash flow as the safety margin between you and the unknown. The more cash flow, the more can unexpectedly occur and you'll still be fine.

Yes, there *are* great deals that require no money down. But don't be seduced by the prospect of a no-money-down deal. Be *sure* your property is cash flowing properly (where have you heard that before?!).

Easy Piece #4: How to Figure Replacement Cost

Whenever you can buy a property below its replacement cost, and the property cash flows in an emerging market, it is usually a good deal.

Replacement cost is simply the amount of money that it would cost you to rebuild the property from the ground up. When an area is in a Buyers Market Phase I, there is an oversupply on the market. This results in a drop in demand and a lowering of prices. Eventually, prices will fall below what it actually costs to build a new property. At this point, new construction virtually stops.

As the market starts to transition into the emerging phase, prices will still be below replacement cost until the market reaches equilibrium. This is a great time to *buy as many properties as you can get your hands on.*

At different times during the later stages of an emerging market (after equilibrium), you may still have opportunities to buy properties at below replacement cost. These situations are also usually very good deals.

I mentioned earlier that some *no-money-down* deals are not worth the risk. The same is true with certain properties you can pick up at below replacement cost. Watch out when you find yourself in a Buyer's Market Phase I, where there is no plan to increase job growth and migration into the area.

This market is in stagnation and you are primarily buying for cash flow. The opportunity for appreciation is not very good.

When I started buying in the Boston area, the market was in a Buyer's Market Phase I. Prices had been stagnant for several years, and there didn't seem to be a turnaround taking place in the near future. But I started buying, because I realized that I couldn't build these properties for what I was buying them for.

As a matter of fact, I was buying them at 50% below replacement value and they gave me great cash flow every month. I didn't even know what I (and you!) now understand about market cycles. It just made plain sense to me to be buying as many properties as I could get my hands on.

Everyone else told me that I was crazy.

I remember buying a six-family building for $65,000, which at the time was very pricey. That building had sold for $225,000 just a few years earlier when the market was in the emerging stage. But during the back side of the cycle, $65,000 was thought to be much too high, and I got a lot of unsolicited advice about how I was making a big mistake for buying it.

I *was* crazy—like a fox. My instincts were right: Within a few years, that property was worth over $300,000!

And you know what they are saying today? "Of course he is successful; he bought the property so cheap!" Keep in mind that at the time, plenty of other investors had the same information I did, and even more resources than I had.

What they didn't understand was the wealth power of market cycles. Not only did they not buy, but they laughed at me when I took action.

Who's laughing now!

Please understand that many of your very best investments will be made at the opposite time from when the great herd of investor sheep want to buy. That means you'll get the whole spectrum of laughs, jeers, raised eyebrows, and warnings.

If you did your homework and followed my advice in this book, then stand your ground! Soak in the criticism with a smile. Because *you* know what *they'll* soon see: You're about to get a lot richer.

Easy Piece #5: How to Determine Price per Square Foot

To determine the replacement cost of a property, you must first determine what the price per square foot is to build the property from scratch.

Do this by going to your local library and opening up the *Means Square Foot Costs Book*.

Materials and labor costs vary from location to location to build new construction. The RS Means Company tracks these variations in almost 1,000 locations around America, and updates their directory yearly. They give you the price per square foot to build a property anywhere in the country. You can even go to www.rsmeans.com and use an online calculator.

Simply figure out how many square feet are going to be in your building, and find the price per square foot in your area. Then multiply the two together and you have a solid replacement cost estimate.

If the replacement cost is lower than the purchase price, you just might have a great deal!

Easy Piece #6: How to Analyze Land and Building Value

Whenever you are analyzing a property, you're always working with two values: the land value and the building value.

Though the nature of the land will always remain constant, the building on the land is called an improvement. The structure improves the value of the land.

Once a building is built, it immediately begins to depreciate, meaning it begins to lose its value. It's just like a new car that leaves the car lot: As soon as it leaves that lot, it's lost a certain percent of its value.

Buildings can last a long time, but they don't last forever. Dilapidated old buildings that are condemned and need to be torn down can actually decrease the value of land. That's because there are expenses associated with the removal of the building.

Sometimes a perfectly good building on a lot will get torn down because it doesn't meet the *highest and best use* of the land. Another building will be erected that can generate more profit to the owner.

There's a free and easy way to determine the value of the land and building: Go to the assessor's office of the city or town where the land is located, and get the property card. This card is full of information about the property: when it was bought, for how much, what type of improvement is on the property, what the property is zoned for, and—most importantly—what the assessed value is of the property.

The assessor will determine the assessed value by adding the land value to the value of the improvements. Since assessed values are usually lower than market values, simply determine what percentage the land and improvements are to the total assessed value.

For instance, let's say a property is assessed at $1,000,000. The land is assessed for $200,000 and the improvements are assessed for $800,000. You now know that the land is 20% of the value of the property and the improvements are 80% of the assessed value.

Simply apply those percentages to the current purchase price of the property you are buying to determine what the land and building values are of the property.

HOW TO PUT IT ALL TOGETHER, TO X-RAY A DEAL!

Okay, let's put this all together to determine if you really want to buy your deal.

1. The first thing you do is determine what type of property this is: A, B, C, or D.

2. Then you want to determine what type of *area* the property is in.

Avoid the D areas, but not necessarily the D properties: If you can get a D property in a B area, you have a possibility of a good value play. You can reposition the property in the neighborhood. But if you have a B property in a D area, you should run from this deal as fast as you can.

3. Then do a quick check on the gross rent multiplier. Is it below 7?

What are the other similar properties in the area selling for, regarding gross rent multiplier? Use this as a quick reference. But remember, the gross rent multiplier should not be high on your list of criteria to determine whether you *really* want this property.

4. Next, look at the cap rate. Buy properties with cap rates at 10 or higher, if possible. But don't be averse to buying a property with a lower cap rate, as long as you can justify the purchase with really good upside.

5. Now take a look at other properties, and determine which cap rates typically apply to each of the four property types in this market.

Remember, if you know investors are buying B properties at a 9 Cap, and you can buy at an 11 Cap, you can turn around and resell the property immediately at a 9 Cap and make a handsome profit.

6. After reviewing cap rates, turn your attention to the cash-on-cash return. This is the ratio that you should really be concerned about: How soon are you going to get your money back so you can go out and get yourself another property?

Get a deal with a cash-on-cash return over 20%, and you've got a good deal!

You also should have some sort of value-added component in this deal—a Value Play. You want hidden equity that you can tap to increase the value of your property quickly and easily. Though there are several value plays to look for, you only need one to turn a good deal into a superb deal.

A secondary criterion that you should look at is whether you're buying this property below replacement cost. If it cash flows and you're buying below replacement cost in an emerging market, that's icing on the cake!

In the Next Chapter

Half empty . . . half full: So much depends on one's perspective. When it comes to due diligence, most people just grimace at the thought. I break out in a big smile. Turn the page and I'll show you why.

CHAPTER 11

How to Make $10,000 or More per Hour (I'm Not Kidding)

"Trust but verify"

—Russian proverb, (later quoted by Ronald Reagan)

Ten thousand dollars per *hour*?

I'm dead serious.

Every single hour you put into the due diligence process could easily make you 10 grand. Maybe much more.

First, let's make sure we're on the same page about what *due diligence* is. That's an investment term that's used when one company is buying another, or is issuing stock to the public. When investors do *due diligence*, it means they are doing their homework on the investment. They are making sure they understand the ins and outs of the investment before finalizing the deal.

Due diligence is an absolutely critical phase of an investment. It has a lot of downside if you blow it off and don't do your homework (as we'll see in a minute.) And it's potentially where you will make the bulk of your profit, if you do it right.

I know that the term *homework* might not bring back warm, pleasant memories. But don't look at it as a negative. Sure, there may be some tedious work. But it's also quite literally a *treasure hunt*. Only with this hunt—and with my guidance—there's a MUCH higher probability of finding gold!

As a rule of thumb, you'll end up spending somewhere between 5 and 40 hours doing your due diligence. But you could very realistically make from several thousand, to several hundred thousand, dollars of additional profit from spending those hours!

That's why I'm not kidding at all when I say these are quite possibly the highest-paid hours you'll ever work in your life!

THE *WRONG* WAY TO DO DUE DILIGENCE

Here's what most people think and do:

"I have to be sure before buying that property. I'm going to do my homework on it, for as long as it takes. After all, I can't afford to be wrong! Only if and when I'm comfortable that it's a good deal will I make my offer. Then I'll really know the right amount to offer."

That's a recipe for working hard and staying poor.

THE *RIGHT* WAY TO DO DUE DILIGENCE

Here's what *I* think and do:

I've found a property, and a review of the numbers tells me it fits my buying criteria. Yes, I have very clear standards for what I'll buy (and you will, too, if you stick with me!). I negotiate a good price, based on what the seller has provided for details on the property. I sign the contract.

Then I turn to the seller, and say "Prove it!" I often have an opportunity to renegotiate. Plus, I uncover hidden value in the property that even the seller probably did not know was there.

Let's go through how these approaches differ.

Many new investors think they have to do all the due diligence work up front. That's a problem for several reasons: First, it's impractical. When you're only a potential buyer, you don't have as much access to information as you do when you have the property under contract. So your analysis is based on less-than-adequate information.

Second, too much number crunching up front takes time. That's resulting in a delay in your making an offer on the deal. That allows me to walk in, put an offer in, and take that deal out from under your nose.

Plus, I don't want to spend too much time on a deal when I have no lock on it. My most precious resource is time. If I'm going to spend a good amount of time, I want to do so only after I have tied a property up, and it can't be sold in an instant to someone else.

Only THEN does the real due diligence kick in: This is where I validate what the seller told me, renegotiate the price if necessary, and find hidden value.

Yes, I ask the seller to prove his or her claims about the property. You have based your purchase price on the income and expenses that the seller stated to be true. Now it's documentation time.

In most contracts, the seller has up to 14 days to provide you with all the paperwork to demonstrate that the income and expenses he or she stated to you during the offering process are accurate.

There's an old story that if you ask a lawyer "Do you have the time?" the lawyer will answer "Yes." The lawyer is responding to your specific question (do you have the time), and not to your intent (could you please tell me the time).

Keep that story in mind in the due diligence phase: The owner only has to provide for those items that you request. No more. So the burden is on you to request the right information. You need to ask for enough to determine if the deal you're getting into is the deal you *thought* you were getting into.

Some investors actually take the owner's word for it! They discover, after the closing, that:

... The income was not as high as they expected;
... Oh, and the expenses were a lot higher than the owner had disclosed;
... Plus there are not as many tenants in the building as the owner said there were;
... And the ones that *are* there, are not paying the amount of rent the owner stated they were!

Of course, all you're left with then is a financial disaster.

To be fair, no doubt some owners honestly tell you what they *think* the real numbers are. But because they do not keep good records, they don't realize there is a large discrepancy in those numbers.

Then there are some owners who are outright deceptive, and will lie to you on purpose. They just hope you will not find out the truth in time to do anything about it.

I truly believe that there is good in everyone and I give people the benefit of the doubt. I also know from experience that deceptive owners exist. If you are dealing with one, and if you don't find out the real information, you may end up with a property you paid too much for. You then won't get it turned around without a lot more of your money on the line.

My due diligence philosophy is "Hope for the best, but expect the worst." I assume every owner I'm buying from is deceptive, and it's up to me to find out where the discrepancies are.

Here is my experience: About 75% of the due diligence I get back is not what I was told it was going to be. Some people think this is bad.

They're wrong.

It's actually good news! I now get the chance to go back to that owner and renegotiate the price! Hey, I based my price on the numbers *the seller* provided to *me*, and that's all I had to go on, at the time. If the person won't renegotiate, definitely move on.

Most will renegotiate, because most people are decent.

THE DUE DILIGENCE PROCESS—AND HOW TO MASTER IT

Remember, the owner of the property will only provide the documentation that you ask for. He or she is under no obligation to provide anything extra.

This being the case, you want to have a system in place to get the process done *quickly but thoroughly*. There's good news here:

1. Regardless of the size of the property, you will be asking for the same information from every deal you go into.
2. You have me to help you know what to ask for! (Unlike when I was starting out, and I had to figure it out myself.)

Here's what you want to see:

- last 2 years, operating statements
- year-to-date operating statement
- ALL leases
- ALL security deposits
- rent roll
- maintenance log
- ALL outstanding contracts
- current mortgage term and condition
- any existing warranties

You are primarily interested in the income and expenses.

Is the income as high as was stated on the information given during the offering process?

Are the true expenses at the level that was disclosed?

LOOKING AT PROPERTY INCOME

You can very easily determine the income by adding up all the leases. Keep in mind that this won't give you an exact amount of rental income, however. Some tenants may have moved out prior to their lease expiring, and other tenants are behind on their rent and are going (we hope) through the eviction process, if they're making no effort to catch up.

Your other income will be from a variety of sources: laundry, other vending, cable contracts, and more.

I like to see variable income such as laundry and vending have a 2-year consistent history before I count it as other income. Other income that comes from the result of a contract (for instance, cell phone tower on the property) can be counted immediately, as long as the contract runs for 5 or more years.

If you don't trust the owner, you may want stronger assurance that the property income is indeed the income. In that case, you can have *estoppel letters* signed by the tenants. Estoppel letters ask the tenants to verify:

- what they are paying
- the terms of their lease
- any security deposits they have on file

A lot of owners want to sell you their property based on what it *could* bring in, if the rents were brought up to market. Or, they want to sell you the property for what the income level *would* be if they could get it full.

Always buy your properties based on *today's* numbers! If you don't, you may never get the chance to get the numbers up to where you *thought* they could be. Why reward the owner with a higher price than the property currently merits?

And don't fall for any *just around the corner* stories: "Oh Dave, I know my rents are a bit low now, but I just know for sure that I'll be able to raise rents on 13 tenants next month. I've talked with them! They've agreed! So it's a done deal, and I should get credit in the sales price for that!"

Do NOT fall for stories. The only thing that counts is results, also spelled M-O-N-E-Y. If the money is coming in the door, it gets counted. If it's any version of *the check's in the mail* song, it is worthless.

If the seller strongly disagrees, you walk away. Simple as that.

First buy low, based on today's numbers. Then reward yourself for a job well done, after you get the complex brought up to current market occupancy and current market rents. Your reward? All that equity and cash flow you just created!

Looking at Property Expenses

When calculating the expenses you may want to take a look at the seller's "Schedule E" form. This is filed with the seller's income tax return.

Warning: Every schedule "E" has a story. Whether you believe that story is up to you.

Why does it have a story? Because the Schedule E is where property owners list their income and expenses for a property. The goal for every investor is to pay as little taxes as possible. To do this, they may have included one of the following:

- loopholes
- creative accounting
- tax preparers that don't know what they are doing
- outdated information
- math errors

People sometimes get highly creative in their determination to lower the income and increase the expenses on this statement.

I usually listen to the story. If it makes sense, I'll give the owner the benefit of the doubt. Regardless of whether I believe him or her or not, I'm still going to get the past 2 years of bills for ALL expenses.

What if the owners do not have these bills? They must be reconstructed. I know it's a pain, but consider this: Best case is that you are dealing with sloppy landlording. Worst case, the person is trying to cover something up.

Before you finalize this deal, you must find out the truth. Get permission from the owner to get the past 2 years' bills directly from the utility companies.

What to Look for, in the Pile of Stuff You'll Get

When you're doing your due diligence, really focus on items that may affect the way you can run your property in the future. And look for items or situations that are not normal.

You MUST review every single lease, because—as luck will have it—the one you don't review will be the one that will give you a problem somewhere down the road.

Of course, there's another, nonluck-related reason: The seller may only conveniently have given you leases that support the sales price; others that he or she would rather that you *not* see are the problem ones.

Upon your review of the leases, you might find a lease that was for 5 years instead of the normal 1 year—and the rent is locked in at below-market levels. If you did see this lease, or if you accept this lease, you're obligated to honor it.

Some people think that there's nothing you can do about bad leases if they're signed and valid. There ARE things you can do: Tell the owner to break the lease (which the owner may or may not be able to do); or say that you want a reduction in price for the difference between the market rent for the 5 years and that undervalued lease.

In most cases, the previous owner has done a friend or family member a favor and created that favorable lease, knowing that he or she was going to sell the building.

You'll run into the same situation with contracts. You must review *every outstanding contract*. With any contract that does not make sense, have the current owner negotiate with the contract provider, either to get out of the contract or set better terms. In most cases, you should just try to be out of the contract completely.

Sometimes the owner will not be able to get out of the contract. The situation that comes to mind most often is the type of contract most owners have with their laundry machine service. There are a couple of major companies that sell and service laundry machines throughout the United States. They are ruthless negotiators, and their contracts run for 10 to 15 years!

I have seen some situations in which the only person making any money from laundry vending is the machine company—and they won't renegotiate the contact. If you inherit this situation, and if the company will not deal, then figure out how much below market that lease will cost you in the long run. Then renegotiate down the sales price of the property by that amount.

Most other contracts can be renegotiated. What you should be trying to spot is the long-term maintenance contract that was given to a friend at a too-friendly rate (especially if it was signed recently, indicating it might have been when the seller knew he or she was selling).

THE CHECKLIST: YOUR BEST FRIEND

You really must have a checklist to work from when doing your due diligence. You will be requesting a lot of information, and it will arrive in clumps. You will need to sort it and check off that you've got it.

Your checklist should have a column for items requested, by whom it was requested, when it was received, if it checked out—and if it didn't check out, what is the issue.

By having a checklist, you can look on one piece of paper and determine exactly where you are in the due diligence process, what you are waiting for, and what needs to be done on your end.

Without a checklist, you WILL miss things. Sometimes those things you miss will cost you money.

FINDING HIDDEN VALUE

When you are going through your due diligence checklists, now is the time to find hidden value in the property.

As you are going through the leases notice how many leases seem to be below market rent. These are the leases that you will be able to raise as soon as they expire.

When you do your property inspection, look for opportunities to increase revenues. Is there extra land on the property where you can build storage facilities and rent them out to tenants or people from the area?

If not, is there unused space in the basement or in the attic that can be used for storage that you can rent to the tenants? Can you use that space to add more units onto the property? Adding just one more unit at $600 per month will give you approximately $7,200 more in income per year and will increase the value of your property by approximately $72,000.

Do you have space on your land or on the roof of your building for cell phone towers? They will lease that space for a very nice monthly fee.

Who's providing the cable or satellite services for the property? The cable and satellite companies are very competitive and will give you a large one-lump sum for the exclusive rights to provide service to the entire building.

I have one student who owns a 110-unit complex and a 170-unit complex. The cable company came in and offered him a free lifetime of unlimited cable for his personal residence if he would give them a 10-year exclusive contract.

He called me up and asked me what I thought of that deal, I told him to go back to that representative and tell him that, unless they get serious, he's going to start negotiating with the other company in town.

They wrote him a check for $81,000 for the rights.

You'll want to notice if there is availability for vending. We've already discussed laundry services, but what about the detergent for the laundry, or soda, snacks, and any other item that you can think of that you can sell to your tenants that they may need or want on a regular basis? This increases your cash flow and the value of your property.

FINDING HIDDEN GOLD IN EXPENSES

As the due diligence comes in, take a look at the expenses. Are they high in any particular area?

Stephane Fymat from Manhattan, NY was doing his due diligence on a 188-unit complex in Baton Rouge, LA. He noticed something peculiar in the maintenance on the property. It appeared to be running at 17% of gross rents instead of the normal 10%.

After further investigation, he realized there were a lot of tenants that were moving in and out in about a year's time. This meant that a lot of money was being spent on making those units ready for the next tenant. In addition, there was lost income from having vacant apartments.

After even further investigation, he learned that the present management company had no screening process in place for new residents; if tenants had first and last month's security deposit, they got the apartment.

Here's the solution: Put in a proper screening process. It should be that the manager only allows people to move in if they've been living at the previous address for 2 years or longer. That will reduce the maintenance expenses considerably, create additional income (from less tenant turnover), and create additional value in the property.

"But Dave, isn't that discriminating?"

No, it's not. Discrimination is when you apply different rules to different groups of people, based on race, religion, and so on. But there's nothing discriminatory when you apply the same rule—up front—to everyone: "I'm only going to rent to people who have lived at their previous address for at least 2 years" does not exclude anyone on the basis of race, religion, or any other key measure. (Except possibly being a deadbeat.)

By the way, don't even *think* about discriminating! It's not folklore, but a fact, that the government employs discrimination *testers*, who call up and see if you are treating one caller differently from another. It's dumb to discriminate, and the penalties are severe.

You'll want to look for other unusual expenses. When doing the due diligence on a property in Birmingham, Alabama, we noticed that the water bill seemed to be really high.

After calling the water company and comparing records with other complexes about the same size, it was apparent that there was a leak somewhere in the system. The previous owner had either not noticed that the bills were getting higher and higher, or didn't care.

We hired a contractor to find the leak and determine what it would cost to fix it. There wasn't just one leak—there were several in the pipes that ran under the buildings. It would cost $14,000 to fix the leaks. The first year's savings on the water bill would be around $11,000. That means the repair would pay for itself in just over a year, and we would add close to $110,000 in value to the property! That was a no-brainer.

Is the owner paying for the water for all tenants, and are you in a city that allows the owner to submeter the water? If so, you could install a meter for each tenant, and have them pay for it themselves. (More on this in a minute.)

Other places to find hidden value are in electrical and heating systems. If the owner is paying for the heat or electricity, you should always be looking for ways to submeter the utilities and put the responsibility of paying those costs onto the tenant.

"But Dave, isn't all this 'sub-metering' burdening the tenant?"

That's not how I see it. If people don't pay for something, there's tremendous waste. This waste drives up the cost for the owner, who passes it on to all tenants. Why shouldn't tenants be individually rewarded for their own conservation?

You'll have to do a break-even analysis to determine if it will be cost effective to do the work. Simply determine how much it will cost to install a new heating system in every unit, or to submeter the electricity. Then determine how much you will save by having each tenant pay for these services in the future.

When doing this calculation, be sure to take into consideration a decrease in the tenants' rent. Because you will no longer be paying for their utilities, you usually have to reduce their rents to the level of market rents without utilities included. You can determine what this rent is by doing a rent survey.

Base your calculations on this new rent, and determine how long it will take for the new systems to pay for themselves. Then figure out how much value you added to your property.

Sometimes it is not cost effective to separate utilities. Each complex is different, so do the numbers.

Using Others as Your Eyes and Ears

Are you one of those people who hates to crunch numbers? Would you rather suffer the bites of a thousand mosquitoes than sort through all the information that's contained in a due diligence package?

I don't understand that position when, as I said, it's like being paid $10,000 per hour. But if you still truly hate the thought of this analysis, fear not: There are a lot of companies that offer services to do the due diligence on your acquisitions for a fee.

Some management companies specialize in the due diligence process. They can be very qualified and motivated, because their entire livelihood is determined by how well they run the numbers on a property.

Because they work with these numbers on a regular basis, they will have a trained eye as to what the reasonable cost of items should be. They'll immediately spot any discrepancies from the norm.

Finding these discrepancies can add real value to your deal.

Of course, their services will cost you some of your profits. Then again, they may find more money than they cost.

I suggest that *you* do the due diligence on your first couple of deals. Only then should you consider hiring another company to do it. This will give you the hands-on experience you can rely on in the future, when you'll need to make decisions.

After you've done it a couple of times, then it's time to delegate it to someone else. That way, you can be out there working on your next deal and creating more cash flow.

IN THE NEXT CHAPTER

Up until now, just about everything about your deal could be done from your desk. Now is when things start to get exciting. We're going on a property walk-through—and we're going to uncover even more hidden profit!

CHAPTER 12

How to Inspect Both the Property and the Investment

You've found a deal!

You put it under contract. Then you did all your due diligence on the seller's information. If that information came back different from what was given to you at the time of the offer, then you renegotiated the price, as I explained earlier.

Now it's time to do the property walk-through.

The Property Inspection

Regardless of how much experience you have, you must have a property inspector do the inspection. A *good*, qualified property inspector will go through every inch of that property. He or she is going to tell you what you need to be concerned about immediately, what to expect in the near future, and what to keep an eye out for further on down the road.

Property inspectors are worth every penny you pay them. The best part about inspectors is that they will give you a report. You can use it to your advantage.

Let's say the property needs more work than you expected, based on what the owner reported to you prior to your agreement with him or her.

Now you can go back to the owner and seek a price reduction for the repairs that need to be done. (Review the "Repair Allowance" in Chapter 9).

You have a professional, third-party opinion, with a written analysis to back you up.

Not only is a property inspector essential, but so is this: You MUST get into *every* unit when you have the property inspection done. Some owners want to let you into every third unit, and sometimes every other unit. *Do not* allow this. You must get into every unit. Why? Because, as I emphasized earlier, the units you don't get into are the very units where you're likely to have problems.

In larger complexes, some investors forgo getting into every unit because of the overall cost to perform the inspection. This is a mistake. Get into every unit! The extra cost will turn out to be a cost savings in the long run.

Property inspectors are good at telling you about the nuts and bolts of a property. Keep in mind, though, that they do not look at the property through an investor's eye; they see it through the eyes of an engineer.

We investors want to know about the nuts and the bolts, but we also have something else on our mind: profit. What is it about a property that will allow us to:

1. Rent it faster?
2. Rent for a higher dollar amount?
3. Sell it quickly? and
4. Command a higher price?

Successful investors and chess masters have something in common: We're always looking ahead. Even before making an offer on a property, we're looking many moves ahead, and asking the four previous questions.

Whether we're anticipating market cycles, or anticipating tenant and contractor issues, the mark of a real estate master is this ability to look ahead and plan—now—for the future.

THE INVESTMENT INSPECTION

We just finished talking about the property inspection, where you're relying on your crackerjack inspector to do the heavy lifting.

Now let's cover the investment inspection: In this section, I'll show you the little things that make a property a good deal. I'll also reveal the flip-side of the coin and the things you want to avoid like the plague.

Note: This inspection can be done even before you have a property under contract. At the very latest, you must do it before you close on it.

Roofs

On most structures, the roofs will either be flat or pitched (tilted). Up until the mid-60s, most apartment roofs were pitched. Then someone came up with the bright idea of using a flat roof to lower the cost of construction.

A flat roof meant less surface area, and therefore less materials and labor to build it.

Flat roofs were finished with either rubber or tar and gravel. This seemed like a good idea at the time. But as time went on, leaks started to develop in these types of roofs. Just small leaks, here and there. So a maintenance person or roofer was called out to make the repairs.

Sometimes the repairs were made on the first visit, but often they weren't. That's because it's very difficult to find leaks on flat roofs. Water will run for quite some distance along a seam in the rubber, or under the tar and gravel. It's very challenging to detect the actual source of the leak.

More time went on. As the roofs aged, more small repairs had to be made. These repairs began to get very costly; in fact, more costly than it would have been to put on a pitched roof in the first place.

That's how flat roofs have gained a bad reputation. As a result, most investors prefer a pitched roof over a flat one.

Does that mean you should pass on a deal just because it has a flat roof? Not necessarily. Take a look at the entire deal with your property inspector, and compare it to the asking price. If that price is good enough, even after you factor in roof repairs, then you may have a solid deal on your hands.

Roof maintenance is one of the major expenses you will incur when owning apartment buildings. When buying, you want to get an idea of how long the current life expectancy of the roof is. Then estimate how long you will own the property.

If you can tell that the roofs are on their way out, you had better get a concession from the owner to replace them. If you feel that the roofs have only 5 more years of life, you better account for that expense when you go to resell the property.

If you do plan to re-roof a property, wait as long as possible! That way, when you eventually put the property up for sale, the roofs will look as new as possible. This *will* be one of your key selling points.

Finding the TRUE Rentable Square Feet

Your buildings have two square-foot calculations: total square feet and rentable square feet.

We are most concerned with rentable square feet. This gives us an indication of apartment size, and whether they'll be competitive in the local market.

Total square feet takes into account the entire wall-to-wall area in the building. You can take a tape measure and walk the outside of the building to determine total square feet.

Inside that building are areas common to all tenants. It's space that isn't leased by any one tenant. Hence the name *common areas*.

Common areas consist of hallways, basement, elevator shafts, and stairwells. To get the total number of rentable square feet, you must deduct the total square feet that these areas cover. Then you'll have total rentable square feet.

Analyzing Traffic Patterns

Is it important to have a lot of traffic going back and forth in front of your property? Yes! Is it an absolute necessity? No. It's a big plus, though. I prefer a property to be on a main road, if possible.

When you're on the main road, you'll get a lot of foot traffic into your complex. It won't matter if you've got a "For Rent" sign out front or not—people will come in off the street and ask if you have any vacancies.

Because tenant turnover is our biggest expense, this is a good problem to have. When you do have a vacancy, just put a couple of For Rent signs out front, and watch as applicants steadily arrive at your door.

Your property may be buried in a residential area, where you need to take four or five turns to get there from the main road. If so, this will be one of the biggest obstacles that you'll face when filling vacancies.

People will get lost trying to find the property, and many of them will give up. You'll have a higher no-show rate for appointments in a property like this.

There is a silver lining, though: Once they DO find the place, they'll usually like the location! That's because it's away from the hustle and bustle. But there are other considerations:

HOW GREAT AMENITIES
ATTRACT TENANTS

Transportation

Is the property close to amenities? If it's out of the main traffic stream, it's also likely to be away from most amenities.

People like easy access to things they want or need to do. One of the key tenant concerns is transportation. It's a definite plus when your property is on a major bus route, near a subway stop, or within walking distance of shopping.

If there isn't adequate transportation, and your property is geared toward blue-collar households, here's what will happen: Two people will work in the household, but they share a car. One of them will rely on public transportation to get around.

If your tenants are lower blue-collar (often the case with C type properties), they may not even have one car. Then they REALLY depend on transportation to get to and from their jobs, and also to shop.

Infrastructure

In addition to good transportation, you should look for good infrastructure in the city.

That means good highways and roads. You should have at least one major route running through the city. This means businesses looking to move to the city will have access to other goods and services they need to run effectively. They'll also be able to get their products out to other markets.

Infrastructure is one of those *upward spiral/downward spiral* things. When businesses move in, the tax base increases and so does infrastructure. When they move out, the opposite happens.

Two other questions concerning infrastructure:

1. Are the roads and bridges in good shape?
2. Are the highways adequate to handle the volume that filters through on a daily basis?

These are important. Many companies are heading South, where traffic congestion is less, and so are the commutes.

I live 16 miles outside the Boston city limits. When I go to the city, it takes me 25 minutes to get there, if it's NOT rush hour. When it's rush hour, I'm looking at 75 minutes for 16 miles.

Boston is like lots of cities in America: They are popular for all the jobs and attractions, but roads have not kept up with the volume.

As apartment investors, we do well when companies want to relocate nearby. When you're doing your investment walk-through, keep this constantly in mind.

Local Shopping

Try to be close to local shopping, for the convenience of your tenants. Even if you don't think of it, they certainly will. It's simple: The closer you are, the easier it will be to rent your units.

If you are investing in *C* class properties, it is imperative that your property be located within walking distance, or on the bus line, of a food store.

Parking

Your tenants are not going to like coming home from a hard day's work with no close place to park. It's even worse if they have to park on the street. And if it's a cold-weather state where the snowplow buries their cars, you're going to have vacancy issues.

People like the convenience of being close to their doors. They love knowing that they always have a spot when they get home. Such happy tenants are tenants that just keep on giving.

You should have at least one space per tenant, close to his or her living unit. These spaces can be numbered and assigned in the lease. That way, tenants know where home is for their cars.

There should also be an area for visitors and the occasional need to park a second car.

In some areas, it's common for parking to be on the street. As a matter of fact, in these areas, sometimes the landlord charges tenants for parking spaces. If this is possible in your area, it's another income stream that increases the value of your property.

Another parking issue to anticipate: condominium conversion. If you're buying an *A* or *B* type property, you just might want to turn it into condos down the road, and create a big windfall for yourself.

A lot of areas require two spaces per condo; most areas require at least one. If you want to keep all your options open and all your tenants happy, be sure you have plenty of parking.

DEFERRED MAINTENANCE

Deferred Maintenance is work that should have been done a long time ago to a property. It may be repairing or replacing the roofs, painting the trim, replacing doors and windows, painting common areas, maintaining parking lots, landscaping, and so on.

You can usually tell how well a property has been run by the amount of deferred maintenance on the outside. It's a pretty good indicator of the amount of deferred maintenance you will find in the individual units.

Deferred maintenance will also give you a good idea of your tenant profile. Most good tenants will move from a place when the work stops being done.

Once you start ignoring your tenants' maintenance requests, you can kiss them and your cash flow good-bye!

Then you'll be left with a complex full of tenants who think it is acceptable to live in a dump. They will run it down even more. These tenants are typically also the late payers. They have no *self*-respect, so they certainly won't have any for your property!

WHAT KIND OF TENANTS LIVE THERE?

Do you know your tenant profile, in detail? You don't? I guess you're okay, then, with leaving a lot of profit on the table.

Typical situation: You buy a property that is underperforming, has low occupancy, and is in need of repair. Because occupancy is low, the owner puts very little money into maintenance, in order to preserve his or her cash flow. That drives occupancy even lower. (In the previous section, it was the city infrastructure that caused upward or downward spirals. The same effect occurs here, but at the property level.)

Once in a while, occupancy starts to decline *before* maintenance starts to drop off. This happens when the tenant profile in an area changes and the owner doesn't recognize it. If even a well-maintained property does not change to meet those new needs, the tenants will vote with their feet.

Another cause of tenant profile change is market movement: You might have a B property on the fringes of a C area, where the path of progress is going the other way. Because of this, the C area engulfs the B property. The B tenants don't like this, and move to another B part of town.

Many owners don't see the subtle changes in tenant profile, or they stubbornly refuse to adjust. Sooner or later, they'll end up selling their properties—at a steep discount—to opportunity investors like you and me.

If you *really* know the types of tenants in the property, you get to do two very profitable things:

1. You can cater to those tenants (and they will love you—and pay you—for it).
2. You can make specific changes to upgrade your tenant profile.

Those are the two profitable choices: Make the property fit the existing tenants; or adjust the property to attract the tenants you do want.

Yes, tuning your property will involve some expense. But not making these adjustments can result in much more expense, in terms of lost occupancy, damage to the property, and marketing expenses to get it full again.

To determine what your tenant profile is, be observant. Check out what kind of cars or trucks are in the driveway. Anything over 10 years old is usually a blue-collar tenant.

What race are the majority of your tenants? What music do you hear coming from the windows? Different races have different housing preferences in terms of color schemes and amenities.

What is the average age of your tenants? Do they have children? Are they single? These are all questions that you want to answer so you can best service your tenants.

Do NOT ask these questions of prospective applicants, or even describe a common tenant profile to them when they are applying! This could easily be seen as a discriminatory act, and there are stiff penalties for discrimination.

What you want to do is the perfectly legal and moral act of paying attention. There's an old saying: "People will move heaven and earth to buy from you, if you give them what they want." It's proven every day, with lines around the block at Christmas for the *hot* toy, or sold-out sports events and concerts. You don't need to be a rock star; you just need to match your property closely to the tenants you want to have, and you'll notice the money move your way.

MAKE FRIENDS WITH THE PEOPLE WHO WILL MAKE YOU RICH!

Take the time to talk to tenants during the walk-throughs. Every time I visit a complex with a partner, we always play a game to see who can get into the most units.

Of course you have to be invited in if you don't own the property yet, so you can't just knock on the door and ask to be let in. If you try this, you will not have much success, because people won't trust you. Try to get invited in.

You do this by talking to tenants as you're passing by. They might be sitting on their porch or their steps, at a window looking out, or just getting out of their car and walking to their unit.

If you give them a friendly smile or a wave and they smile and wave back, they have just given you an invitation to build rapport. Pretty soon that rapport will turn into an invitation to enter their unit.

Now it's interrogation time. A very nice interrogation, mind you. But still, you should ask a lot of questions:

- How long have you lived here?
- Do the tenants get along?
- How is management at responding to your requests?
- What kind of problems are in your unit?
- Is the plumbing and electrical okay?
- Are there any water leaks?
- Are there any tenants dealing drugs?
- How much do you pay in rent?
- Has rent increased in the last year?

These are the kinds of questions that are going to tell you a lot about a property, its tenants, and its owner.

Ask these questions as they are showing you around their unit. While on the tour, look for deferred maintenance. You'll start to get an idea of how many repairs may be needed in this unit and most of the others.

"But Dave, Why Would the Tenants Possibly Want to Answer All My Questions?"

The tenants will *happily* answer these questions and show you around their units! That's because you will be going in under the guise of an insurance agent.

There are two times you will be going into a property under the guise of being an insurance agent: The first is when you are doing the property walk-through *with* the owner, but the owner does not want the tenants to know he or she is selling.

The second is when you are at the property, taking a look around, and the owner is not there.

I'm not saying to trespass onto the property. But if an owner is looking to sell a property and has listed it, then it's only natural to take a drive to see the property. If so, you may find yourself pulling in and taking a walk around the parking lot.

As soon as you start walking an arc that does not go directly to a doorway, you will arouse the suspicions of the tenants. They may ask you what you are doing. Never tell them that you are interested in buying the property and are just looking around. The owner may have not told the tenants. If you tell them, the owner will be very upset. He or she just might not sell to you, even if you're willing to pay the full asking price. (I learned this one the hard way!)

If the tenants do know, the owner may send you over by yourself. In that case, I tell tenants that I may possibly become the new owner, and I'd like to take a look at their unit, and then I ask if that would be okay. About 99% of the time, it's okay with them. After all, who wants to upset the new owner?

Neighboring Properties—Are They an Asset or a Liability?

You walked the outside of the property. Then you got into a few units to get a solid feel for the inside. Now it's time to walk the neighborhood.

- What are the neighboring properties like?
- Are they residential apartments?
- If so, then what type are they?
- Will they compete directly with you for tenants?
- If so, how does your property stack up?
- Do they have bigger units?
- Do they have more amenities?
- Are the common areas in better shape, with more room for activities?

All these questions are going to affect the amount of rent that you'll be able to charge.

As mentioned previously, it's best to have a property situated on a main road for high visibility. If it is on the main road, though, there are other issues we need to consider.

For instance, how many additional apartment units are on the street? Is it a heavily congested residential area? Will you compete—day-in, day-out— for the walk-ins? Or are you one of only a couple of properties and the competition is low?

If the neighbors are mostly businesses, what kind are they? If you've got a B property and the majority of the businesses are attracting C clients (liquor stores, convenience stores, lounges, used-car lots), you're going to have a problem. Your tenant base is going to turn into Cs.

The surrounding businesses must attract the type of tenants you want living in your units.

In addition, watch how those businesses are trending. If better and better companies are leasing the available space, your property will be in a position to prosper. If the most recent businesses are the less-affluent types, you may be on the other side of the path of progress.

I like to see offices and office parks. If you own nice apartments near office parks, wouldn't it be convenient for the employees of those businesses to live in your apartments? You may even be allowed to advertise in their personnel departments, because this is a real win/win arrangement.

Hazards You Must Avoid

The other benefit of office parks and business centers is they mainly *house* people and not things that are for sale.

Here's the situation that you want to avoid: A business—your new neighbor—looked quiet and innocent enough. But it was storing hazardous material in drums way out back. Those drums are starting to leak. The hazardous materials are seeping into the ground and have made their way to part of your property. Your grounds are now contaminated.

If one of those mini-storage facilities is nearby, the risk goes up even more. That space is rented out to 50 to 100 individuals, who—by definition—do not want to store their stuff at their own property. Most of it is probably old furniture from a past marriage. But it only takes a unit or two of bad stuff to cause serious headaches for you.

Underground oil and gas tanks in nearby gas stations are also an issue. If your property is within a couple of blocks of a gas station, you absolutely need an inspection of your soil, to ensure no waste has leaked out and found its way to your property.

Check to see if there are any underground oil tanks on your property. If there are, you should insist on having those removed by the current owner *before* you buy the property.

Underground oil tanks have a nasty habit of developing holes. Each time the tank is filled, more chemicals leak into the soil.

Even if the tank is not now being used, it could have leaked for years. If this is the case, decontamination of the soil could get very, very expensive.

If the property has asbestos wrapped around the pipes—or if it's found anywhere else on the property—have it removed before you take ownership. Asbestos particles look like tiny little fish hooks. When they enter your lungs, they hook onto the tissues and they never come back out.

Most lending companies will not lend on a property that has asbestos. Even if you find one that will, have the current owner remove the asbestos before you buy. If you don't, *you* will be the one required to remove it, when it's time for you to sell the property.

Lead Paint

The federal government has a law that prohibits children under 6 from living in units where there is lead paint that's not in compliance with the laws.

Compliance basically means that there are no *mouth-able* surfaces below six feet, and all the paint is intact (not flaking or peeling). Why do kids eat the lead? Because—aside from their habit of putting just about everything in their mouths to begin with—lead paint is sweet.

Most insurance companies will not insure you if a child becomes poisoned in your unit. You will have to pay for all of the child's medical bills and for any long-term consequences. Stop and imagine the cost of that.

If you buy a building with units that have two or more bedrooms, get lead paint certificates that state the units are in compliance.

Most child poisonings do not come from eating flaking paint on walls. They are usually a result of the child breathing in dust particles from lead paint on the window frames. The windows going up and down causes the dust, and wind blows the dust into the room.

A good number of children are poisoned from playing in the dirt at the playground or right outside in the yard. All those years of burning leaded gasoline in cars has contaminated the ground in many areas.

Lead poisoning also comes from playing with old toys that contain lead paint. This could happen at the day care center where the child is playing or over at a friend's house.

Here's the cold, hard truth: If a child is diagnosed with lead poisoning, and your units are not de-leaded, it doesn't matter where the kid got it—*you* will be at fault.

Get your de-leaded certificates.

Toxic Mold

Toxic mold has been around for a long time. Recently, though, it's received a lot of attention, and rightly so: Toxic mold is poisonous to human beings. If inhaled, it makes people very sick.

Toxic mold is usually black, but that doesn't mean all black mold is toxic. Actually only a small percentage of mold that is found in properties turns out to be *toxic*. If you're doing a property inspection and uncover mold, hire a certified mold specialist to come in and determine what type of mold it is.

Mold grows because of the presence of moisture and poor air circulation. This problem can often be fixed simply by removing the infected areas and stopping the moisture from accumulating.

Even the toxic variety of mold can be removed and the area repaired without major expense. If done right, there will be a low probability of it happening again.

The real issue is how to stop the moisture source. If you cannot remove the moisture source, the mold will come back.

I was doing a property inspection for a 92-unit complex in Oklahoma City. We noticed excessive moisture in the carpets in the basement units. When we pulled up the corners of the carpet, we noticed that mold had been growing below the carpets.

Upon further inspection, we confirmed that mold had grown on some of the walls, too. We had a specialist come in and he informed us that it was toxic mold and it was creeping closer to the ducts that supply air to all the units.

We knew that we could remediate the toxic mold, but we weren't sure if we could prevent the water source. That's because the mold was created by water seeping through the foundation. The ultimate cause was a high water table. The only way we could hope to prevent the water from coming in was to install a "French drain" system around the perimeter of the buildings. We weren't sure if this would work, because the water would also be touching the bottom of the foundation that the property sat on.

We couldn't install the drains under the property, so we would never really know for sure if the water would continue to penetrate the foundation. Besides, the owner was not willing to pay for the work.

That property was defective. It was up to the owner either to make it right or give us a discount on the price. A property will sell for market value only when it meets the current conditions of the market.

When we first negotiated the property, it seemed that it met the current market conditions. That's what we based our negotiations on. When we did the inspection, it became apparent that this was no longer the case.

The toxic mold was a surprise to the owner, too. But it needed to be rectified by that owner. We walked away from the deal.

Water

Water is the source of life. Without good, clean water, we all know what happens.

You must do a water inspection to make sure it's not contaminated.

You'll never know if something has found its way into your water source until you have an analysis done. Of all the things that could contaminate the water source, lead is one of the most common, especially in urban areas.

For many years (actually, for thousands of years, since the Romans), water departments of many cities used lead pipes to carry water from streets into dwellings. Eventually the lead works its way into the water.

As you know, high lead in the water is toxic to small children.

To be on the safe side, you should test your water every year or so. That gas station nearby was not a problem last year during your test, but any leaked chemicals have now had another full year to spread to other properties.

IN THE NEXT CHAPTER

Does all this sound like a lot of work? Even though you do need to analyze a property thoroughly before buying it, there are two great points to keep in mind:

1. You're going to be paid handsomely for your effort.
2. You don't have to do all the work yourself, by any means! I'm all about building a *Dream Team* to delegate the work to. And that's exactly what the next chapter covers.

**Special Offer for Readers of this Book:
As mentioned on the cover, you can claim
bonuses worth more than $375.00 for free.
Simply go to: www.MarketCycleMastery.com
and type in the words "Reader Bonus" for details.**

CHAPTER 13

HOW TO RECRUIT YOUR DREAM TEAM

"The best executive is the one who has sense enough to pick good men to do what he wants done, and self-restraint enough to keep from meddling with them while they do it."

—Theodore Roosevelt

REMEMBER: YOU'RE THE CEO

When you invest in multi-family properties, it will be in one of two ways. Either you will invest like a CEO (chief executive officer) or you'll invest like a landlord.

Landlords deal with tenants, trash, and toilets. They buy properties while intoxicated with the thought of easy income. Then they proceed to spend their time handling tenant issues, doing repairs, and every other daily duty at the property. It's no wonder the average landlord follows a downward spiral to burnout in 2½ years.

By contrast, a CEO buys properties and delegates. He or she delegates the repairing of toilets to maintenance people; delegates tenant issues to the manager; and delegates daily operations to specialists in each area of service needed.

With all that extra time freed up, the CEO investor follows the upward spiral of finding new deals, creating more cash flow, and cashing more checks.

What's the key difference? The CEO investor has taken the time to surround him or herself with a team. They're a hand-picked group of specialists who are great at what they do. They make it easy for the investor to get into more and bigger deals.

WHO'S IN YOUR DREAM TEAM

1. Real Estate Broker
2. Assistant
3. Banker
4. Attorney
5. Demographer
6. Property Inspector
7. Contractor
8. Manager
9. Accountant
10. 1031 Specialist
11. Mentor

Now let's look in more detail at each team member.

1. BROKERS: FINDING ONES WHO WILL REALLY WORK FOR YOU!

It's vital that you establish a relationship with a good commercial broker to start feeding you deals.

In most areas of the country, commercial brokers do not have a multiple listing service like that of residential brokers. Therefore, commercial brokers have lots of *pocket listings* (that appear on no website, but only in their pockets).

When commercial brokers get a new listing, the first thing they do is contact their private list of people to see if they want to buy the property. This is done before they let anyone in the office know about the listing. There's a simple reason: They want to earn a commission on both the *buy side* and *sell side* of the transaction.

Commercial brokers usually have a list of 100 to 500 potential buyers. After exposing the new listing to their entire list, if there are no takers, then they show the listing to all agents in their office.

Those agents then expose the listing to their own lists. If there are 10 agents in the office, this means that up to 5,000 buyers have now seen this listing. If it still doesn't sell, then the broker starts to advertise it in the classifieds and puts it on some of the commercial Internet sites.

Can you see how important it is to establish relationships with commercial brokers? If you rely on the Internet or classifieds to get your deals, you're looking in the bottom of the barrel. They have been picked over by hundreds—maybe thousands—of other investors who have *all* rejected them for one reason or another.

Usually brokers will get even more selective and first offer a new property to investors at the very top of their private list. After all, if it's a hot property, they don't want multiple takers from the list and have all but one of the buyers mad at them.

So it's not only important to get *on* the brokers list, but to get up, *high up* that list.

How to Approach a Broker

First things first: Let's get you introduced.

When you first meet a broker, tell him or her who you are, what you do, and how you like to invest—just like the other 500 investors that the broker has met. It's best if you can do it in person, but if you've got your sights focused on an emerging market that's 200 miles away, you will be doing this by telephone.

What you do next will determine if you create a new team member or not. *You must follow up.* I like to follow up with a personal note and a gift—something made of food.

People love food! I send mail-order cookies, brownies, or fruit. Don't be cheap; send the good stuff. There are a lot of good mail-order companies that send some real quality gifts. (People send them to me all the time, and I'm grateful!)

This will create an impression. Then you follow up at least once a week.

When the broker sends you a deal, if the numbers work, then great! You got your first deal. If the numbers don't work, then it's time to pick up the phone and explain to the broker why those numbers don't work for you, and re-explain you criteria for investing.

You're doing two things by following up like this: You're training the broker on how you invest; and you're building rapport by getting quality time with that person.

Most investors make the mistake of simply disregarding any deal that doesn't make sense. Major mistake! They don't respond, and then sit back and expect to get the next good deal!

Look for many creative ways to build rapport with your brokers. They certainly are key members of your team. A good broker will feed you deals for years to come.

How to Be on That Broker's Short List

There are two ways to get up high on that list:

1. Be a known quantity—where you did a deal with the broker that went quickly and smoothly. If you just made contact with the broker, of course this isn't possible. Now you must resort to the second method:
2. You must establish a common bond with the broker and build rapport. Be in constant contact. Find reasons to call the broker so that you are on his or her mind. Always remember that "The squeaky wheel gets the deal."

Notice I said "find reasons to call." This is important. If you just call with no reason—other than you want a deal—you'll be seen as a pest. But in your rapport building you should have discovered SOME common ground. Maybe the broker likes to fish, golf, shop, eat ... whatever. Your job is to find something in the news, or on the Web, that is a conversation opener.

"Fred, I'm just calling to tell you I saw a great tie just like the ones you told me you love to wear. It was at this website ... " If Fred has a moment, he'll chat, and then he might just bring up the topic of real estate. Don't worry: He'll remember that you are looking for deals. However, if he doesn't, you could say at the end: "Oh, by the way, have you heard anything more about what's going on over at the East Side? ... "

Fred maybe has no news for you. But you've gracefully stayed in touch. And you've also separated yourself from those 499 other investors who would love to be *in tight* with Fred.

2. YOUR ASSISTANT: NOT AN EXPENSE, BUT A PROFIT MULTIPLIER

Many people overlook an assistant as a key member of their teams. Don't make that mistake. It's your assistant who will:

- keep track of all the members of your team;
- make sure the direct mail campaign continues without interruption; and
- do all the running around and checking up, so your business continues to run smoothly.

That enables YOU to:

- find more deals;
- create more cash flow; and
- cash more checks!

The sooner you hire an assistant, the sooner you will get to the next level.

I remember when I started my investing business in my small three-room apartment. I was up to my sixth multi-family property and I was collecting rent, opening mail, answering the phone, paying bills, and working with contractors. I did it all.

It was an exciting time because I was growing. For the first time in my life, I was making some real money and was finally starting to taste financial independence.

At first, I didn't mind doing those tasks. Then I realized that the more of them I did, the less time I had to find more deals.

The more money I thought I was *saving* by doing everything myself, the more money I actually lost. I hate to think of the cash flow and equity appreciation I could have had if I weren't busy with administrative tasks.

I finally put an ad in the paper and hired my first assistant. I set up an "office" in my very small living room, and put my assistant's and my desks in there.

My assistant answered the phones, dealt with contractors to make sure they were on site each day, opened the mail, did the paperwork, and ran errands. She took away all the stuff that I didn't like to do—and the things I shouldn't be doing—as CEO of my tiny company.

Within the first week, I closed another deal that gave me enough cash flow to pay for the assistant for an entire year! My business exploded and yours will too when you get yourself a good assistant.

"But Dave, I'd do that, too, if I had six deals under my belt, like you did!"

You may be saying to yourself "Dave, I can't even pay my OWN salary, never mind an assistant's."

As they say, "I've been there, done that."

Here's the answer: At first, you need to do all that stuff on your own. That's just the real world. But *sooner than you think appropriate*, you need to get someone to take these tasks off your hands. It could be a relative, or a kid. It could be just one task for a few hours a week. Just *start* the process of delegating. If you do, it will multiply your effectiveness. If you don't, you'll muddle along until you burn out.

3. BANKERS: HOW TO BORROW AS MUCH MONEY AS YOU WANT!

The next team member you need to recruit is a banker or mortgage lender.

It's obvious that you need financing when just starting out because you don't have any money of your own. But the funny thing is, you'll always be looking for more money. That's because when you have a lot of your own dough, you'll be doing lots of deals. By getting more financing, you can do even more deals.

Donald Trump's fairly wealthy. Yet even he is constantly looking for financing!

There is a huge financing-related benefit to investing in multi-family properties: The lender will take 75% of the net operating income of the property and *add it to your income* when qualifying you for a loan.

That means if the property has a net operating income of $100,000, the bank will credit you with $75,000 of income on your application. This makes it easier to qualify for loans. Think of it: The bigger the deal you get, the easier it is to qualify!

Lenders tend to specialize in certain markets. Therefore, you need to establish relationships with lenders in not only your local market, but all other markets you're focusing on.

When you're looking to recruit a lender in an emerging market, get out the phone book or go to the Web and search for all the savings banks in that area. They are the lending institutions most likely to do loans for apartment buildings. They also tend to be the most flexible.

Talk with a loan officer and explain what your plans are in the city. Then ask that person what steps are involved in the preapproval process.

Being preapproved or prequalified at a lending institution will help you get into a lot of deals. It will show the seller that you're qualified and prepared to buy. When it comes down to a decision between you and your competition—and you're both offering around the same price—the seller will go with the person who has the best possibility of closing that deal. That person will be you.

4. ATTORNEYS: WHEN AND HOW TO USE THEM

A good real estate attorney will both save you, and make you, a lot of money.

To find good real estate attorneys in an emerging market, get referrals from commercial real estate brokers, property managers, and savings banks.

You need a good *local* attorney on your team to review all documents.

We may be the United States, but you'd never know it from some of the state laws. Different states were highly influenced by Britain, France, and other countries when those states were first settled. Therefore, the flavor of different states' laws is as distinct as Cajun cooking is from Philly cheesesteak subs. Make sure someone with local knowledge is protecting your interests in the appropriate local version of a purchase and sale agreement, or a contract.

If you're an experienced investor in your own area, and you've been through the process several times, you may feel that you don't need an attorney for all aspects of the closing. I suggest you think again. Just one overlooked clause could cost you your deposit on a deal you thought you had every right to walk away from.

I like to use two attorneys: one in the market where I'm investing, and my own hometown real estate attorney who also reviews the documents. It's a security measure to ensure that I'm protected against any irregularities.

When you are interviewing attorneys, always ask them what their usual fees are. Most real estate attorneys will charge you between $2,500 and $7,000 for a multi-family transaction. Their responsibilities would be to review the purchase and sale agreement and the closing documents.

As the deal gets bigger, the transaction fee gets higher. Rarely does it exceed $7,000. Some attorneys are used to working with large real estate investment trusts. In that case, their responsibilities are much broader. Even though they have created systems and have the paralegals do most of the work, they charge fees of $15,000 and up.

Very often you'll get quoted this higher fee. When you do, simply let them know that such a fee is excessive for what you're looking for. Then watch how fast they drop their pricing!

5. Demographers: How They Can Pinpoint Emerging Markets!

Throughout this book, I've revealed different ways of finding emerging markets. Most of these methods will cost you little or no money.

As with everything else—except making offers and cashing checks—you should eventually delegate the task of finding these markets to a consultant.

Many companies specialize in *demographics*, or the study of population segments and shifts. For a fee, they can quickly and easily point you to markets with:

- the largest job growth in the last 2 years;
- the highest population increases in the last year; and
- the most household formations in the last year, or whatever period you choose.

After receiving this information, plug it into your due diligence process. That will tell you which market to put your money in.

Most demographers get their information from the United States Census. As you know, the complete census is done every 10 years, with certain data updates every few years in between. The census is a great source of information.

But like drinking from a fire hose, the problem comes from having too much of a good thing. You must know how to decipher it quickly and easily, or you'll grow old analyzing it.

Your demographer will have models with certain filters attached that have been proven to produce certain results. The trick is to put the right combination of filters in place in order to find emerging markets.

The filters are threshold measurements. For instance, a demographer may be looking for cities:

- with populations over 100,000; and
- that have had a 4% or greater population growth the previous year; and
- that are experiencing annual household formation growth of at least 3%.

These are examples of filters.

Like a prize-winning recipe at the county fair, demographers do not give out their successful filter *recipes*! Otherwise, you could potentially fire them and do the analysis yourself.

Fortunately for these analysts, most investors have absolutely no desire to go through those numbers, so they just pay the demographer. (Of course, most investors don't do this kind of thorough analysis of markets in the first place—and that's why you and I are way ahead of the game!)

When I first started out, I found the majority of my emerging markets by keeping my eyes and ears open. I read business periodicals and subscribed to free news services on the Web. After getting leads for job growth, I would follow up by contacting key individuals in those cities.

I found some good cities to invest in that made me a lot of money. When I finally decided on a city where I was going to invest for 3 to 5 years, I would spend between $300 and $500 on a demographics report, just to be sure my research was correct.

These days, I don't just invest in properties, but I also develop apartment buildings, condominiums, and townhouses in emerging markets. When I'm buying a tract of land in another market, I hire a demographer to tell me exactly what type of building is most needed in that area. This is called *finding the highest and best use.*

For instance, a student partner, Rose Morris, and I bought a parcel of land in Columbus, Ohio. Through a demographic study, we learned that the highest and best use of the property was to build two-bedroom townhouses in the price range of $79,900 to $99,000. In other words, this was the greatest need in that area.

At the time of this writing, we are selling those townhouses—and they are selling like hotcakes! We've been able to raise the prices with each phase, and total profits on the project will reach well into several million dollars.

Building or buying the right property in the right area will make you money fast! Building or buying the wrong property even in the right area is a recipe for lost profits. Demographers are worth their fees, many times over.

Through the years I have worked on my own demographics program and have laboriously experimented with many different combinations of filters. I have created a model that identifies emerging markets about a year prior to their taking off.

This means that we are into these markets in the very early stages of a Buyers Market Phase II. That is well before most other investors around the country have any idea what's going on in that market.

6. Property Inspectors: How to See the Invisible

When I started investing in real estate, I'm pretty sure I knew less than you know now. I was clueless about property inspections, how to do estimates, or how to fix anything.

So I'd go to Home Depot on many nights, when they would hold free sessions on how to lay tile, install a sink, and other skills. Whenever I hired contractors, I'd offer my labor for free so I could see how things were done.

When I bought a new property, I'd follow the property inspector around. I'm sure I was a nuisance, because I would interrogate the inspector about what things to look for and how they worked. Through this slow process, I learned a lot about what's good and bad on both the inside and outside of a property.

I proceeded to do so many rehabs that I got my General Contractor's license. I then got so used to going through properties, I stopped hiring property inspectors and started doing my own inspections. Big mistake!

Every now and then, a problem would come up on a property that I hadn't seen before. But because I wanted the deal, or was in a rush, I wouldn't raise a red flag the way a third-party inspector would.

Those unforeseen problems usually cost me a lot of money. A lot more money than if I had just hired an inspector. Of course, you also see the other mistake I was making: I didn't delegate this task. Here again, I could have made more money doing more deals (and making fewer costly mistakes) if I had simply relied on my team.

Some people use a friend or relative who's *in the business*.

Want to know the absolute fastest way to lose that friend or relative? Have that person do a property inspection and find out later there was a major defect that the person missed. Trust me: Do NOT mix friendship/family with business, or you will, indeed, be sorry.

Another reason to have a good property inspector on your team: Every part of the country has little quirks that show up on a property inspection. For instance, here in New England you've got to make sure that all water pipes are insulated from the weather. Otherwise, in the winter, the pipes may very well freeze. That causes splits in the pipes from expanding ice.

If you live in a warm-weather state, you might find an emerging market in New England. Without a local inspector, you may miss this potential problem.

Texas soil is made of mostly clay. During the dry season, if you don't keep the soil irrigated, the clay shrinks. This causes buildings to slide off their foundations! I certainly didn't know this—until a property inspector showed me a building that had begun its slide.

Remember what I said earlier: When you and your inspector are going through properties, go into *every* unit. But let's say you're having an inspection done on a large number of units—say, 300 to 400. What's the rule then?

Go into *every* unit.

Do not listen to the owner who strongly suggests that a *survey* of every second or third unit is plenty. Do not listen even if your property inspector says it's not necessary to look at every unit. Listen to Old Dave, who graduated from the School of Hard Knocks.

You can thank me later.

7. Contractors: How to Get Great Work at Low Prices

Contractors.

Just saying the word sends shivers down the spines of the strongest men!

Everyone has a story about working with a difficult contractor, either at home or in a business setting. Fortunately, I have a unique perspective: I've not only been an investor, but I'm also a contractor. I'm one of very few people that have seen both occupations, up close and personal. And I've found a way to coexist with contractors.

There are two tricks to working with contractors:

1. Finding good ones; and
2. Staying in control of the process.

When you're in a new area, you may be tempted to open up the phone book, call some general contractors, and begin establishing relationships.

Don't be fooled by first impressions. They could have the best-looking trucks, the nicest equipment, all their teeth, and still do a terrible job, at a bad price, when they finally decide to show up and work.

On the other hand, a guy might pull up in a 20-year old truck, have hands as rough as a fisherman's, and be filthy—but he does great work at a great price.

Instead of relying on impressions, you must rely on referrals.

Some of the best referrals will be from the brokers and property managers already on your team. These people are established in the area. They specialize in multi-family properties, and probably get asked about contractors all the time.

They also realize that their reputation—and future business—is at stake. Because your Dream Team only consists of experienced professionals, that experience will work for you here, too. Your team has no doubt referred several contractors to others in the past. Some were good, and others were not. You'll get the benefit of tested-and-proven recommendations.

When choosing a contractor, make sure the person is local to the area. Also, you would be wise to choose a smaller company over a larger one.

The smaller company does not have as much overhead, and can be a lot more competitive with its prices. You will also be a larger customer to that smaller company, and it will be more responsive to you needs.

A larger company may work well for you for a while, but big companies are always looking for big jobs. If they land that big job, you will quickly drop down (or off) their ladder of priorities.

Align yourself with a *Goldilocks* local contractor, who's not too small, and not too big, but just right. They are your best bet to respond quickly to emergency repairs; it's also easy for them to finish any *call backs* after the job is complete. (A *call back* is when a contractor completes a job; then a week or month later, you realize that something was not done right. You then call the contractor and tell him or her to come back to the job and make it right.)

If the contractor is local, the call back usually won't be a problem. If the person has to travel any distance to get to the site, you may find it difficult to get him or her back. Just another reason to find proven contractors through word-of-mouth from your Dream Team.

Always work with contractors who are licensed and insured. All contractors should carry workman's compensation insurance. This protects their workers in case of a job-site accident. If a contractor's employee has an accident on your site and the contractor does not have workman's compensation insurance, then the employee's lawyer will come after you and your insurance company.

If for some reason you don't get good referrals from your broker or property manager, there's still hope: Go to the local companies where tradespeople get their supplies.

This is where a bunch of guys meet in the morning over coffee, and talk about what's happening in the town. They hear all the stories about every contractor. They know the good, the bad, and the ugly ones! This is a great resource for finding good contractors at great prices.

Ask the people behind the counter for names of good contractors. Sometimes they'll not want to play favorites because they want everyone's business. In that case, ask different people at different times of day. Eventually you'll hear the same names repeatedly. Those are your targets.

8. MANAGERS: YOUR LONG-DISTANCE EYES AND EARS

The property manager is one of the most vital members of your team. These people oversee the daily operations of your property. They're your eyes and ears, while you comfortably sit hundreds of miles away, putting more deals together. Therefore, they have the most influence over your profit and loss, once you own the property. In short, they can make or break you.

In Chapter 7, we talked about how to find quality companies to manage your properties. To recap, the www.irem.org website is a great shortcut to finding a solid manager for your team.

It's important that you screen them thoroughly before hiring them. Make sure they specialize in the property type you are buying. If you follow the recommendations in this book, you'll pretty soon have more than one property manager working for you in a city.

Property managers who specialize in C properties should manage your C properties. If you own more than one type of property, and hope to have a *one size fits all* manager, you're asking for trouble.

Interview two or three property management companies, and choose the one that best meets your needs. Through years of experience and countless property manager interviews, I've developed a list of questions that I ask to ensure I'm getting a good one.

Most of the questions have double meanings. For instance, I always ask: "How many properties do you own that are like mine?"

Naturally, most managers think I'm asking this question to see how much experience they have with my type of deal. And they answer accordingly.

Here's why I'm *really* asking it: I want to know if I'm going to be in competition with them for good tenants! I've learned the hard way what happens when a management company owns properties like mine. You guessed it: When we both have vacancies, they're going to get the good tenants, and I'm going to get the leftovers.

I never hire a property management company that *owns* properties like mine. I only hire those that *manage* properties like mine.

After you close on the property, the management company will begin to run it. Be very active and involved at the beginning. You've got to let them know that you are watching their performance, and they will be held accountable.

It doesn't take much effort. If you don't do it at the beginning, they'll think you are like the majority of property owners—absentee landlords they very rarely hear from.

Management companies are no different from every other service company: They do their best work when they know they're being watched and held accountable for results.

It's a good idea to stir things up at the beginning and make a little noise. They will oversee your property more thoroughly, and you can start to relax and put the process on cruise control.

9. ACCOUNTANT: FINDING ONE WHO CAN SAVE YOU SERIOUS MONEY

Accountants are just like doctors and lawyers these days: They're specialists. Maybe it was different a hundred years ago, but now there is far too much information for any one person to stay on top of.

If an accountant tells you he or she is covering all the bases, don't use that person! Any doctor who claimed to be a brain surgeon, AIDS researcher, and gynecologist—all at the same time—would need his or her own head examined.

Be sure your accountant specializes in real estate investments. There are many tax and structural strategies available to real estate investors that most accountants have no clue about. An experienced one will know what questions to ask you, what to look for in your property financials, and the latest IRS rulings on ways apartment owners can save money. Such specialists are worth far more than their fees.

I started out like most people do and did my own taxes. Hated every minute of it.

Every year starting in *April*, I went through boxes of receipts, trying to remember what half of them were. I attempted to reconstruct the paper trail on deals I was doing. What a pain in the butt!

Then I got smart! I brought them to an accountant—you know, the tax types that you go to in the strip mall. He trained people every year in January to do his clients' taxes. Turns out they weren't much better than me! I still had to show up with the receipts and try to explain everything.

The second year, it was getting close to the April 15th deadline, and my taxes still weren't done. He was waiting for a key piece of information that I had to find and bring to him. I finally found it on the 15th and rushed it to his office. When I got there, I found a note on the door that said he was gone for vacation and would be back in 2 weeks! The IRS smacked me, and I was searching for a new accountant.

I was referred to another guy from a member of my real estate group. This guy was a former IRS agent and supposedly knew every legal loophole in the book. The relationship worked great for a few years, until I started owning hundreds of apartment units. Then I think he looked at my taxes like some nasty chore he'd get around to doing... someday!

He kept putting me on filing extension after extension, even though I had given him all of my information.

I finally got tired of the extensions, so I sought referrals for yet another CPA. Instead of asking other members of my club, I started asking real estate attorneys. Because they were in the business, I figured they would really know who was a hero, and who was a zero.

The same name kept coming up. I interviewed this guy and after a free review of my taxes, he showed me how I could get over $14,000 given back to me from an overpayment I made from my last year's taxes! He was hired in under 1 nanosecond.

I hired him not just because he got me that $14,000. It was also his references.

He was working with quite a few real estate investors and owners of real estate brokerage offices. Everyone gave glowing reviews about how much money he had saved them through the years. Not only that, they were happy with the good advice he had given through the years, and all said that he was a key member on their teams. He's been a key member of my team ever since. I meet with him once a month to go over what's going on, and what I plan on doing in the future.

10. 1031 Specialist: Get One, and Defer Your Taxes as Long as You Want!

The IRS has a rule called a *1031 Tax-Deferred Exchange*. Using this section of the Internal Revenue Code allows you to sell a property and use *all* of the proceeds from the sale of that property to buy a bigger property.

You pay NO current taxes on the sale. That means . . .

> . . . You have substantially more down payment money for your next deal. Which in turn means. . .
> . . . You can afford a bigger property, and that means . . .
> . . . Bigger cash flow for you!

Then you can sell that second property and do the same thing again: Take all the proceeds from that property, defer all your taxes, and use all the profits to buy an even bigger property, with even more cash flow.

1031 exchanges don't wipe-out your taxes; but they defer them to the next deal. And there's no limit on how many *next deals* you can line up.

1031 exchanges explode your wealth because you're not giving any current profits to the government; they're all going to buy bigger and bigger properties.

Eventually, when you sell the last property and you do not buy a replacement property, you must pay all taxes on the gains you made through the purchase and sale of all previous properties. Yes, the tax bill might be big. But think of the position you'll be in! Your portfolio (and cash flow) will be even bigger!

One more bit of good news: If you die, your family does not have to pay taxes on any of the gains you got during the time you were alive! (I haven't taken advantage of that final tax break.)

The sooner you start using 1031 exchanges in your investing, the faster you'll become obscenely wealthy.

One other bit of good news: The government requires you use an intermediary to handle 1031 transactions. This means you don't have to do any of the paperwork. Remember, you're the CEO.

11. MENTORS: A PAT ON THE HEAD, A KICK IN THE PANTS

The most important member of your team is your mentor. This is a person who has done what you want to do. With his knowledge, you'll avoid making a lot of key mistakes, and get wealthier, faster.

You'll have a one-on-one relationship with some of your mentors. You'll know others from a distance. Still others will exist only in books and tapes. (I laugh at the losers who make fun of *book learning*. After all, books are written by real people who may have achieved astonishing success. To learn directly from them—through their books, tapes, or courses—is an amazing gift and advantage.)

By reading this book, you can consider me to be one of your mentors. I've been sharing with you the very techniques I've used to make myself very successful in real estate. They'll work for you, too.

You no doubt noticed that this book also contains many mistakes I made along the way. They're just as important for you to understand and avoid.

That's an extremely critical function of your mentor: to tell you when you're off course. You might not like to hear that kind of *support*, but you should take it to heart. A little bit of *tough love* might save you countless dead-ends and wasted money.

My first mentor was a man who lives on Cape Cod. An attorney referred me to him because I was looking for some money to borrow. Mark was a hard-money lender. (See Chapter 9 for a description of how *hard money* lending works.) He was also an investor, who once owned many thousands of units, five commercial real estate brokerage companies, an insurance company, and a hard-money lending firm.

By the time I met him, he had sold all of his other businesses but the hard-money one. He still owned some real estate, but focused mainly on hard-money lending. I was told he only worked 3 days a week. That's because he spent his time playing golf the other days. And he would only do business with people that he liked.

I gave him a call, put on my best suit (I thought all successful investors wore suits), and sat down with him to chat. I brought my portfolio along, and we discussed it. We talked about where I had been, what I was doing, and where I planned on going.

Mark was a very easy man to get along with. He had a great sense of humor and a constant twinkle in his eye that made you feel at ease when you were in his presence.

I must admit, I was very nervous. Here was a man worth many, many millions of dollars. And here I was, just starting out.

We hit it off, and began to do business together. Not only did we do business, but he was always willing to answer any questions I had about investing, and even about life.

We would periodically review my portfolio, look at the market cycles, and determine what I'd keep and what I'd sell. His advice was—and still is—invaluable.

Mark gave me a piece of advice I've always remembered.

At our very first meeting he said, "Dave, being successful is easy, as long as you follow the simple rules. Success is like a checkerboard. When you're playing checkers and you're marching over into the other player's area, what is your sole objective?"

I said, "to become a King."

"That's right," Mark said, "and when you become a king, what can you do?"

"You can go anywhere around the board, forward and backward, and you can do what you want."

"That's right," Mark said again. Then his face got stern, but still had that twinkle in his eye. "And the reason most people don't become successful is because they act like kings before they *are* kings. Because of that, they never *become* kings. Always remember that."

Mark, I always have. And I've lived my life accordingly.

I've accumulated many mentors through the years. I keep in regular contact with the live ones, and regularly reread the books and materials of the others.

Mentors are a phenomenal shortcut to success. If you want to become successful quickly, get a mentor. We'll talk more about mentors in Chapter 16.

IN THE NEXT CHAPTER

We've been covering a great many details for investing in real estate emerging markets. Sometimes it's important to step back from the trees and look at the whole forest.

That's what we're going to do in the next chapter. It's about how all my methods for identifying, financing, managing, and profiting from emerging markets can, in fact, be done long distance.

CHAPTER 14

How to Scout, Buy, and Profit From Properties— Long Distance

If you've stayed with me the throughout the last 13 chapters, I have no doubt you'll be successful in real estate. How do I know?

Most people are dabblers. They taste and poke at the buffet items, to see what pleases them the most. World-class athletes sit down and eat a complete meal that gives them the fuel they'll need to win. So far, I've served up a pretty complete meal of profit-making information. If you've digested it all, you *will* be that winner!

Even so, with all the new information I've laid out in earlier chapters, it can seem daunting. It's time to pause in this chapter, and make sure you have the right picture in your head about investing in emerging markets. Let's just quickly step back from the details we've been talking about, and look at the big picture.

DON'T MAKE THESE NINE MISTAKES

I've prepared a comparison for you. It goes through nine significant steps to making your fortune, and shows both the conventional (wrong) thinking, and the successful (right) approach. As you read them, *please note how much of the work can be done sitting at home, in your spare time, or by other people.*

1. Wrong Way: Take advice from your brother-in-law about whether to invest in real estate.

Successful Way: Only take real estate advice from people who are already highly successful in real estate. After all, you wouldn't take medical advice from someone who flunked out of medical school and is now down on all doctors, would you?

Be careful whom you tell about your investing goals. Almost everyone knows somebody who got into real estate on a whim, and just as quickly got burned. You're doing the right thing by reading books written by professionals.

Oh, and don't be discouraged when someone sees you reading this book, and says: "You'll never learn real estate through *book learning.*" I can assure you, I'm a real, live, active investor. The secrets I'm giving you in this book are what I use today to make millions. Those secrets are no different if you read them in my book or I whisper them into your ear.

2. Wrong Way: Listen to the newspapers about when to invest in real estate.

Successful Way: First, get to know the four market cycle phases that all real estate goes through. We discussed them in Chapter 2. You then can laugh at the journalist *experts* who print big headlines like: "Investors: Get Out NOW!" You'll understand that the only headlines that count are the ones on the local newspapers in the area you're investing in.

3. Wrong Way: Cross your fingers and hope your local market is in the right stage.

Successful Way: You become absolutely liberated by the thought that it doesn't matter what stage your local market is in. That's because, at this very moment, there are dozens or hundreds of markets across the United States that are sitting on the launch pad, fueled, and ready to take off.

You've read Chapters 3 and 4, so you know how to identify these markets around the country. Remember my earlier tip: Given that you can choose from many of these markets at any given time, why not pick one that's a nice vacation destination? Then, when you go there to look over a property that's made it all the way to your own personal investing *finals*, you should be able to write off some or all of that trip as a tax deduction!

4. Wrong Way: Find properties by driving to work, keeping your eyes open, and hoping you'll luck out someday.

Successful Way: Connect with real estate brokers and burned-out landlords in the way I describe in Chapters 4 and 7. Just one good broker in one city is all you need to have a successful real estate career! Imagine when you follow my advice and have a whole stable of them around the country!

The beauty of using my system is you can be sitting in your den, 1,500 miles from your target city, and be finding deals that the locals in that city will not see. They don't know my secrets of how to hook up with brokers, and how to grab burned-out landlords at their moments of greatest pain. You do.

5. Wrong Way: Delay investing because you really don't know how to analyze a deal with confidence.

Successful Way: In Chapter 12, I showed you the way the pros do deals, and how you can follow the same system. We discussed the clear standards for what makes a good deal, and what doesn't. The next step is to tie up the deal for long enough to do your *due diligence*. That way, you can focus on the deal, without worrying that a competitor will grab it out from under you. Only when you are satisfied that the deal is in fact solid do you go ahead with the investment.

This is a very crucial difference between the wannabes and the pros: The former group either doesn't do deals, or they rush around in a frenzy, hoping to analyze and bid on a property before the competition takes it. The pros find lots of deals that the competition doesn't even know about; then they lock up the best ones for long enough to analyze them without rushing. Which approach would you rather take?

6. Wrong Way: Postpone investing because you haven't raised the down payment yet; and besides, you won't qualify for a big bank loan.

Successful Way: After reading Chapter 9, you know that money will not hold you back any longer. There are many sources of financing for your deals besides banks and your life savings. One of the best sources is all the private citizens whose IRA investments are plodding along at lousy money-market rates of return. Once they discover that the right IRA can hold real estate investments, and that those investments are backed by the property as collateral, they'll be knocking at *your* door.

That's just one alternative source for funds. There are many others. The bottom line is that there are literally dozens of ways to invest in real estate without a down payment.

7. Wrong Way: When you finally own a multi-family property, you keep a toilet plunger in the trunk of your car, because you never know when you'll get the next "clog call" from a tenant.

Successful Way: Your investment property can be next door, or 2,000 miles away—it doesn't matter. You care very much about your tenants; after all, they are working all week to send you about 30% of their paychecks in rent.

But the great thing is that you've never met them! You have a property manager do *all* the tenant work for you. In Chapter 4, I explained how to find tested, proven, professional management companies. By *only* doing deals that can support such managers, you're saving yourself 50 blood pressure points of aggravation. Plus, you're making the whole country your profit playground!

8. Wrong Way: Cross your fingers when you try to raise rents, and cross them again when you try to sell the property.

Successful Way: This is a science. There's no *art* or hoping involved. If you treat your tenants well, you can steadily raise rents.

I'm not talking about heaping luxuries on your tenants. Instead, just think back to when you lived in an apartment: Wouldn't you be delighted if your landlord:

- kept the property in good shape;
- tolerated no drugs, loud parties, or other nonsense; and
- made repairs on a timely basis?

(Remember, *you* are not doing these things; it's your professional property manager that's running the property.)

If your property is run this way, then tenants practically expect a rent increase of some amount each year. And given that your property is run better than 90% of rental units around town, you can also charge more than average rents. In fact, you're likely to have vacancies filled quickly, as tenants tell their friends about a unit that's just opened up at your property.

Because rental properties are valued based on their income, each time you raise rents, you skyrocket your property value. The rule of thumb I mentioned in Chapter 7 was that renting one single additional apartment for $600 per month will raise your property value by roughly *72 thousand dollars!*

9. Wrong Way: Having invested the wrong way, you swear that you'll never invest in real estate again. Now you've become someone else's brother-in-law, and can discourage that person from ever investing.

Successful Way: No pain, *more* gain: That's the feeling you'll have when you invest on a remote-control basis across the country, in the right markets.

As revolutionary as my emerging market system for real estate investing is, in one sense it's nothing new. Just think about your supermarket: It used to be that seasonal fruits like blueberries or grapes were available only a few months out of the year. Now, those markets have developed reliable methods for finding ripe fruit across the globe, and long-distance systems to deliver it to your store, quickly and profitably.

I've done the same with real estate: In your hands, you have a reliable method for identifying the markets that are reaching their peaks of ripeness. Then my remote-control systems for analysis, financing, and management allow you to deliver those profits right to your local checking account.

IN THE NEXT CHAPTER

There's no question about it: Real estate investing involves some level of risk. (Of course, so does everything else in life.)

But only a fool takes *unnecessary* risks! Fortunately, there's a major way to reduce your risk when investing in real estate. The next chapter shows you how.

**Special Offer for Readers of this Book:
As mentioned on the cover, you can claim
bonuses worth more than $375.00 for free.
Simply go to: www.MarketCycleMastery.com
and type in the words "Reader Bonus" for details.**

CHAPTER 15

KNOW YOUR EXIT STRATEGY, BEFORE YOU GET INTO A PROPERTY

For thousands of years, the Polynesians and other ocean-going people would steer their boats by the stars. And the most famous star of all was Polaris, the North Star.

There's also a North Star of sorts in the world of real estate. It's called your *exit strategy*. It's the most important decision you will make, prior to buying a property.

Your exit strategy is:

1. How long you plan to keep a property;
2. What you plan on doing to the property; and
3. What your target profit is.

Knowing these aspects of a deal will give you a tremendous advantage. They will guide you to make the right decisions both before and during your ownership of the property.

Here are the main exit strategies you'll use.

FLIPPING PROPERTIES

The Wrong Way to Do It

The word *flipping* has a negative meaning in some areas. That's because the term is used to describe a scam. A team of people would buy properties and sell them to each other very quickly (sometimes within days) to increase their value. They would *flip* the properties back and forth to each other. To conceal their activities, they would use different buying entities (trusts and LLCs) to hide their identities. After building up the value artificially, they would finally flip the property to an unsuspecting investor for a grossly inflated price, and then split the profits.

The scam required lots of people to be crooks: Investors, appraisers, attorneys, and mortgage bankers were all part of the team. When these scams were uncovered, lots of people were awarded matching pairs of silver bracelets (held together by a small chain) and all-expenses-paid rooms to stay in for a few years.

The Right Way to Do It

There's a totally honest and valuable service that also comes under the term *flipping*. It's exactly what we covered in Chapter 5. You find motivated sellers who just want out of a property. They might have inherited a property out of state, or maybe they are getting a divorce. Perhaps the property has just become a headache, what with taxes and up-keep. If you follow my steps, you can buy that property at a decent price, and then turn around and sell it for more. It's completely legal, because no two people are conspiring to cheat a third person, and everyone is free to walk away from the transaction.

You can flip apartment buildings just as easily as you can single-family homes. There is one big difference, though: You get much bigger checks when you flip apartments. I've done both kinds, so I speak from experience.

Depending on how good your *value play* is, how fast a market is appreciating, and how much below market you bought a property, the potential profit to flip a mid-sized apartment building is around $200,000. That's no typo—I said *Two Hundred Grand*.

The profit (again, in my experience) on single-family property flips is from $5,000 to $20,000. Of course I'm going to do an easy single-family home deal that drops in my lap, and so should you. (By the way, if you keep your marketing up, as I described earlier, good deals WILL drop into your lap.)

But *really* keep an eye out for the apartment flips: You can do one single, solitary deal in an entire year and live quite nicely!

Most apartment flips involve buying a property that needs upgrading of some sort: raising rents, increasing occupancy, or doing repairs.

Other flip opportunities occur when you can buy at a capitalization rate that is higher than what the market normally merits. (Remember, a higher cap rate means a property is cheap.)

For instance, let's say you bought a B property for $1,000,000 at a 12 cap. You knew that B properties in that area are selling for a 9 cap. (You know this from my techniques in Chapter 10.) You could now buy that property, resell it quickly, and make a nice profit. How nice of a profit? If you bought at a 12 cap, and resold the property at a 9 cap, the gross profit would be $333,000.

That's right. A third of a million bucks. And these types of deals have been done, all around the country, by me and also my students. (Go back to Chapter 11 for a refresher on these calculations. Or find out more about my software at www.MarketCycleMastery.com and type in the keyword: "Software." It automatically calculates cap rates and dozens of other factors.)

Keep in mind that you did *nothing* to this property, except take title and transfer it, as soon as you found another buyer.

"But Dave, why would a good property be undervalued?"

The seller might just want out of the property. Or that person has not kept up with local market conditions, and has set the sales price lower than market. In my career, I've come across dozens of reasons this happens. Here's the important point: It happens. And you can become wealthy if you know how to find these deals, the way I show you.

Interior Repairs.   Most repairs on multi-unit properties are quoted on a per-unit basis. A quick cosmetic repair where you replace carpet, paint some walls, and change a few appliances will cost between $1,000 and $3,000 per unit.

Once you start going over $3,000, you're dealing with a more extensive rehab.

Exterior Repairs.   The best scenario that you can hope for is the interior is in good shape, but the exterior needs some tender loving care. This can be a great opportunity to buy below market value.

As many times as I've done it, I still can't get over it: Just by putting a few thousands of dollars into the right improvements, you can increase the value of a property by TENS of thousands of dollars, or even more.

Perhaps the paint is peeling, or the vinyl siding has holes in it. Maybe the entry doors need repainting. A lot of trim might be rotted and needs to be replaced.

The most common exterior improvement that can add quick equity to your property is landscaping.

A nicely landscaped property is going to give your property curb appeal. If you have overgrown shrubs in the front, consider pulling them out and putting in new ones. When you buy the new shrubs, don't go cheap, and get small shrubs that need years to mature. Spend your money on the medium-sized mature shrubs, so they look like they fit right into the landscaping.

Anything you can see from the street should be groomed. Install mulch beds and flowers, and put in rock formations.

If a courtyard is not being used, can you put in a recreation area? How about a few picnic tables and raised mulch beds with more shrubs? Take it from a former landscaper: A few bucks spent here will come back to you, multiplied many times over.

Make sure the name of the property is prominently and proudly displayed. Put it on the side of the building, or even create one of those standalone signs surrounded by a small flower bed at the front entrance.

Can you see how you might be able to specialize in flipping? It's called being a *turnaround specialist*. Having an eye for minor improvements that can generate big value gains—it's one of the most profitable things you can do!

Buy and Hold: Is this Strategy Right for You?

Think cash flow.

Think more cash flow automatically coming into your house—month in and month out—than you make in your current job. Think two or three times more monthly cash flow.

If you have that image firmly planted in your mind, you'll start to see what has made me so excited about apartments over the last decade. I started out doing apartments when I was broke; and they've made me rich. Of all the types of real estate investing I can do—and I can choose anything I wish right now—my favorite is the apartment *buy and hold* strategy.

Flipping multi-family properties IS a great way to get huge chunks of money—no doubt about it. But when you get really lazy about things, you start to ask yourself: "You mean, I have to flip another property in order to get another fat check?"

I know. Real tough work there, having your Dream Team do most of the work, while you get most of the profit. Still, this book is about my journey through real estate, and the shortcuts I've found to becoming rich.

Here's the next shortcut to consider: Don't flip the property; keep it and milk it for cash flow, month after month.

Play your cards right, and your monthly income from properties you own (and other people manage) will equal and soon exceed the amount you got in one of those fat *flip* checks.

Even if you never bought another property in your entire life, that money would continue to come into your house, month in and month out. That is true financial and personal freedom!

Here's how it happens:

1. You start getting passive income from the first few properties you buy.
2. That gives you extra money coming in at the beginning of each month and it becomes easier to pay your bills.
3. As you continue to buy more units, your passive income grows.
4. You now have extra money to start doing the things on your *Wish List*.
5. As more units come into your portfolio, you get to the point where your passive income equals what you earn at your job.
6. Then you have a choice to make: Do you continue to be a full-time employee/part-time investor? Or do you dump the job, and become a full-time investor?

Some people really love their jobs and they just don't want to quit. That's maybe 1% of the population. The other 99% were ready to cut off the ball-and-chain J-O-B yesterday!

The benefit of becoming a full-time investor is you'll have much more time to do more deals, and you'll really accelerate your wealth.

ANOTHER BUY-AND-HOLD BENEFIT

Don't forget that while you're enjoying monthly passive income, your property will also be appreciating, and you'll be creating equity. You can become wealthier every day.

If you follow the advice in this book and invest in emerging markets, you will attain appreciation at a much higher rate.

When I invest in emerging markets, I always purchase based on some form of positive cash flow. But my *real goal* is to get the greatest appreciation in the shortest time.

I then take that newly created appreciation and transfer it into another property in the same market, using the 1031 exchange strategy (more on this in a minute). Or I move it to a new market that is getting ready to take off.

If you're in a market that has given you a great deal of appreciation in a short period, you can make that money work harder for you if you transfer it into another property.

1031 Exchanges: How to Master Them

You'll make a quantum leap in your investing career and in your wealth when you start doing 1031 tax-deferred exchanges. We talked about this in an earlier chapter. But it's so absolutely critical to making you a fortune, I want to cover it again.

A 1031 exchange allows you to sell Property A, and defer all of the taxes, as long as you put the proceeds into a similar-type property B. It needs to be a *like kind* property, but it can be bigger. That gives you even more cash flow.

You can then sell Property B and in effect take all the profits from Properties A and B, and buy Property C. When you realize that the profit from one property can become the nontaxed down payment on another property, you start to see the wealth multiplier effect here.

Time for an example: Let's say you sold Property A in less than a year and realized a profit of $100,000. You would pay taxes based on the short-term capital gain rate of 30%. That means $30,000 comes off the top for Uncle Sam, and $70,000 goes into your next investment. (Just hold off buying that yacht until I make you much richer, okay?)

Let's assume you put 20% down on your next property. That means you'll purchase a property for $350,000. ($70,000 is a 20% down payment on $350,000.)

If you did a 1031 exchange, you could *defer any tax payments to the government on the entire $100,000.* Now you have a 20% down payment available for a property worth $500,000, instead of $350,000. Not only will you have a property of greater value in your portfolio, but you'll also be creating more cash flow.

(Ain't the IRS great! I think so, because this is all 100% legal, ethical, and done every day, with the *blessing* of the IRS—no tax loopholes necessary.)

If both properties increased by 20% the $350,000 property would now be worth $420,000 and the $500,000 property would now be worth $600,000. Yes, you just made $180,000 more.

You may say, "Sure, Dave, you made the 1031 exchange look better compared to short-term capital gain taxation. But what if I hold it for more than a year, and pay the lower 15% rate?"

Good question. Bottom line answer: Yes, the long-term capital gains rate is better than the short-term rate. But you still can't touch the ZERO current taxation of your profits when you do a 1031 exchange. They could reduce long-term tax rates to 5% and the 1031 strategy would still be better.

The same amount of effort goes into both traditional and 1031 investing. The only difference is using *all your money*—instead of *some of your money*—to buy the next property.

The beautiful part of this entire situation is the government does not limit the amount of 1031 exchanges you can do, or the amount of wealth you can create.

Sure, you eventually pay taxes on all the gains you create. But you're paying taxes on a much larger pile of money, with much more left over for you! Not to mention the massive amount of cash flow you'll enjoy along the way.

PROFIT BY THE RULES

There are some rules you must follow to do 1031 exchanges. Here's a rough summary of them (check with your tax advisor for specifics in your case).

When you sell Property A, you have 45 days to identify a *replacement property* (the next property you will buy).

You usually can identify up to three properties, but you have to purchase at least one of them.

That purchase has to take place within 180 days of selling Property A. (If you close on Property B on the 181st day, you're out of luck. You will now pay taxes on any gain that you realized on the sale of Property A.)

You must use a qualified intermediary. That is someone who facilitates all the paperwork and handles the money from the sale of Property A. You are not allowed to take possession of that money at any point. If you do, you have just blown the exchange.

I saw a situation in which an investor's attorney told him that the attorney would hold the money so they could complete the exchange. Big mistake. An attorney is not a qualified intermediary. That money then became taxed at the regular rates, and the investor lost the right to do an exchange.

Common question: Can you take some of the profits out of an exchange, and still do the exchange? The answer is *yes*, but you'll be taxed on whatever amount you take out of the exchange.

There are many variations available within the 1031 exchange rules. Be sure to contact a qualified intermediary and explain your situation. A good intermediary will have seen it all and can advise you on the best approach.

1031 tax-deferred exchanges are *the* vehicle of choice, if you want to create a vast amount of wealth in the shortest amount of time. I just can't emphasize this enough.

IN THE NEXT CHAPTER

Even though I've stuffed this book full of tips, techniques, secrets, and re-sources, there still are plenty more where those came from.

In the next section, we'll talk about how you can pursue anything you've found interesting in this book. The resources and help are there, waiting for you!

Special Offer for Readers of this Book:
As mentioned on the cover, you can claim
bonuses worth more than $375.00 for free.
Simply go to: www.MarketCycleMastery.com
and type in the words "Reader Bonus" for details.

CHAPTER 16

Your Next Steps to a Fortune in Real Estate

"Fools say 'Experience is the best teacher.' I prefer to learn from other peoples' experience."

—Otto Von Bismarck, German Chancellor

There are two ways you can go forward with your real estate investment career.

APPROACH #1

You definitely can adopt the trial-and-error method. You'll make lots of mistakes, but as long as you learn from those mistakes and don't repeat them you'll do okay.

In one sense, this method is inexpensive. No courses to take, no books to buy—you just go out there and start bumbling around.

In another sense, it's an expensive way to acquire skills. For one thing, it burns up a lot of time. You can always earn more money, but your time is gone forever.

It also creates lots of scars. But if you're looking for some great *war stories*, this is the way to go!

For the first couple years of my investing career, I did lots of trial and error, and I made countless mistakes. I still did pretty well for myself, so this is one possible method.

Fortunately I did something critical to success: I was smart enough to create systems every time I made a mistake. I didn't make the same mistake twice. So—aside from the burned-up time, and physical/mental scars—I did fine. I accumulated properties and created some nice cash flow.

APPROACH #2

1. Find someone who has already made those mistakes, and created those systems.
2. Plug them in.
3. Make your fortune faster.

After 2 years of doing the trial-and-error approach, I became a big believer in the second approach. I then began to soak up other real estate investors' advice wherever I could. Sure enough, my progress became faster. In fact, in my third year of investing, I did three times the business I did in the first 2 years.

The "My Situation Is Different" Syndrome (and the Biggest Secret of this Book)

I want to tell you a profoundly important secret right now: Don't fall for the *my situation is different* excuse!

Let's just get this out of the way: Of course your situation is different! You're a unique human being, and no one's ever been down the exact path that your life has taken you. Fine; we've acknowledged it, right up front.

The key to the secret is this: Your situation is *not different enough* to prevent you from succeeding at real estate. You maybe walk on two legs. You probably can speak and read. You most likely live in a town, near a larger town.

And you have one other extremely important ingredient: Because you're reading this book, you have a desire to improve yourself.

There's an excellent chance that you can get on the road to real estate success, whenever you set your mind to it.

Here's what happens with the *my situation is different* addicts: They see someone else succeed. They then rationalize how it was easy for that person to get ahead, and how they can't, because of some difference they dredge up.

As we established at the beginning of this section, it's not hard to dredge up a difference, because there are hundreds of them, if you look hard enough.

Future Losers look for reasons NOT to model themselves after a successful person.

But here's where millionaires are made: Future Winners look for the parts that they CAN adopt from the successful person!

This is an incredibly important distinction! Sure, Future Winners can see all the differences, too. But they use the adoptable parts as rungs in the ladder toward success.

If you've gotten nothing else out of my book, please take this advice to heart: Look for ways you can selectively adopt winning techniques from people who've succeeded before you.

They don't have to be *my* techniques. I think I have a lot of good ones, but so do other real estate investors. Just see things clearly, identify what you CAN adopt. . . and then take action!

How to Speed Up Your Progress in Becoming a Real Estate Millionaire

When you are looking for advice to adopt from successful people, be sure to find role models who are fanatical about systems.

Some people are great successes, but they got there by flying by the seat of their pants. That's not terribly helpful to the aspiring tycoon (you). What you need are people that not only have become successful, but have done so in a way that's copyable.

By *systems*, I mean you want to see steps and checklists. It's incredibly helpful to be able to pull out a tool that tells you what to do, in what order (procedures). It then tells you if you skipped a step (checklists).

The last airplane flight you took might have been captained by a pilot with 30,000 hours of experience in the cockpit. But that pilot still ran through a checklist before taking off. Those types of carefully created systems truly separate the amateurs from the professionals.

One big step in your investing career is to find a mentor who is successful in what you want to do. I have mentored and continue to mentor thousands of people across the United States, and in many other countries.

Some people are mentored through my books and home study systems. Others come to live events. Both approaches are effective. The only difference is how fast you want to become successful. When you're at a live event, you can have all your questions answered on the spot. You also get the benefit of current case histories, and how to adapt your investing to current situations.

I even have a limited program in which I work with students one-on-one to buy and sell in emerging markets through a unique coaching program I established.

This is one of the key roles of mentors. When you're in a situation, good mentors will be able to analyze it quickly. They should be able to tell you three or four different options that you could choose. They will range from the "very good" to the "you should avoid this at all costs!"

It's this type of feedback that gets you where you want to go, very quickly. It also helps you to avoid that one big blunder that could turn you off to doing any more investing.

I wish there had been courses, live events, and mentoring on multi-family investing when I was starting out! Even though I was set for life after only 3½ years, you're luckier: You can progress faster because you don't have to make all the mistakes I did.

You can find out more about these programs by going to my website at www.MarketCycleMastery.com and typing in the keywords: "Live Events."

A Free and Fantastic Way to Benefit from Distance Learning

In this age of new technology, there are many different ways to get information from a mentor. My organization provides monthly and bi-weekly teleconferences that cover the details of investing in emerging markets and in multi-family properties. We also have programs that explain exactly how to invest in single-family properties and other types of real estate.

Teleconferences are simply fantastic tools: No matter where you are in the country or even in the world, you can discover the techniques of successful real estate investors just by picking up the phone and listening. (You'll get the most out of these calls when you take good notes!)

The Best Books and CDs

In my humble opinion, the best manual and CDs available today on multi-family investing is my *Apartment House Riches* Home Study System. It's a 172-page manual, plus many CDs and special reports. They take you from the very basic principles of multi-family and emerging market investing, right through to advanced strategies.

You go step-by-step through the entire process of:

- Getting started;
- Attracting deals;
- Writing offers;
- Understanding market cycles;
- Negotiating the deal;

- Completing the due diligence to make sure the deal you *think* you're getting is the deal that you *are* getting; and
- How to put large checks in the bank by using the right exit strategies.

This home study system gives you all of the simple-to-use, fill-in-the-blank forms necessary to successfully buy and sell multi-family properties *without dealing with a single tenant.*

I'm so confident in my systems that I give a *one-full-year, 100% money-back* guarantee that they'll make YOU a fortune.

In fact, because you've read this far, you're in a different, higher class from the *big talkers* and wannabes out there. I want to reward your *go-getter* attitude.

I have a special web page link that's ONLY published right here, deep in my book, where few people ever get to. If you go to that page, I'm making a special offer that's better than what the rest of the world gets. Hey, you read this far, you deserve it. Go to www.MarketCycleMastery.com and type in the Keywords: "Hidden Offer."

The Power of LIVE Instruction from an Emerging Markets Expert

A different level of accelerated learning takes place when you attend one of my live seminars. We work together side-by-side. Your understanding is enhanced, and your questions are answered immediately.

We go through the process of analyzing markets and deals in a systematic process. You then get to take that process home, and use it over and over again to make big profits in emerging market investing for the remainder of your life.

You get to network with a room full of like-minded people. They come from all over the United States and usually several foreign countries. You create friendships and business relationships that will last a lifetime.

Through my years of teaching live seminars, I've noticed that the students who attend the live seminars become wealthier faster than the students who get the home study system.

Don't get me wrong: There are people around this world making a ton of money with the home study system! But the students who attend the live events are taken through a series of case studies of deals that are on the market right now.

They are shown how to analyze those deals, what makes them good, what makes them bad, and what we can do creatively to put the deal together. We start with very small deals—two- and three-family properties. By the end of the seminar, all of the students are comfortable analyzing and creating offers for properties with values of over eight million dollars!

I believe the reason my students are so incredibly successful is because when they leave the live event and do their first deal, they say it's like they are doing their seventh or eighth deal. That's because of all of the case studies they did during the live event.

Students who attend the live events are more comfortable with the bigger numbers—so they do the bigger deals earlier in their investing careers. That's how they become wealthier, faster.

For more details on my next live event, just go to the website at www.MarketCycleMastery.com and type in the keywords: "Live Events."

How to Have an Emerging Markets Expert Hold a Seminar in Your City

Are you a member of a real estate investment association or landlord association? Or do you hold a convention or have some other related seminar or organization?

If so, and if you would like to have an emerging market presentation done in your city, call my office at 781-878-7114.

Because I and my senior staff constantly travel throughout the United States, there's a possibility that we could schedule something near to you.

The Importance of Taking Action Now

If you've read even just portions of this book, you most likely are fascinated at the prospect of creating great wealth by investing in emerging markets. You now have an excellent understanding of the process it takes to become successful.

It is now time to take action.

Fortunately, you don't need to make any big decisions to take action. All you need to do is apply the concepts I've given you in this book.

Whatever you do, don't let your enthusiasm grow stale! Keep it fresh—and keep moving toward your goal of complete financial freedom—by taking action NOW.

See you at the top!

INDEX

1031 tax-deferred exchanges, 21–22,
    35–38, 125, 201–202, 215–217
Adams, Jeff, 30–31
Accredited Residential Manager
    (ARM), 35. *See also* Property
    management
Acquisition cost and cash-on-cash
    return, 156
ARMs. *See* Accredited Residential
    Managers
Asbestos, 183
Avoiding investor mistakes:
  adequate employment base, 115–116
  capitalization rate (*see* Cap rate)
  cash-on-cash return (*see*
      Cash-on-cash return)
  debt–service ratio, 121
  identifying a good deal, 114–115
  market diversification, 121–122
  overbuilding, 122–123
  pollution problems, 118–120
  selling, 123–124
  taxes, 124–125
  timing, 116–117
  unit surveys, 117–118

Bren, Donald, 4
Brokers, commercial:
  approaching, 189
  overview, 188–189
  participation of, 142 (*see also*
      Financing)
  short list, 190

Buffett, Warren, 83
Building value, 159
Buy and hold strategy:
  appreciation, 214–215
  cash flow, 213–214
Buyer's Market Phase I:
  example of, 93–94, 157–158
  investing in, 15–16
  overbuilding, 122
  overview, 12–14
  See also Emerging market, and job
      growth
Buyer's Market Phase II:
  investing in, 18–19, 124, 195
  overbuilding, 122
  overview, 16–18
  See also Emerging market, and job
      growth
Buying below replacement cost, 32
Buying right:
  compiling the data, 160–161
  overview, 132–134
  rating a property (*see* Types of
      properties)
  types of areas of a city, 149–150
  types of properties (*see* Types of
      properties)
  See also Cap rate; Cash-on-cash
      return; Gross rent multiplier;
      Replacement cost; Value plays

Cap rate (capitalization rate):
  calculating, 153–154

understanding, 120, 151–153
See also Buying right, compiling the
    data; Net operating income
    (NOI)
Cash-on-cash return, 19, 121
  and rating a property, 156
  See also Buying right, compiling the
    data
Certified Property Managers (CPMs),
    35, 58. *See also* Property
    management
Comparable method of appraisal, 151
Confidentiality agreement, 53
Conventional mindset, 29–30, 33
CPMs. *See* Certified Property
    Managers
Creative financing, 84–85, 144–145

Deal flow, 133–134. *See also* Financing
Debt service and cash-on-cash return,
    156
Deferred maintenance, 99–100,
    178–179
De-leaded certificate, 184
Demographics, 193
DINKs (dual income no kids), 146
Discrimination, tenant, 170, 180
Dream team:
  1031 specialist, 201–202 (*see also*
    1031 tax-deferred exchanges)
  accountants, 200–201
  assistants, 190–191
  attorneys, 192–193
  bankers, 192
  brokers (*see* Brokers, commercial)
  CEO vs. landlord investor, 187
  contractors, 197–198
  demographers, 193–195
  inspectors, 195–196 (*see also*
    Inspections)
  managers, 198–199 (*see also* Property
    management)
  member list, 188

mentors, 202–204
Due diligence:
  demographics, 193–195
  expenses, 170–171
  hidden value, 169–170
  investment inspection (*see*
    Inspections, investment)
  overview, 162–163
  paying for analysis, 171–172
  philosophy, 164
  process of, 165
    checklist, 168–169
    leases, 167–168
    outstanding contracts, 168
    property expenses, 167
    property income, 166–167
    property inspection, 173–174 (*see
      also* Inspections)
  right way, 163–165
  wrong way, 163

Echo Boomers and population growth,
    115
Efficient market, 154
Emerging markets:
  approaches to investing, 218–221
  barriers to entry, 27–28
  buy and hold strategy (*see* Buy and
    hold strategy)
  buying plan, 44–48
    beginning, 46–48
    cash flow, 45–46
    direct mail campaign, 48–52
    financing, 60–62 (*see also*
      Financing)
    Internet properties, 54–56
    market research, 56–58, 59–60
    property management (*see*
      Property management)
    real estate agents, 52–54
    time management, 48
  characteristics of, 26–28, 56–58
  courage to invest, 33–34

Emerging markets (*Continued*)
due diligence (*see* Due diligence)
example of, 6–8, 27–28
exit strategy, 210
flipping property (*see* Flipping
property)
vs. hot markets, 39
investor mistakes in (*see* Avoiding
investor mistakes)
and job growth, 14–15
mistakes to avoid, 205–209
multi-family investments (*see*
Multi-family investments)
overview, 25–26, 40–43
population growth, 115–116
profit use, 82–83, 103–104
rent increase, 110–111
research methods, 221–223
single-family investments (*see*
Single-family investments)
vs. stock market, 8–9
team building (*see* Dream team)
and transportation infrastructure,
39–40
value plays (*see* Value plays)
wealth creation, 46
See also 1031 tax-deferred
exchanges
Equilibrium, 122–123, 157
Equity Protection Formula, 25
Equity sharing, 101–103, 137, 141
Exclusive Buyer's Agency Agreement,
53–54

Financing:
creative (*see* Creative financing)
four-step system
buying right (*see* Buying right)
finding investors, 138–143
reducing outside financing,
134–138
using credit, 143–144
leverage, 131–132

myths of, 126–129
reasoning behind, 129–131
Flipping property:
exterior repairs, 212–213
interior repairs, 212
right way, 211–212
wrong way, 210–211
Frew, Kristy and Kevin, 93–94
Fymat, Stephane, 170

Gross rent multiplier (GRM), 155. *See
also* Buying right, compiling
the data

Hard-money lenders, 141–142. *See also*
Financing

If-then formula, 33
Immigration and population growth,
115
Inefficient market, 154–155
Inspections:
hazardous situations
contaminations, 183
lead paint, 184
toxic mold, 184–185
water inspection, 185–186
investment
deferred maintenance, 99–100,
178–179
infrastructure, 177
local shopping, 178
overview, 174
parking, 178
rentable square feet, 175–176
roofs, 175
tenant profile, 179–180
tenant turnover, 176
transportation, 176–177
unit inspection, 180–182, 196
neighborhood, 182–183
property, 173–174, 195–196
See also Property management

Institute of Real Estate Management (IREM), 35

Land value, 159
Lead paint, 184
Limited Liability Company (LLC), 137

Mann, Oliver, 105
Means Square Foot Costs Book, 158
Morris, Rose, 61–62, 195
Multi-family investments:
  advantages of, 85–87
  creative financing (*see* Creative financing)
  due diligence (*see* Due diligence)
  economies of scale, 79
  equity sharing (*see* Equity sharing)
  forced appreciation, 111–112
  income method of appraisal, 151–152
  low risk and larger returns, 81–82, 84
  overview, 76–77
  part-time investing, 79–80
  pollutants and, 118–120
  positive cash flow, 77–79
  profit use, 82–83, 103–104
  property management (*see* Property management)
  unit surveys, 117–118
  value-added components, 82 (*see also* Value plays)
  See also Emerging markets; Value plays
Multiplier effect, 18

Nesbitt, Sandra, 55
Net operating income (NOI), 108, 123
  and cap rate, 153–154
  and cash-on-cash return, 156
No-money-down deals, 156–157
Nuisance rent increase, 109

Path of Progress, 4–5, 58–59
Pocket listings, 188
Positive cash flow, 31–32
Price per square foot, 158–159
Private placement, 140. *See also* Financing
Pro Forma, 108
Profit multiplier, 108–109, 190–191
Property management:
  attracting tenants, 107
  and emerging markets, 44–45, 58
  and multi-family investments, 80–81, 198–199
  nightmares, 95–96
  red flags of
    deferred maintenance, 99–100, 178–179
    dishonesty, 100–101
    higher than average vacancy, 96–97
    increase in notices to vacate, 97–98
    long "make readies," 98–99
    permanent vacancy, 101

Real estate blind spots, 5–6
Real estate investment trusts (REITs), 3
Real estate market cycle:
  local investments, 30–33
  out-of-area investments, 34–35
  phases of, 2–3 (*see also* Buyer's Market Phase I; Buyer's Market Phase II; Seller's Market Phase I; Seller's Market Phase II)
Reg D offering, 140. *See also* Financing
Repair allowance, 136, 173–174. *See also* Financing
Replacement cost, 157–158. *See also* Buying right, compiling the data
Resolution Trust Corporation, 23, 24–25

Roof inspection, 175
RS Means Company, 158

Seller's Market Phase I:
  investing in, 21–22, 124
  overbuilding, 122
  overview, 19–20
  See also Emerging market, and job
    growth
Seller's Market Phase II:
  days on the market, 24
  foreclosures, 23
  investing in, 24–25, 124, 215
  job growth, 23
  overbuilding, 122
  overview, 22–24
  supply, 23
Single-family investments:
  assigning contract, 74–75
  comparable method of appraisal, 151
  finding buyers, 73–74
  out-of-town owners
    targeting, 64–65
    finding, 65–66
    letters of intent, 66–67
    screening deals, 67
    answering the calls, 68–70
    making the offer, 70–73
    overview, 63–64
Sub-metering utilities, 171
Sutton, Willy, 129

Tenant profile, 178–179. See also
    Discrimination
Tenant turnover, 176

Threshold measurements, 194
Total vs. rentable square feet, 175–176
Toxic mold, 184–185
Trump, Donald, 60
Types of properties:
  type A, 146–147, 178
  type B, 147, 178, 179, 182
  type C, 147–148, 177, 178, 199
  type D, 148–149
  rating a property, 151
    building value, 159–160
    cap rate (see Cap rate)
    cash-on-cash return (see
      Cash-on-cash return)
    gross rent multiplier, 155
    land value, 159–160
    price per square foot, 158–159
    replacement cost, 157–158

Units, Jack, 7

Value plays:
  burned-out landlords as:
    characteristics of, 89–91, 92–93
    finding, 91–92
    dealing with, 93–94
  example of, 93–94
  high vacancy as, 106–108, 176
  low rent as, 109–111
  management nightmares (see
    Property management)
  as profit opportunity, 88–89
  repositioning as, 103–105
  See also Buying right, compiling
    the data